OSCAR SLATER: A KILLER EXPOSED

by Brenda Rossini

"Oscar, Oscar, Oscar..." Felix Unger

First edition published in 2023
© Copyright 2023
Brenda Rossini

The right of Brenda Rossini to be identified as the author of this work has been asserted by her in accordance with the Copyright, Designs and Patents Act 1998.

All rights reserved. No reproduction, copy or transmission of this publication may be made without express prior written permission. No paragraph of this publication may be reproduced, copied or transmitted except with express prior written permission or in accordance with the provisions of the Copyright Act 1956 (as amended). Any person who commits any unauthorised act in relation to this publication may be liable to criminal prosecution and civil claims for damage.

All characters appearing in this work are fictitious. Any resemblance to real persons, living or dead, is purely coincidental. The opinions expressed herein are those of the author and not of MX Publishing.

Hardcover ISBN 978-1-80424-178-3
Paperback ISBN 978-1-80424-179-0
ePub ISBN 978-1-80424-180-6
PDF ISBN 978-1-80424-181-3

Published by MX Publishing
335 Princess Park Manor, Royal Drive,
London, N11 3GX
www.mxpublishing.co.uk

Cover design by Brian Belanger

DEDICATION

To all the female victims of violence by strangers. If you survived, you never forget. For those who died, you are not forgotten.

TABLE OF CONTENTS

LIST OF ILLUSTRATIONS 7
LITERARY LIST 10
CHAPTER 1 The Murder of Marion Gilchrist 13
CHAPTER 2 Scotland, Empire, and Marion Gilchrist 17
CHAPTER 3 The World of Oscar Slater 20
CHAPTER 4 Why Oscar Slater? 23
CHAPTER 5 Scotland is Nigh 31
CHAPTER 6 The Gilchrist Jewelry 36
CHAPTER 7 Dramatis *Personae* 45
CHAPTER 8 Slater's Two Scottish Partners 75
CHAPTER 9 Précis of the Plot 80
CHAPTER 10 The Place: Gilchrist Flat, 2d Floor, 15 Queen's Terrace 82
CHAPTER 11 A Case Old and Cold 87
CHAPTER 12 Anti-Semitism 93
CHAPTER 13 Oscar Slater and American Citizenship 97
CHAPTER 14 Oscar Slater's Return to Glasgow 100
CHAPTER 15 Timeline to Murder 106
CHAPTER 16 Glasgow Donjon 123
CHAPTER 17 A Tale of Two Diamond Brooches 139
CHAPTER 18 November Pause 149
CHAPTER 19 Oscar Slater's Nightly Strolls 158
CHAPTER 20 The Trio Coordinates 166
CHAPTER 21 December 21, 1908—The Day of the Murder 169
CHAPTER 22 Slater Prepares for Murder Night 172

CHAPTER 23 Oscar Slater Enters 15 Queens Terrace **174**

CHAPTER 24 Tricks About the Time **188**

CHAPTER 25 Oscar Slater, the Killer **192**

CHAPTER 26 Motive: Diamonds Worth Thousands **206**

CHAPTER 27 Oscar Slater's Inglorious Escape **210**

CHAPTER 28 "That's When Your Heartaches Begin" **212**

CHAPTER 29 "That Man Has Done Something to Miss Gilchrist" **222**

CHAPTER 30 The Investigatory Team of Police **225**

CHAPTER 31 A Dogged Investigation **227**

CHAPTER 32 A Puzzling Motive **232**

CHAPTER 33 A Murderer's Ensemble **235**

CHAPTER 34 From Plans to Panic **245**

CHAPTER 35 Hunting a Killer **247**

CHAPTER 36 Lightning Strikes December 25 ....**260**

CHAPTER 37 The Heat is On, December 26 ....**267**

CHAPTER 38 Flight **270**

CHAPTER 39 Detective-Lieutenant John T. Trench **278**

CHAPTER 40 The Sinking of Oscar Slater on Board the Lusitania **282**

CHAPTER 41 Oscar Slater Enters the American Criminal Justice System **288**

CHAPTER 42 Verisimilitude in Oscar Slater Descriptions **291**

CHAPTER 43 Gilchrist Jewelry Back in the News **301**

CHAPTER 44 Extradition Hearings **303**

CHAPTER 45 On Scotland's Soil **310**

CHAPTER 46 The Burden of Proof **313**

CHAPTER 47 Trial: May 3 to May 9, 1900 ....**321**

CHAPTER 48 Parsing the Evidence **330**

CHAPTER 49 The Verdict **341**

CHAPTER 50 A Disquisition 351
CHAPTER 51 Trench and the Course of an Innocence Campaign........... 355
CHAPTER 52 Trench Turned Inside Out... 360
CHAPTER 53 An Appeal for the Misbegotten 366
CHAPTER 54 Windswept Gloom 372
CHAPTER 55 Authors as Sleuths.. 375
CHAPTER 56 Arthur Conan Doyle's *"Je t'accuse!"* 379
"The whole of Slater's story is a tissue of lies."
CHAPTER 57 Oscar Slater in Retirement 382
BIBLIOGRAPHY 386
INDEX 392
ACKNOWLEDGEMENT 405

LIST OF ILLUSTRATIONS

For the Love of God, Damien Hirst 12
Marian Gilchrist at death 16
Queen Victoria's Jubilee Certificate 18
William Roughead portrait 25
Gilchrist dining room 33
George's Square 34
Marion Gilchrist, age 80 37
Brooch #1 39
Brooch #2 40
Hamburg, Germany Flea Market 48
Hamburg, Germany Gentleman's Club 49
Leith, Edinburgh shore 51
Scottish Highlanders 51
Oscar Slater in 1895 52
Sauchiehall Street 60
Central Station and Highlandmen Umbrella 63
Arthur Conan Doyle at the pool table 66
Leicester Square 70
Empire Theater 70
Empire Theater Promenade Room 71
Carfin and Holytown map 77
Bookies at the track 78
Irish terrier 82
14 and 15 Queen's Terrace 83
Gilchrist flat stairs and door 84
Arthur Adams 85
Dumbarton Road 110

Ayr seaside	113
Marion Gilchrist at Ayr	114
Sauchiehall and Charing Cross Mansions	124
St. George's Road	128
Kitchenette	130
Sleeping Quarters	130
Victorian fireplace	131
Slater's Hammer	134
Toffee hammer	135
Mademoiselle Andrée	143
Victorian jewelry box	144
Victorian tray and velvet compartments	147
Padlocks affixed at the left of the front door	153
Edward VII gold half-sovereign	177
Grandfather Clock	179
Patrick Nugent wedding photo	186
Patrick Nugent	187
Victorian kitchen	194
Spare Bedroom	201
Runaway matchbox	202
Oscar Slater in his Ayr garden	203
Queen's Terrace outdoor streetlamps	212
For Whom the Bell Tolls	215
Oscar Slater prison photo	217
Edwardian Era Men's Coats	220
Newsboy caps	236
Edwardian soft cap	236
Arthur Conan Doyle, cap and pipe	237
Defendants and soft caps	237
Fawn waterproof coat	238
St. George's Cross Road	242

Children at River Kelvin 244
Mary Barrowman and parents 249
Thomas Cooke Travel Office 258
St. John's United Free Church 260
Glasgow Central Police Station 263
North Western Hotel ledger 271
Oscar Slater letter to Max Rattman 272
Cunard Line ticket application 274
Cunard liner 275
Detective-Lieutenant John Trench 278
Oscar's Luggage 286
Manhattan Courthouse, Bridge of Sighs, Tombs Prison 288
Oscar Slater arrested on Lusitania 289
Oscar Slater letter to Hugh Cameron 305
Edinburgh High Court 310
Evidence for Trial 322
Helen Lambie at the trial 329
Judge Charles Guthrie 343
Oscar Slater after sentencing 347
Crowd at Oscar Slater sentencing 348
Peterhead Bay cormorants 373
Marion Gilchrist tomb, Necropolis Cemetery 385

LITERARY LIST

"Adventure of Abbey Grange," Arthur Conan Doyle

"Adventure of Black Peter," Arthur Conan Doyle

"Adventure of the Copper Beeches," Arthur Conan Doyle

"Adventure of the Creeping Man," Arthur Conan Doyle

"Adventure of the Empty House," Arthur Conan Doyle

"Adventure of Shoscombe Old Place," Arthur Conan Doyle

"Auld Lang Syne"

Bleak House, Charles Dickens

Crime and Punishment, Fyodor Dostoevsky

Cyrano de Bergerac, by Edmond Rostand

Dombey and Son, Charles Dickens

"Henry V, Part I," Shakespeare

Hound of the Baskervilles, by Arthur Conan Doyle

Ivanhoe, by Sir Walter Scott

"Julius Caesar", Shakespeare

"The Mouse," by Robert Blake

"Much Ado About Nothing," Shakespeare

Oliver Twist, Charles Dickens

"Othello," Shakespeare

Persuasion, by Jane Austen

Richard III, Shakespeare

"Rime of the Ancient Mariner," by Samuel Taylor Coleridge

"Scandal in Bohemia," by Arthur Conan Doyle

The Sign of Four, by Arthur Conan Doyle

A Study in Scarlet, by Arthur Conan Doyle

"That's When Your Heartaches Begin," the King, Elvis Presley

"To a Louse," by Robert Burns

"221B," by Vincent Starrett

Zadig, by Voltaire

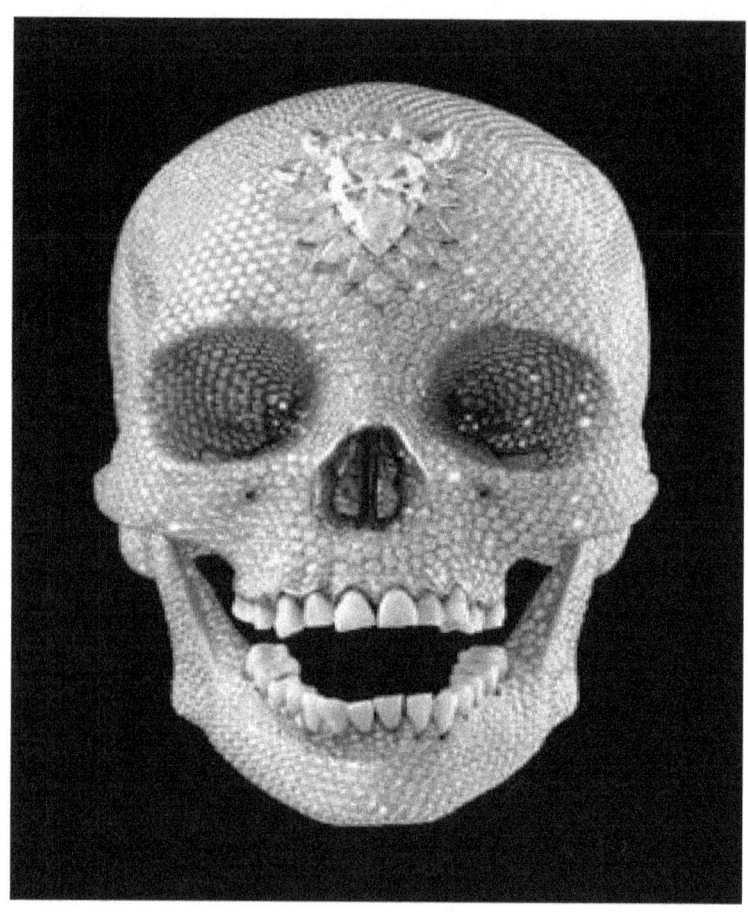

Damien Hirst, "For the Love of God." There are over 8,000 diamonds encrusted into the grinning skull. The message of death and gem-greed add a fitting and fantastical element to Oscar Slater's murder of Marion Gilchrist. (©Damien Hirst and Science Ltd. All rights reserved/DACS, London/ARS, NY).

CHAPTER 1

The Murder of Marion Gilchrist

In the late 1800s, Oscar Slater (fka Oskar Leschzinger and Leschziner) migrated from Silesia to Scotland along with a great exodus of Jews from eastern Europe. In Glasgow, he connected with two Scottish scammers and fellow indigents, Helen Lambie and Patrick Nugent. The trio conspired to rob an elderly, wealthy lady of her diamonds, and in the course of which burglary, Oscar Slater murdered her in the Christmas season of 1908. All, not some, authors and sleuths who researched the 1909 conviction emphatically supported Oscar Slater's innocence.

The Man Who Showed No Mercy

On the rainy night of December 21, 1908, the assailant's fawn waterproof coat swished as he trod silently into Marion Gilchrist's flat. He walked towards the kitchen, headed directly for the rear dining room door. The wood floor creaked. If he left wet footprints, no one identified nor examined them. After the murder, there were so many wet feet on the premises that the intruder's footprints were lost in the shuffle. His soft cap was pulled down low over his forehead.

The dining room door from which the man entered was to the left of the fireplace. Helen Lambie, the maid, told the police, as she previously informed the intruder, that when she ran out on an errand, Miss Gilchrist had been sitting with her back to the fireplace, reading a magazine. On the table, the maid had left behind a half-sovereign for later errands that evening.

This information was communicated to the intruder before he slipped into the flat at 6:40 p.m. He knew what to expect.

6:45 p.m.---The rear dining room door was to the left of the fireplace. With his right hand, the intruder readied the hammer in his pocket. He bought the hammer on November 10 when he returned to Glasgow. He had intended to land a blow to the back of Miss Gilchrist's head sufficient to stun her. A swift act of a minute. The blow would also have been enough to kill her, but that wasn't his concern. His concern was to render her unconscious while he plundered a locked wooden jewelry box in a spare bedroom. It contained diamonds.

Instead, as the door slowly opened, Marion Gilchrist was standing upright and warming herself before the fire. This was confirmed by the medical examiners. The intruder came face to face with a very tall, very frightened Scottish lady. This would prove the first of his Robbie Burns' surprises.

TO A LOUSE

Oh, would some Power give us the gift
To see ourselves as others see us!
It would from many a blunder free us,
And foolish notion:
What airs in dress and gait would leave us,
And even devotion!

She turned towards him, terrified. Fear does dull the senses. Its effects are indescribable and particularly so when a woman is met by the lethal force of a cutthroat. There is terror as one's body contracts awaiting the worst...pain, inability to ever again see one's family, and death.

There were no screams nor shouts. She gagged. She perceived the end of life. She would have known there would be no goodbyes. She would have felt surrounded by silence, and in her aloneness, she was fated to die at the hands of a virulent poltergeist.

She was elderly and her defenses negligible. She grabbed tight hold of a wooden chair beside her as if she could fend off the madman.

6:50 p.m. to 7 p.m.---He was no less stunned to see her staring wide-eyed. In that instant, what could he do? She had turned towards the door and looked right down into his face. The intruder could not now think of an easy escape. Panic set in. His face was distinctive. She could identify him. He would be done for and led to the gallows.

Instinctively, his reaction was to kill. The defenseless do not inspire fear. Oscar Slater was strong and accustomed to punching and fighting. His life had been punctuated by vicious fistfights.

He turned the hammer to its claw edge, stepped forward, reached up and plunged the hammer into the right side of her face, through her eye and into the skull. In turning towards him from where she stood, the right side of her face was the logical target. He wasn't as tall as the old woman, but the long handle of the hammer allowed an expert reach. As the bloodied and gouged Marion Gilchrist fell backwards, Slater, the hammer, and the chair fell over her. The chair she'd groped for as protection curbed the splatter of blood onto the intruder's clothing. **Thud #1**.

His muffled grunts were unhinged; her torn face, grotesque. Blood gushed. He pushed the chair hard and hammered away at her face, this defenseless old woman, through the skull, through the eyes and mouth, disfiguring her with all his inhumanity, lying heavily atop her body with the chair. **Thud #2**.

Had he sensed a breath of life from the victim? Did he hear a death rattle or the whisper of a remembered prayer? Her pain and her elderliness were meaningless. His malignancy continued. There could be no witness as Lord Guthrie, the judge presiding, would grimly conclude at trial. Slater knelt on that wooden chair, using its legs and his weight to crush the fragile ribs of the 82-year-old. Her breastbone was broken in half. **Thud #3**.

He had been panicked, yes, but tension had built up over the past weeks and he exploded in rage. The plan had been to be swift, certain, and successful. He expected to leave the flat with a cache of diamonds worth thousands.

Marion Gilchrist at death

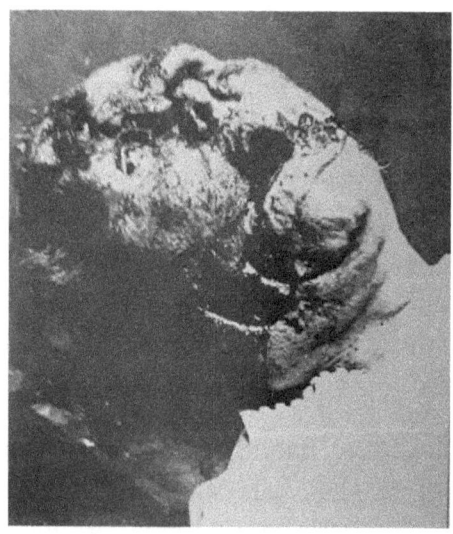

CHAPTER 2

SCOTLAND, THE EMPIRE AND MARION GILCHRIST

In 1897, newspapers the world over touted the pomp and circumstance of Queen Victoria's Diamond Jubilee. Millions of British attended the six-mile procession to see the Empress in an open landau head for Westminster Abbey. With spectacular flourish, the flower of the Empire's colonies and possessions marched alongside—military men from Kabul to Kandahar, Cyprus, Trinidad, Borneo, Natal, and Hong Kong. From the Raj were Sikhs and Malays along with members of the Imperial Camel Corps. The Queen in her resplendent carriage rode slowly through cheering crowds—in an era of "august, unchallenged and tranquil glories" as Winston Churchill proclaimed. Across the sea and the Continent, stretching towards eastern Europe, keening populations of pauperized masses heard the accounts with awe and longing.

Certificate of Queen Victoria's Jubilee

By 1908, the late Queen Victoria's affable, card-playing and libertine son, King Edward VII, had been sitting on the bequeathed throne for seven years. The former Prince of Wales, "Bertie," was crowned monarch at age 59. No more the familial admonitions: *O tempora! O mores!* The new king escorted Great Britain into the Edwardian era and the 20th century. Corsets and collars were relievedly undone due in no small part to Bertie's example of prodigality, gambling (within a tight clique of aristocrats), and deep-sixed scandals. His reputation and habits were not so objectionable to the British public, upending Victorian morality and self-discipline.

Even more defining upheavals rent Queen Victoria's legacy. Social and cultural divides buffeted the kingdom--urban industrialization, income inequality, tenement life, suffragette clamor, and a mass immigration of foreigners, primarily from eastern Europe.

The Empire's diamond mines in South Africa and India brought diamonds to the market in unheard of numbers. People, among them the nouveau riche derided by novelist Anthony Trollope, were able to buy and the women to wear diamonds.

During the heyday of South Africa's diamond discoveries in the mid-1800s—Jews could profit, just not as prospectors, nor god forbid, as owners. Smithing had been a centuries-old Jewish occupation. *My father may have been an Aramean but he was also smithing horses until the assembly line Model T Ford put him out of business.* Whether blacksmithing, or the more advanced skills of smelting, metallurgy and ore analysis, Jewish smiths had long mastered the procedures which took patience, acumen, and rigor. The skill was passed from generation to generation, even in Oscar Slater's Silesia.

Queen Victoria, once she unfurled the velvet curtains to display the vast colonial deposits of diamonds, herself designed a diamond necklace. She wore faithfully the diamond tiara gifted her by Prince Albert, and added it to the Royal Treasury collections for future successors to the monarchy. Her favorite crown, a small purple Imperial crown encrusted with over 1200 diamonds, was placed atop the bier at her funeral procession.

CHAPTER 3

THE WORLD OF OSCAR SLATER

Oscar Slater was a Jewish refugee from Beuthen, a small town in Silesia, a region intermittently under the occupation of rival powers. Intensely anti-Semitic Silesia sat abreast of dysfunctional, anti-Semitic Russia and Poland and militaristic Germany —havens of mobs and fanatical elements. Is it a wonder that individuals bred in this psychotic world would carry in their souls a grim bitterness and melancholia?

Refugees Escape Chaos

In Russia, the tsars ignored civil and humanitarian niceties towards their Jewish subjects, hostages in a nation of historical barbarism. The government, with its armed and mercenary troops, forced conscription, confiscated property, deported populations to the bitter wasteland of Siberia, or caged them within the borders of "the Pale of Settlement," turning a blind eye to the murder of Jews en masse.

The modern usage of "pogrom" is devoid of the calumnies committed against a people who had lived in Russia for centuries. Soldiers converged on Jewish villages in the middle of the night, evicting frightened families from their beds, out of their homes and towns. They savaged mothers, wives and daughters. They hanged rabbis from trees. And it was all countenanced by the Tsarist state soon to be replaced by Stalin, the successor barbarian.

A mighty exodus to freedom began: from Russia, through Poland, then Germany, and, finally, to the portside ships headed for the Baltic and the

North Sea—waves of emigrés as numerous as the cresting waves.

Oscar Slater's Odyssey to Scotland

On the European continent proper, anti-Semitism had been inbred over centuries, learned from childhood in schools, churches, and families, and from state-sponsored restrictive policies. In eastern Europe, Jews lived in *shtetls*, set apart, linguistically, culturally and socially, from the gentile, largely peasant population. Particularly targeted were the *Ostjuden* (Jews from the East)—medieval-garbed strangers said to be taking advantage (at last) long denied them by ancient and petty disabilities: property ownership, licenses, and professional and academic opportunities. A political, ruthless, anti-Jewish enmity met the bewildered Jews fleeing their uneasy lives to settle in Continental cities

In France, *liberté* and *fraternité* confronted their ethnic limitations. Napoleon's intention had been to assimilate his empire's Jews with the 1809 Emancipation Declaration. His Christian public hadn't connected to the absorption. It was content without the emancipated French Jew or the emigrating Jewish refugee.

An assimilated activist, Theodore Herzl detected the malevolent breadth to anti-Semitism, the implacable bigotry, and the hysterics of France's 1894 trial and conviction of Alfred Dreyfus. Germany, too, boasted its Christian bona fides. Belonging to the *Heimland* meant dual devotion to God and to the armed forces. Herzl's radical address in August 1898 before the World Zionist Congress was a call to his people to uproot from the continent of Western and Eastern Europe and to return to the historic Jewish homeland across the Mediterranean. Jews did so, going on the run not so much to Palestine as to Great Britain and to America. Oscar Slater chose Great Britain, beginning with Scotland.

The Dreyfus Dilemma and Oscar Slater

From the outset of Slater's May 1909 trial, writers compared Slater's conviction to France's 1894 Dreyfus case--an example of anti-Semitic falsification with the Gallic nation's endorsement. Fractious the world may have been, and the influx of refugees troubling to homogeneous populations, but the Slater murder trial was not reminiscent of Dreyfus'. Slater wasn't of Alfred Dreyfus' mettle. Though Slater's case took place in Scotland of 1908-1909, the Scottish public had not been braying for a Jew's execution but for the execution of a guilty man who happened to be Jewish. After the conviction and sentencing, the Scottish public took a turn—becoming convinced by renowned authorities that a man had been unjustly convicted because he was Jewish.

Had the Oscar Slater prosecution been provably exhaustive, and had the police investigation preserved evidence and vigorously examined the plot and the participation of Helen Lambie and Patrick Nugent, the conviction of Oscar Slater would not have been open to a hundred years of specious thoughts and prayers.

Scotland's Oscar Slater had dark hair and a mustache. He was well-dressed, and generally wore a bowler hat and gloves. He was not tall but was broad-shouldered. Slater was not targeted by the police and the Crown because he was Jewish nor because he was Jewish-looking. Four days after the murder of Marion Gilchrist, a witness came to the Glasgow police with his suspicion that a fellow gambler, diamond dealer and fence was the murderer. He described him as "a German Jew" named "Oscar." Only then did police supplement what had been appearing in the headlines as a suspect with a crooked nose.

The police gathered descriptions from a healthy supply of witnesses. Impeaching eyewitness testimony is the job of the defense. It proved ineffective in disputing witness descriptions of the distinctive-looking Oscar Slater.

CHAPTER 4

Why Oscar Slater?

"There's the scarlet thread of murder running through the colourless skein of life, and our duty is to unravel it, and isolate it, and expose every inch of it."

A STUDY IN SCARLET
by Arthur Conan Doyle

Pro tempore

Margalit Fox's book, *Conan Doyle for the Defense*, published in 2010, resurrected the miscarriage-of-justice hosanna in the Slater murder conviction.

This book reaches an opposite conclusion. Oscar Slater was guilty of beating an old woman to death with a hammer on December 21, 1908. His motive was a diamond theft from a woman who was a lifelong diamond collector. He had never met the woman. In mid-1908, he learned about the jewelry collection from her maid, Helen Lambie, and her friend, Patrick Nugent, a fellow Glaswegian bookie.

Initially, the furor had been over the Christmas murder of an old lady and the police bureau's delay in catching the criminal. On the day Slater absconded to Liverpool for passage on board the Lusitania for America, Scotland's news headlines had been angry: "Wealthy old lady clubbed to death;" "Shocking Glasgow tragedy;" and "keen and widespread interest, mingled with anxiety, which has been aroused by the brutal murder of Miss Marion Gilchrist at her fireside."

- **Was Oscar Slater wrongfully convicted?** Only so far as an inadequate prosecution. It left people shaking their heads.

- **Was he innocent?** No. Reviewing the incident with attention to Slater's partners, the evidence, the motives, and relevant circumstances should convince the reader.

For a time, the clothing and physical evidence remained in Glasgow Police archival storage. It was not destroyed until 2007. In that time, there could have been even a rudimentary DNA test upon which police in Britain began to rely in 1986.

Photographs of the physical evidence should have been taken and preserved. They weren't. Painfully absent were photographs of the stained fawn waterproof, Slater's stained trousers, and the diamond brooch he pawned. Since then, select archival libraries and museums in Glasgow and the Peterhead Prison Museum took custody of surviving papers and photographs. Physical evidence exists only through the photos, archival reports, and correspondence.

A Welcome Mat for Oscar Slater

Secondary evidence is abundant. Subsequent books and articles followed the blueprint laid by William Roughead, author of *The Oscar Slater Trial Transcripts*, published in 1910, a year after the trial. Slater anticipated a swift reversal as he assured his lady friend, Mademoiselle Andrée, when she last came to visit him in prison December 1909. Roughead too expected a reversal. Stymied, he updated his Oscar Slater book, in 1915, 1925 and then in 1951.

> "I have a pretty soft heart and time and time again, when the judge has put on the black cap

and the condemned man or woman has howled in terror,
I have felt almost sick."
WILLIAM ROUGHEAD

William Roughead portrait, National Gallery of Scotland

William Roughead Esq, Author, , Edward Drummond Young
Creative Commons - CC by NC

Roughead was not a practicing lawyer. His accounts of the Slater trial included his post-trial opinions and unsupported conclusions. He was a trial transcript annotator and condenser. So long as the case was in the news, it likely interested a reader's market. Publication brought income. That he was daily present at Oscar Slater's trial is questionable. He was not photographed in the audience. He had no assigned seat. No personal annotations seasoned his accounts contemporaneously.

Roughead studied law for three years but did not complete the fourth. He did not practice in a courtroom. According to the *Dictionary of National Biography*, Roughead "excelled in that peculiarly Scottish province of the kingdom of letters, the recounting of criminal trials, not as a criminologist, still less as a psychologist but, like Robert Louis Stevenson, as a *tusitala*, a teller of tales."

What is considered in this retelling of the Oscar Slater trial and conviction was Roughead's participation with Detective Lieutenant John Thompson Trench in an ignoble pact to sell books. Was William Roughead so insincere? What were Trench's motives? These deserve light in exposing the "Innocence Campaign" for Oscar Slater.

The Slater case was not Roughead's only iniquitous trial tract. His probity about ethnicity rang hollow. In 1931, he published *Bad Companions* about a case of slander brought by two school mistresses who had been accused in a complaint by an Anglo-Indian student. She described their sexual activity with one another while she, young Jane, was in bed with them, and that this conduct also occurred in another girl's bed. Roughead's estimation was hardly the product of a meticulous law historian. Young Jane Cumming, who was illegitimate, faced racial prejudice. She was understandably hostile towards the British. Had she been the legitimate, fully British granddaughter of Dame Cumming, Jane's story may have been believed by the Edinburgh judges.

Roughead wrote of Jane Cumming as an "evil child," the "Dusky damsel from the East," and that her story about the women teachers was "the black girl's blacker charge." He also chided the child's grandmother for having accepted "as gospel the revelations of the half-caste."

Joyce Carol Oates, in a 1999 essay for the *New York Review of Books* in which she reviewed three books about the murder of Jon Benet Ramsay, wrote this about Roughead:

> "Roughead . . . wrote in a style that combined intelligence, witty skepticism, and a flair for old-fashioned storytelling and moralizing; his accounts of murder cases and trials have the advantage of being concise and pointed, like folk tales..."

Though she cited some of the cases about which Roughead wrote, there was no mention of dishonorable Oscar Slater.

As Roughead began writing his book after the May 1909 trial, he requested court stenographers' transcriptions, interviewed police, solicitors and barristers and the judge himself, Lord Charles Guthrie, and he read the newspaper trial accounts.

Roughead began with an agenda, appropriated from Rabbi Eleazar Phillips who successfully petitioned the King to commute Slater's death sentence. The Rabbi remained unstintingly loyal to Oscar Slater, a lapsed member of the Tribe. No Jew raised in a relatively observant household would commit such a crime.

Roughead and Detective Lieutenant John Trench became as determined as the Rabbi to restore Slater to good odor. Their version was that Glasgow's police force too hurriedly focused on one suspect, Oscar Slater, a poor refugee, haphazardly described by deluded witnesses and police prompting. The substitute theory offered by Roughead and Trench was that in the heat of public sentiment to convict a Jew, police ignored the victim's greedy, dangerous relatives who had a motive to steal from aunt Marion Gilchrist.

Roughead wrote that "a conviction was obtained by the Crown upon identity evidence based on "corroboration supplied by the circumstantial evidence, *though containing elements of strong suspicion...strange and suggestive elements."* (emphasis added). These suspicious and strange and suggestive elements failed to persuade Roughead. He rejected them because they "added nothing conclusive of the prisoner's guilt."

Enter Arthur Conan Doyle

Arthur Conan Doyle, creator of the Great Detective, Sherlock Holmes, became involved in the Slater campaign in 1912, influenced by suddenly famous local author, William Roughead.

Oscar Slater, imprisoned in Peterhead Prison, believed a reversal of his conviction imminent with enough publicity. His warders censored his correspondence. Where law enforcement was concerned, Slater was ever ingenious. In order to get a note to Conan Doyle, Oscar asked a prisoner, who had served his sentence and was leaving the good times behind, to conceal the note within his false teeth. Conan Doyle received this moist plea and was hooked. Peterhead Prison was no less enthusiastic that a man of such preeminence was corresponding with their notorious prisoner.

The tender supplications of a man, confined wrongfully within the stone-cold walls of Peterhead, induced Conan Doyle to work not only for his release, without pay, but to solve the murder as well. He decided that Slater's defense team had been at fault and that Slater was innocent of the murder of Marion Gilchrist. Slater wrote letter after letter expressing his gratitude to Conan Doyle.

Public concern grew with successive headlines about Oscar Slater: "Infamous." "Miscarriage of Justice." "Scandalously Inaccurate." Conan Doyle's participation enervated the public. He published his book about the case and peppered newspapers with articles about the outrage committed against Oscar Slater, a foreigner and a Jew. How could Conan Doyle be in error?

Conan Doyle, positioned into the defensive spot of Oscar Slater's wrongful conviction, turned his attention, justifiably, to Patrick Nugent and his friend, the young housemaid, Helen Lambie. At least Doyle hadn't been gulled by Detective John Trench into accusing Marion Gilchrist's relatives against whom evidence had been imagined and fabricated. Four years after the murder, Doyle wrote that there could be no solution "without Helen Lambie's *confession*" (emphasis added), unambiguously attributing guilt to the insider, the maid Helen Lambie. Neither she nor Patrick Nugent replied to the putatively libelous accusations.

Lambie married and relocated after the trial to Peoria, Illinois. As to Patrick Nugent, Doyle suggested he likely passed information about wealthy Marion Gilchrist in the gambling haunts of Glasgow: the Sauchiehall (pronounced "Sookiehall") streets. It was an area frequented by Slater, a mecca of entertainment with clubs and music halls, dancing girls, pubs, cafes, hot pies, money lenders, and stolen goods.

Philosophizing on Detective Work

Voltaire, philosopher of reason, was obsessed with and disparaged Jews yet applied their misfortune in writing a novella, *Zadig* (1747; Hebr. *tzaddik*, a good man). Parsing biblical accounts, wandering Zadig emerged as a paradigm of reason, a detective and forensic scientist. His journey should have served as a template in 1909 for what was required in a criminal investigation, a prosecution, and so far as post-trial critiquing.

This book's premise is that the identification of the murderer can be drawn from the timeline, the plot, the motive, the parties, and the witnesses—both then and now. Every single one of the Oscar Slater authors was dead wrong. He did it. The police never doubted it. Following Slater's 1927 appeal hearing and his release from prison, and after all his years of support, reality struck Conan Doyle in the pocketbook. A year after Slater's release, London's *Daily Mail* published Doyle's remorseless verdict: ***"Everything he says is a tissue of lies."*** (September 14, 1929).

Oscar Slater's release in 1928 was marked by complacency and indifference about the "unsolved" murder of Marion Gilchrist. On November 13, 1927, in anticipation of what he expected to be a successful appeal hearing for Slater, Conan Doyle published in the *Empire News*: "Who Did Murder Miss Marion Gilchrist?" He couldn't quite say, though he made no secret of his disparagement of Helen Lambie.

CHAPTER 5

Scotland is Nigh

The Victim: Marion Gilchrist

The murder victim was Marion Gilchrist, age 82 (born January 18, 1826). The word "brutally" hardly conveys the shock, battering, pain and suffering endured by a helpless, elder lady.

She was a moneyed spinster, in the legal parlance of the day, and comfortable, thanks to an inheritance left by her father. The money enabled Marion to collect jewelry, her particular, expensive passion. As was customary among the Victorians, she wore jewels throughout her life befitting her dignified attire. She may have drawn inspiration from only-daughter, jewel-bedecked Lizzie Greystock of *The Eustace Diamonds* written by Anthony Trollope in 1873.

When Marion made purchases, she dealt with established jewelry shops, one of which was owned by William Sorley who was her primary jeweler. Sorley would testify for the Crown at Oscar Slater's trial.

She attended St. John's United Free Church services on St. George's Road, walking the short distance from her residence. It was one of the oldest Free Churches in Glasgow, dating to 1845. In 1905, it advanced a strong anti-gambling campaign in response to the street traffic and betting shops littering the streets that crisscrossed the Church, including St. George's Road, St. George's Square, Sauchiehall Street and further.

Marion may have joined the hurly burly who walked around the park of St. George's Square, named for King George III, where the giant monument to Sir Walter Scott dominated the skyline outside the Central railroad station.

She kept dental appointments, made regular bank deposits, and met with her solicitor and her stockbroker. She went shopping. When she stopped at Sorley's in March 1908, she also did some banking. She may have paused for tea at the Ingram Street Tearoom, a newly established business created by Catherine Cranston who opened dining for unaccompanied women. Surprisingly, it was Glasgow that set the standard for British tearooms.

Until her murder, December 21, 1908, Marion lived in a large flat of seven rooms on the second floor of 15 Queens Terrace. It was a peaceful and quiet community. Her neighbors were stockbrokers, dentists, lawyers, and other respectable Scots.

Her flat fulfilled the era's Victorian credentials with antiques, dark wood furniture, horsehair chairs, oil paintings, figurines, animal rugs and sterling silver tableware used in the bygone days of luncheons and dinner parties. Even the curtains were ornate, decorated with jeweled butterflies. One author, Richard Whittington-Egan, charmlessly titled a chapter of his book, *The Oscar Slater Murder Story: New Light On a Classic Miscarriage of Justice*, "Blood on the Antimacassar," as if the "unsolved" murder were a cozy mystery: An antimacassar, a Victorian lace doily, was placed atop furniture to protect it from oily hair. The blood in this case splashed, spattered and dripped from the battered body of Marion Gilchrist.

Gaslight was laid throughout so the flat was well lit. The kitchen played a minor role in the murder. There was a coal-fired kitchen stove, a sink and wooden fittings on which to hang laundry. The kitchen window lent a modicum of light. The fireplace was a necessity. Scottish air was heavy with dampness. It leached through walls and windows and seeped into the hardy bones of Scotland's citizens.

The Dining room –oil paintings hang on all the walls. Above the mantlepiece is a large portrait of the young Marion Gilchrist.

After all her years in the community, there was a quiet acquaintance and recognition of Miss Gilchrist. She was a walker and a shopper. People—or, more likely, the housemaids-- gossiped about Marion's money, family, and jewelry. Helen Lambie chatted up a maid from across the street, keeping her informed about the treasures in the house and the relatives who visited.

St. George's Square—Honoring Scotland's Luminaries

Poet Robert Burns' statue stands at St. George's Square. Sir Walter Scott's towering statue dominates.

GLASGOW GEORGE SQUARE AND MUNICIPAL BUILDINGS.

The poet "Rabbie" Burns was Scotland's hero, celebrated annually, revered as well by Jewish citizens who referred to him as Rabbi Burns. Sir Walter Scott, author of romantic historical fiction, described Scottish defenders as brave, lusty, tartan-clad Highlanders. If Slater supporters believed that anti-Semitism convicted him, they hadn't read nor appreciated *Ivanhoe* and its Jewish heroine, Rebecca, whose patience and resolve united two foreign races.

Marion Gilchrist attended services regularly and was a reliable spoke in St. John Free Church's philanthropic efforts. St. John's minister said of her that she had a kindly smile which came from a kindly heart. Like many of the old Scottish ladies, she lived her religion rather than spoke of it.

At her funeral services on December 25, neighbors and fellow congregants mourned in a great chorus about God's goodness and mercy. They wept and wondered why He had been absent at the hour of Marion's greatest need. No telling where He was for the 120 years that Marion's murder went unsolved. Her urn of cremated ashes was situated atop the Gilchrist family tombstone in the mossy Necropolis cemetery. Here, Druid priests once worshipped trees and sacrificed criminals by burning them alive in a human-like wicker cage.   -

CHAPTER 6

The Gilchrist Jewelry

In Marion Gilchrist's collection were gems in every hue: sapphires, emeralds, garnets (her birthstone), rubies, pearls and opals. Surprisingly, though saltwater pearls were the bounty of the Indian Ocean, Scotland was also a source of freshwater pearls whiter in hue. For a time, pearls were even more expensive than diamonds. These too were collected by Marion.

King Edward and Queen Alexandra hosted balls where guests in their finery made the palace sparkle almost as much as the Queen's jewels. The Queen, among the most beautiful of princesses, often wore a unique pearl "dog's collar" necklace or a sapphire and diamond brooch given her by the King as wedding gifts or an act of contrition. She was admired for her sense of style and women imitated the trends she set. The monarchy may have glittered in riches and jewels, but for low-rent characters in Glasgow, riches led to a hearth and security.

Primarily, Marion purchased diamonds. Diamond necklaces, diamond rings, diamond brooches, diamond bracelets and diamond pendants. In the Edwardian age, diamonds were in high demand, in lace-like gold designs to show off the stones. Oh, how her jewels lit the fire of desire in the dead hearts of tricksters come to call. A vapid trio, for whom diamonds meant, not fashion nor status, but riches...decided, like Othello, to "Put out the light, and then put out the light."

Even more intriguing and unexplored in the investigation and in the surplus of Slater books was a tray of diamonds discovered by the police "in a hidden corner" of the Gilchrist flat two weeks after her murder.

Detective-Inspector John Pyper confirmed that a large cache of jewels was found in the flat. Police had eagerly continued to search for weeks after the murder, as if they knew there were diamonds not yet uncovered. Or, they did so before the Inventory Appraiser, David Dick, began his job of collection, valuation, and the filing of an official report.

Marion Gilchrist, age 80. She wears a fur-lined coat and a fine fur hat with a filigreed, heart-shaped brooch attached.

Miss Marion Gilchrist

According to Helen Lambie's testimony, whenever Miss Gilchrist went out, whether on visits, shopping, or tea, she wore jewelry. She wore rings on both hands. When Miss Gilchrist went out for tea, "she would wear a better brooch." Thus, there was more than one brooch.

Introducing Two Evidentiary Brooches

Included in Miss Gilchrist's treasure chest were several diamond-encrusted brooches. The significance of the two brooches associated with the murder was misunderstood by the police and the prosecution.

The police erroneously concluded that a brooch pawned by Slater with Liddell's Pawnbrokers on November 18, 1908, a month before the murder, belonged to him. As such, it wouldn't be returned to the estate of Marion Gilchrist for distribution. It left one wondering whether after the trial the brooch at Liddell's came into the possession of yet another slippery fellow.

The prosecution never produced two diamond brooches into evidence at trial. Nor did it establish ownership and whereabouts--which lay at the heart of the conflicted charges and trial. Miss Gilchrist's jeweler of 20 years, William Sorley, testified about the "substantial in size" diamonds in Brooch #1. Slater began selling small diamonds immediately upon his return to Glasgow in October 1908. This evidence was omitted. The inference here propounded is that Helen Lambie gave one of Marion Gilchrist's diamond brooches (Brooch #1) to Patrick Nugent and Oscar Slater. Slater, the master fence, removed the diamonds from the brooch, and sold them each separately that October.

If, as Helen Lambie and Jane Duff Wilson testified that Miss Gilchrist had few visitors, how was it that two brooches (#1 and #2) became the essence of the case within the space of the two months that Slater found his way back to Glasgow?

No reckoning of the physical two brooches having been made, and no investigation of a tray of hidden diamonds or a missing diamond necklace having been undertaken, still the Procurator-Fiscal and Glasgow police decided to proceed against Oscar Slater as the murderer of Marion Gilchrist with no convincing motive.

Following this lead, William Roughead and successive authors accepted the prosecution's theory that a jewelry heist hadn't been the motive for the murder. Only one brooch was reportedly thefted that night—the brooch with one row of diamonds (Brooch #1). Other jewelry was left behind by the murderer.

Conan Doyle and the assembly of Oscar's crime-solving authors ascribed the motive as solely one of murder. In so restricting the motive, Slater's connection to the crime was axed; there was no evidence he knew Marion Gilchrist and no reason to enter her flat and murder her.

Not the authors, nor the police and Crown poked holes in the shell game of the brooches in which Lambie participated, as an accomplice in the crime, misleading the police the day after the murder.

BROOCH #1 – a-crescent-shaped brooch with 1 row of diamonds.

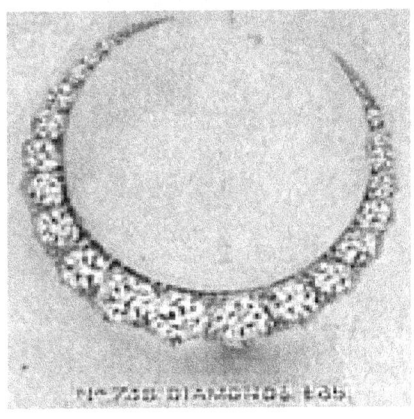

Brooch #1 was the brooch that Marion Gilchrist's housemaid, Helen Lambie, reported to police the day after the murder as the one stolen. That is, her concoction was that the murderer brutalized Miss Gilchrist in order to steal one brooch. Brooch #1 was never located though police scoured Glasgow's pawnbrokers. At Slater's trial, William Sorley produced the above sketch of a lookalike brooch from a catalog. It was the brooch, he said, that he cleaned for Marion Gilchrist in March 1908. He testified she had no other brooches but that brooch with one row of diamonds. This was alarmingly unsupported testimony which will be further discussed.

Brooch #2 Formal portrait of a young Marion Gilchrist wearing a brooch, with 3 rows of diamonds in a circle, pinned to the center collar of her dress. She wears 3 rings and in her hair she wears a jeweled pin. The lace mantilla was in vogue.

Look closely at that brooch pinned to the neck of the dress. The formal photograph is of a young Miss Gilchrist circa 1875. She adorned her mantilla around this brooch—a circle of three rows of diamonds each encased separately in gold. Was this the brooch pawned by Oscar on November 18, a month before the murder? It did not appear in the inventory of her collection taken after her murder.

William Sorley testified that the police and the Liddell Pawnshop clerk brought to his shop for identification Brooch #2, the brooch with three rows of diamonds (the one that appears in the photograph of Marion Gilchrist, above). Sorley testified that Brooch #2 was not the same one as Brooch #1 of the catalog sketch. He further believed that Brooch #2 couldn't have been Miss Gilchrist's because she...a collector...owned only the one brooch.

An inventory of her jewelry in preparation for trial clearly disputed Sorley's recollection. The list drafted after the murder by David Dick, Auctioneer and Valuator, revealed a number of jeweled brooches still remaining in her collection.

Marion Gilchrist's Jewelry Inventory, May 1909

Gold bracelet.

Silver card case.

Morocco manicure case.

Silver necklace, brooch and earrings.

Silver solitaires.

Pair gold eyeglasses and chain.

Brass button hook.

Lace pin.

Curb bangle.

Gold bangle with pendant.

Half hoop ring with 5 diamonds.

Half hoop ring with 6 emeralds.

Half hoop ring with 5 sapphires.

Half hoop ring with 5 rubies.

Scent bottle with silver top.

Silver guard and pencil case.

Pair gold spectacles.

Rope of pearls.

Set 3 diamond star brooches.

Gold onyx pearl and diamond brooch.

Gold onyx pearl and diamond bracelet.

Lace brooch and pair earrings with topaz.

Small ring with diamond and rubies, and gold enamelled ring.

Gold bangle with 3 rubies.

Gold watch with black dial, and albertina and seals.

Single stone gipsy ring with diamond.

Gold bangle, 9 carat.

Signet ring.

Two keeper rings.

Pair gold sleeve links.

Emerald and diamond ring.

Ruby and diamond ring.

Pair diamond earrings.

Circular diamond brooch pendant.

Diamond necklace.

Two pairs gold earrings.

Gold catch with diamonds.

Pair gold solitaires.

Thin gold eyeglass chain.

Two small plain gold rings.

Gold keeper ring.

Cameo brooch with gold mounts.

Two silver bracelets.

Silver pebble brooch.

Gent's gold watch with gold fob, seal, and key.

Florentine brooch with gold mounts.

Gold-mounted brooch with hair.

Pair gold eyeglasses.

Silver shaving brush holder.

Pair pearl and onyx earrings and small brooch.

Gold bangle with pearl and turquoise.

Garnet and ruby lace brooch, "arrow."

Pearl and ruby brooch.

Gold eyeglasses.

Gold necklace with onyx, pearl, and diamond pendant.

Pair cameo earrings with gold mounts

Two diamond bracelets

SUM £1382.12.0

For a woman who collected jewelry and diamonds for nearly 60 years, too few items appeared in the inventory. Itemized valuations of each piece of jewelry was omitted, as, for example, the number of carats in the diamonds--a probability that the inventory was significantly undervalued.

Even more troubling was Miss Gilchrist's niece's objection. She said her aunt owned a diamond necklace with "diamonds the size of peas" which matched the two inventoried diamond bracelets. Even a small, one-carat diamond was worth a £1,000, such as those small diamonds sold separately by Oscar when he arrived back in Glasgow in October 1908. The diamond necklace was not in the inventory. Nor was a diamond brooch in the shape of a bird. Diamond jewelry was suspiciously missing. Either the jewelry had been stolen during Lambie's employ or the jewelry disappeared after the murder and before Dent's inventory

Only two emeralds remained in the inventory. A month before the murder, Oscar wrote to his diamond dealing colleague, David Jacobs, that he suddenly had the inside track on emerald sales to Ireland.

Marion had been especially conscientious about her collection and her estate because she intended to leave a generous portion to her former maid and lifelong friend, Marion Galbraith Ferguson, and her family. Mrs. Marion Ferguson left Miss Gilchrist's employ when she married Alex Ferguson. Miss Gilchrist treated Mrs. Ferguson's children as her own grandchildren. The friendship was a close one over many years. Both visited each other's homes until Miss Gilchrist's death.

CHAPTER 7

Dramatis *Personae*

The Partners: 1. Oscar Slater

He was born Oskar Jozef Leschziner (*lesh zinner*) aka Leschzinger, Jan. 8, 1872 in Opole, Silesia and raised in the town of Beuthen in Upper Silesia (of Prussia/Germany/Poland). The family was Jewish but in stages of assimilation which would not save them in years to come. They were not of the bourgeoisie. They were Germans of the Jewish faith.

His father, Adolf Leschzinger, was a baker but disabled, and his mother, Pauline, was a housewife. Adolf was an observant Jew. In Pauline's prison letters to Slater, she wrote of Adolf's daily prayers and of his uttering a *bracha* (blessing) whenever he uttered his son's name. In the "Oscar-was-innocent" narratives, it was repeated that Slater regularly sent money to his parents. The only support for his filial generosity was a £5 note sent December 24, 1908 as he arranged his shipboard scuttle to America.

His brother, Georg, was presumably converted, enabling him to buy land and to prosper. Neither father nor brother wrote to Slater in prison. Of his two sisters, Malchen, a Yiddish diminutive for Amalie and Euphemia, nicknamed "Phemie," it was Phemi who took up correspondence with him in 1919. She said before her parents' deaths, she did not have permission to write. Slater's parents and Georg died before 1919 while Oscar was still in Peterhead prison. Years after Slater's release, both his sisters would meet their end in the death camps.

He would have attended cheder as young Jewish boys did because his father was devout, and at 13, been bar mitzvahed at the massive synagogue built in 1869 and which stood in the Friedrich Wilhelm Platz. Polish schools were restricted to Catholic Slavs, so German was the Leschziner family's spoken language, sprinkled with Yiddish and Hebrew.

Oscar was educated by Jewish academicians at the high school in Beuthen for Jewish boys who, at 18, were expected to graduate and move on to university, usually in Berlin. Oscar would have studied German, history, geography, the sciences and mathematics. Athletics were rigorous and competitive which would account for Slater's robust fitness. Oscar excelled as a sharp shooter. In the distant future, at a street shooting parlor in Scotland, he won a competition with a near-perfect score. Religious studies would have accounted for Oscar's truancy, and, finally, his taking leave.

In the old country, Jews were barred from land ownership. They worked in small shops as merchants, tailors, cobblers, blacksmiths, and an enviable concern, that of diamond dealer. Jewels were the assets of choice--portable, easily hidden and put in a sack when Jews were sent on the run. Oscar apprenticed with an uncle in the diamond trade, learning to cut, polish and shape precious stones and to distinguish quality. Though Oscar learned to shape diamonds, even more promising was his talent at resetting. This was an intricate process which required removing a gem from its old setting and replacing it into a new one. It hid the origin, making it particularly marketable for an underworld fence. However, shaping gemstones required weeks of dedicated cutting. There were countless hours of whirring instruments and inhaling dust in a stifling storefront. It did not suit. The diamond's glitter and its financial promise were no less provocative than the garish flavor of the underworld. These two allurements defined Oscar Slater.

In 1893 at age 21, Oscar Leschziner emigrated, taking the Prussian fast train to Hamburg. He never again set eyes on his family nor on his birthplace, shaking off the garb of a poor Jewish émigré, wearing a flat, German-military style cap, a coarse-haired suit and leather shoes handmade by the local cobbler.

In life, he would continue to swear by his Germanness, never his Jewishness, though he kept his landsmen close and gentiles at a distance. For a while in prison, with a supportive Rabbi, Slater inclined to his Judaic self. He reflected upon it in correspondence with Jewish lawyers, reporters and authors. This way, he kept these dedicated souls close to the Slater Innocence Campaign.

In his prison letters as well as those after his release, Oskar demonstrated his facility in languages. He was acceptably handy in written English and German, with an ample vocabulary. He even took up the study of languages in prison.

In 1893, Hamburg was a hugely successful, tax-free, democratic, self-governing, commercial region of Germany. Ships docked from every global port to store the world's commodities in Hamburg's warehouses...rubber, coffee and spices, to name a few, and portside, hordes of refugees.

Oscar Leschziner was transitioning from the small town barter economy to a money society...a consumer society. He found work as a bank teller, a stable but monotonous job. A bank teller was an important position putting Oscar into a special class of Germany's civil servants. He would have had to provide proof of graduation, serve three-months of provisional training, and then sit for an exam. The trouble lay in evading conscription, there in the heart of Germany. Oscar had no desire to be baptized nor to wear a spiked helmet in Wilhelm's army. Men by the thousands emigrated from Germany rather than serve in the Kaiser's military adventures.

From bank teller, Oscar Leschziner gravitated toward crooked alleyways and street commerce as bookie and gem peddler—an independent world of tricksters and rats. But rats begat flies and flies begat plague. The plague came in the form of violence, assaults, brothel-keeping, thieving, police surveillance, arrests, courts and lawyers. He became an inveterate law breaker with a streak of violence.

Hamburg *Flohmarkt*

Where Oskar preferred to fence and sell his gems was within the camaraderie and possibilities at Gentlemen's clubs. Membership, however, was not so easily acquired for a young man of 21 or 22 who said he was German but looked very Jewish.

Hamburg Gentleman's Club

Hamburg was overrun by prostitutes as well as by guardians of the "native" people, the German Morals Police. Prostitutes and pimps changed addresses several times in a year to elude charges and arrest. Oscar Leschziner routinely resorted to this gambit in keeping police at bay.

The police in Hamburg, with hundreds of pimps in the city, found it impossible to curb their activities. The commercial entertainment, cheap concert halls, cafes, beer cellars, and the rundown Alley Quarter kept the police at nonstop enforcement of the women and their pimps. The public demanded action but regulation and criminal penalties proved ineffective. By 1895, there was a national call for corporal punishment for convicted criminals. A more emphatic anti-Semitism appeared in newspapers. This was the year Oscar Leschziner chose to leave Hamburg.

Auf Wiedersehen Hamburg. Oscar Relocates to Great Britain

In 1895, Oscar Leschziner left Hamburg, joining his landsmen (fellow Jews) emigrating on steamer ships from a calamitous eastern Europe. This ancient Jewish community would vanish from history in the coming years. Oscar debarked at the port of Lieth in Edinburgh, Scotland. He was not quite fluent in the English language which he spoke with a discernible foreign accent and had a foreign look about him. His declaration upon disembarking was that he was fleeing conscription from the German army—Britain's sworn enemy. It made perfect sense.

New quays accommodated the shipping traffic and thousands of refugees. In the distance from the port rose Arthur's Seat, a great hump of green hill sitting atop a long dormant volcano. Here at the Picts' ancient marshes, Oscar Leschziner set foot and there and then anglicized the spelling of his given name of "Oskar" to "Oscar."

Edinburgh, where Conan Doyle was born in 1859 and educated, was a city of horse-drawn carriages, tartan kilts, bagpipe players, ruddy Scots faces, sharp wits, strong whisky, and the smell of distilleries in the air. Crammed with residents and tourists, it was never too early (nor late) to duck inside a pub or whisky bar. The town was a natural byway for tourists on the windy path to the pure, invigorating air of the Scottish Highlands or the Firth of Forth.

Leith, Edinburgh shore outside the harbor

Scottish Highlanders

Visitors in the city of *Auld Reekie* were bested with an olfactory miasma off the port and the waters of Lief that competed with the land odors of malt and yeast from its breweries and distilleries. Edinburgh's living space, enclosed in fortress walls, was built upwards. Consequently, the odoriferous was trapped making it a most stink-filled city.

Oscar lived in Edinburgh for a brief year during which he revived his Hamburgian livelihood as gambler and procurer. He was an excellent billiards player. Billiard rooms were frequented by men with considerable cash and thus a hypnotic target for bookmakers. Slater's slippery habits with gambling and betting left him feeling insecure in a yet strange city. He took to walking the streets with two great boarhounds, the sort of mastiffs trained to hunt boars and wild pigs as well as to guard German noblemen. He preferred the aggressive stance. He was German in all respects save one.

Oscar Slater, 1895, seated on rattan—a fashionable import from the colonies; nose unsullied.

In a formal portrait, a youthful Oscar Slater bears the mien of a sophisticated gentleman. No pouches under his eyes. Not a strand of his thick black hair out of place. Beneath his stylish mustache, he smiles with the confidence of a cat who ate the canary. His shirt and three-piece suit are immaculate. He is not yet wearing a watch.

In Edinburgh, sooner than later, Slater made hazardous acquaintance with the police to whom he'd identified himself, at first, as Oscar Schmidt. The police knew him as a pimp whose main girl was Annie Hansen. They lived together as a married couple at his house of prostitution. The assumed marital relationship was a front to prevent charges that the residence was a brothel.

In April 1896, Slater took a breather from Edinburgh and left for Great Britain's capital. Train service throughout Britain was efficient and cheap. Trains had little in the way of competition since roads, built for country travel, were slow and in poor condition. Trains raced with breakneck speed alongside wild moorland, green hills and slopes o'erstepped by time and upon which strode kilted shepherds with their crooks, flocks and collie dogs. Slater may have taken pastoral notice but his greater interest was drawn to the green site of a sporting preserve.

He took great pleasure in this new reality. There were no constrictions, no barriers, no policing of travelers. Freedom led Slater to bold and unlawful extravagances. What souvenir did Slater bequeath London upon his arrival? On April 10, a charge of the malicious wounding of fellow Yidden, Isaac Levy, over a betting dispute. There is no record of Levy appearing at trial and thus Slater was acquitted. The court took judicial notice that Levy's bone-crushing fist left Slater with a permanent reminder of the incident--a disfigured nose.

In 1899, he traveled back to Edinburgh. Around June 6, Annie Hansen reported him to the police, telling of Slater's violent temper and having beaten her and blackened her face. Slater had a predilection for smashing a woman's face; its softness attracted a pummeling. Annie did not show for court.

On November 4, 1899, Slater was arrested for being drunk and disorderly in a brawl over cheating in a gambling hall. In another charge, involving his assault of a police officer, Slater was a no-show. Slater was unafraid. He ignored the courts and the police and simply moved away. Packing his luggage was habitual and efficient.

With the growth of a refugee and an underworld population, police duties included walking neighborhood streets to become familiar with criminals by sight. Otherwise, police had few reliable ways of verifying identities. When a suspect was arrested, more often than not, he would give out an alias. If a policeman began to recognize the comings and goings of a particular thug, it was preferable that the target change his residence before giving police the opportunity.

Slater returned to London. He didn't live in its overcrowded slums such as London's Whitechapel where needy prostitutes trolled the streets (a number of whom, in 1888, fell victim to Jack the Ripper/Aaron Kosminski; "An Indisputable Jack the Ripper Identification," by Brenda Rossini).

Slater lived in fashionable, commercial areas. There, his ladies of pleasure and their customers were comparatively safe from interference. Among his London addresses was 41-45 Newman Street, Marylebone, a terracotta building of elegant flats refurbished by the Scottish-born architect, John Slater—a surname Oscar assumed.

The building led to a side cobblestone alley, Newman Passage, through which narrow thoroughfare a higher standard prostitute could saunter. Or, she and Slater might venture into a hotel where she could steal anything of value from the wardrobes or cafes and vanish with him into the night and the alleys.

Oscar Leschziner became Oscar Slater. Leschziner was difficult to pronounce for native English speakers. "Slater" smoothed a business transaction, even though most took place across the green baize of a gaming or billiards table.

Slater may have enjoyed a leisurely smoke beneath the Doric columns of 44 Newman Street, elegantly suited and coiffed, musing over the evening business. A Yiddish proverb could not have been far from his thoughts: "When you have money in your pocket, you are wise, you are handsome, and you sing well too."

Across the square from Slater's London flat stood another improbable foreign import: *La Guillotine*, a beheading machine. It had been repainted from satanic black to the patriotic French colors of blue, white, and red, and donated to Great Britain once executions were done: impassive and armed with a blade that held human life so cheap.

Oscar Slater and the Jewelry Trade

During 1901 and 1905, Slater traveled a great deal between Glasgow and London. In London, he'd met Max Rattman, aka George Schmidt (to Slater's aka, Oscar Schmidt) at The Travellers Society, 12 Denmark Street, a club off Charing Cross where the two gambled. In England, the "travelers" nomenclature applied to gypsies, seasonal folk who passed through towns in horse-drawn carriages. In every country, the public considered them thieving menaces. Max eventually relocated to Glasgow after serving a fraud-related term in a London prison. He would testify as Slater's friend and alibi witness in the May 1909 murder trial.

Slater did business with London jewelry dealer, Robert Rogers of 36 Albemarle Street. He used that address for a business card that read "dentist A. Anderson." Another business card was for "Oscar Slater, Dealer in Diamonds and Precious Stones. 33 Soho Square, Oxford Street, W." A gentile pseudonym carried a respectable cachet. Business cards were an important part of an operation. When his gems traded hands, the business card pledged an agreed price and authenticity of the article.

Slater was a fence and back-door dealer of gems. He didn't have a jewelry shop and he didn't sell jewelry from behind a glass case. He passed around gems likely wrapped in a handkerchief. He also dealt through brokers, fences, and other dealers.

Slater became well-enough versed in the English language that he wrote business and personal letters, signed leases, opened savings accounts, read horse racing tip sheets, bought ship tickets, and signed hotel registries. It was nonsense of authors like Thomas Toughill to characterize Oscar Slater as a rude Jewish peasant who could "barely read English."

The Art of the Jewelry Deal

Slater was an aggressive salesman, cultivating contacts in the resetting, brokering, or fencing of jewelry in New York, London, Edinburgh and Glasgow. A gem salesman like Slater would be excessively attentive to the well-heeled stranger, offering him a cigarette from his gold cigarette case and a drink, and putting before him, in a pressed handkerchief, a gem or a small diamond. A gem's provenance wasn't part of an under-the-table deal. One presumed Slater dealt in gems of questionable derivation. His eyes were dark, but they could calculate clearly the gentlemen he would choose as his customers as well as partners for his ladies, the "penny-joes" of the evening.

Slater brokered diamonds and high-end "colored" gemstones (trade jargon for precious stones other than diamonds). He knew value and set the selling price. He re-cut, re-set, and then redistributed for sale. Resetting legerdemain was useful in order to eliminate the engraved inscriptions on the gold or platinum encasing the stones.

"Hallmarks" were inscribed into the metal of jewelry to establish authenticity. This compulsory mark would be struck by an accredited goldsmith prior to the display and sale of the jewelry.

On December 26, 1908, what if anything did Liddell's Pawnbrokers, the police, and William Sorley observe on the brooch pawned by Slater on November 18? Marion Gilchrist's jewelry would not have borne hallmarks. The marks were not made compulsory until the 1920s. Thus, it was important that a purchaser, such as Marion Gilchrist, a serious collector of many years, should feel confident in a jeweler's reputation. He could never be a man from off the street.

At times, Slater sold individual stones. These were generally not of interest to women who preferred fashionably designed jewelry with an exclusive metal... gold. Gold was *noble par excellence* and incorruptible.

The individual stones in Miss Gilchrist's horseshoe-shaped/crescent brooch with one row of diamonds (Brooch #1) were separately sold--a more profitable gambit than selling the intact brooch. The gold in which the brooch's gems were encased were repurposed and the cast-off gold setting sold by Slater to another dealer.

Gems were costly, diamonds even more so. How did Slater buy them? Or own them? At the time he was charged with the murder, Slater's claimed jewelry collection included **1.** the diamond brooch he pawned on November 18, and **2.** a gold watch which demanded constant repairs, and which, lacking cash, he had to use to pay his lawyers.

Life in Glasgow

Glasgow, Scotland's biggest city lay on the Firth of Clyde. The River Clyde was among the deepest of the Britain's coastal waters, and portside were streams of merchant ships, fishermen, and sailors. Glasgow was no longer a shipping hub nor commercial force of the British Empire though it once had been rich on the sugar and tobacco imported from the colonies.

One would presume that Scotland's big cities promised comforts to the underclasses who worked in the distilleries, factories and mines. What the poor found instead was tenement life, overcrowding, long work hours, and disease. County Lanarkshire in Glasgow was known as the Black Country. Here were the coal mines and coal production. The miner's working conditions were very, very hard and their families suffered along with the breadwinner. People lived in view and breath of the coal ash and smoky emissions from the stone quarries, satanic mills, and factory chimneys.

What Oscar Slater looked for and found in Glasgow of the 1900s—as he did in London and in Edinburgh—was a large working class from which prostitution emerged and thus the growth of the city's entertainment and gambling district.

Had he the inclination to open a shop and do business across a counter? Conceivably, it may have been complicated to open shop as a Jew. It was also likely that Slater lacked the inventory, the credit, and the reputation. A jeweler's reputation was everything. In Glasgow, there was a jewelry shop located at St. Enoch Square, the "James McMenamin Jewelers." It was in fact owned by Jewish Philip Margolyes but kept acceptably Scottish and legitimate by its shop name.

Trust wasn't a word used to describe Slater in any of his history. It was Slater's lack of trustworthiness that kept him a *persona non grata* at certain Gentlemen's clubs such as Glasgow's Sloper Club or the Motor Club. His Scottish acquaintance, Hugh Cameron, the Sauchiehall area "Moudie," had to intercede on Slater's behalf for membership. To have a poor reputation limited Slater's market. But, as discussed below, a criminal defendant's character—such as his lack of trustworthiness—

could not be used at a murder trial. There were exceptions.

Slater also pawned or sold accoutrements. Edwardian gentlemen wore jeweled finery such as gold stickpins, cuff links, rings, watches and chains. They carried engraved cigarette cases, snuff boxes, or the invariable medal. These were easy targets for a femme partner at a dancing hall or while in mutual déshabillé. The pimp lurked in the background, perhaps even within the room. He could leap out and beat and rob the customer. If the woman wasn't sufficiently proficient, the pimp might maltreat her as well. Coins, if pilfered by the ladies, or those with which a gent paid for a lady's services, went into Slater's pockets.

Slater's prosperity was a fickle partner, requiring constant care and feeding, yet he was able to avoid creditors and court fines, traveled, and kept himself and his ladies housed, fed, and costumed.

Was Slater's rootless lifestyle a credential for labeling him a murderer of an elderly woman? It is difficult to give him a measure of doubt. Look to his degenerate, aggressive manner towards women, his assembly of schemes to obstruct the police investigation: the brooch at Liddell's, the reconnaissance of the Gilchrist neighborhood, the false business ventures, or the meticulous breaking-and-entry during Helen Lambie's errand run. The squalor of his life defined him. It was preparation enough for this crime. One cannot be remotely tolerant towards such a menace.

PAWNBROKERS

Slater's particular pawnbroker—one who figured in the pawn of a brooch with three rows of diamonds in November 1908—was Alex J. Liddell, 8 Sauchiehall Street. Pawn shops operated close to the pubs and gambling houses where customers were losing money or trying to raise some. In wry symbolism, three gold balls hung outside pawnbroker shops. They were meant to honor St. Nicholas who helped three poor young maidens—who could have been forced into prostitution-- with three bags of gold to find suitors. For the streetwalkers of Sauchiehall, the same legend held out hope.

Sauchiehall Street

Pawnbrokers were essential to Slater's business. A reliable one handled stolen goods and was close-mouthed. There were scores of pawnbrokers but Liddell's was Slater's choice.

Glasgow's pawnbrokers were often harangued by regulators and constables. Officials could be no less devious than thieves who off-loaded merchandise with a pawnbroker. The rule of pawnbroker play was that once a pledge was made, and a cash-draw loaned to the customer, and the item was not redeemed within a fixed number of days, that item belonged to the pawnbroker. Slater took no action as he prepared his escape to New York after the murder. He had no money. If his lady friend, Mademoiselle Andrée, had any ownership interest, she made no attempt to redeem it. The only conclusion that can be made about the brooch (Brooch #2) was that Liddell kept it. Rightfully, it belonged to the Gilchrist estate.

Edwardian Gentlemen's Clubs

Ronald Adair was fond of cards -- playing continually, but never for such stakes as would hurt him. He was a member of the Baldwin, the Cavendish, and the Bagatelle card clubs. It was shown that, after dinner on the day of his death, he had played a rubber of whist at the latter club. He had also played there in the afternoon. The evidence of those who had played with him-Mr. Murray, Sir John Hardy, and Colonel Moran -- showed that the game was whist, and that there was a fairly equal fall of the cards. Adair might have lost five pounds, but not more. His fortune was a considerable one, and such a loss could not in any way affect him. He had played nearly every day at one club or other, but he was a cautious player, and usually rose a winner. It came out in evidence that, in partnership with Colonel Moran, he had actually won as much as four hundred and twenty pounds in a sitting, some weeks before, from Godfrey Milner and Lord Balmoral.

The Adventure of the Empty House by Arthur Conan Doyle

The Life of a Gambler

In one of London's gambling halls, Slater met Mary Curtis Pryor, a

Scotswoman born in America, also a prostitute and alcoholic. In 1901, the two set out for Glasgow which offered a wider variety of entertainment during Glasgow's Great Exhibition (May 2 to November 9, 1901). Two railway centers made Glasgow accessible to Britons and tourists. Rival trains occasionally indulged in races at top speed along two different trunk lines to the delight of passengers, gamblers, and the press.

It was also in 1901 in Glasgow that Hugh Cameron testified he first met Oscar Slater. He knew him as a fellow bookie and gambler, but also a gem cutter and dealer. Though Slater lived in the same Glasgow vicinity as he would in late 1908, he had no connection in the earlier years to Marion Gilchrist. Helen Lambie did not begin work for Miss Gilchrist until late in 1906.

Cameron carried a title, that of "Moudie," Scottish for "molecatcher" brought into Scottish folklore by Robert Burns' "Moudiewort." Like the molecatcher who made a living working for farmers, the Sauchiehall Moudie monitored gamblers, recommending for membership those who were reliable, and if not, in the style of the fur-fixated molecatcher— ended the efforts below ground *where no one could hear them scream.*

Cameron also held the role of Master in card rooms, holding the bank when stakes were made and assuring there was ready money behind bets. He scrutinized players and bettors for their worth. He customarily wore a gold-buttoned, heavy frock coat befitting his prominent position, outshining even his dapper pal, Oscar Slater. When they weren't gambling, Cameron and Slater frequented a roller-skating rink. Both agile, young and fit, with free time on their hands, they skated to a fiddler's tune such as that Scottish and Hugh Cameron favorite, "Moudiewort."

Since Slater's arrival in 1895 in Edinburgh, he'd had a few years of improving his English, and between Edinburgh and Glasgow, he mixed and gambled with his Scottish-Jewish, diamond-dealing pals, acquainting himself with bettors, pawnbrokers and shop clerks. Circumstances kept him in Scotland where he was to remain all his life and where he rose to prominence as a man wrongfully convicted of the murder of an elderly spinster, to Scotland's profound dishonor.

When he wasn't living with a prostitute in Glasgow, Slater paid for rooms at the Central Hotel located in Georges Square. He chose not to live in the Jewish Gorbals tenements—overcrowded, pestilential, poor, and meddling. The hotel stood in the center of Glasgow, an annex of the Central Railroad Station with an elegant mall of shops, telegraph office, and transit. Among the station's architectural features, underneath a glass-walled bridge, was the "Highlandman's Umbrella," a place that allowed cover for travelers and itinerant salesmen.

Central Station and Highlandman's Umbrella

For Slater, St. George's Road was a convenient stroll to Sauchiehall Street, a welter of streets where the dice was never idle, the wheel always turning, and gaslight lit to welcome all-night customers. Prostitutes openly operated in these commercial districts.

Glasgow proved less competitive for bookies than London. In Glasgow, bookies made a decent living by taking bets on dog runs, competitive football, and the foot races which even brought American runners to town. Slater's tips and information extended to those working in factories and warehouses-- the handicap, the weight, the owner, the money won, and so forth.

Horse races were a long-established spectator sport in Britain and betting on the horses held the rabid interest of thousands, whether wealthy or poor. Off-course cash betting was illegal, but Slater, ever the gambler, ignored the prohibition. He liked the horses. A law that was arbitrarily applied to a leisure sport, conspicuously dividing the social classes (credit betting for the wealthy), was undeserving of duty.

Slater took bets from working men which was why the Transcript Record found him in company with warehouse men. He visited their places of employment to deal in his goods or take their wagers, as he did when he attempted to sell a piece of jewelry to Jacob Jackson in 1908 during that brief, dangerous hiatus in Glasgow.

Pubs, barbers, boatmen at the riverside, and newsagents could all be relied on to place a bet with Slater. The ubiquity of the bookie, and his manner of dress, made him recognizable.

Oscar Slater looked the part of a commercial gent, as future witnesses would recall. He maintained that persona throughout his free life. His clothes were professionally laundered. Slater's shorter torso, wide chest and broad shoulders—as witness Agnes Brown observed—required his shirts be tailor-made to insure the right fit. He was often shaved twice daily by a barber because of his heavy beard but his thick mustache was only lightly trimmed. This is an important factor when one considers that Slater himself shaved off his mustache a few weeks prior to the murder, and then how quickly it grew back.

He wore gloves, the accepted fashion. Men removed their gloves when dining or at the gaming table. Judges wore gloves on the bench. Butlers wore gloves. Jewelry salesmen wore gloves to protect the pieces being displayed to customers. Marion Gilchrist wore gloves, according to the testimony of her former maid, Miss Jane Duff Walker. Slater wore gloves when the American police took him off the Lusitania. In his retirement years, Oscar Slater Leschziner still wore gloves.

Oscar Slater, the Nine of Diamonds

"Pope Joan" was a card game popular during Slater's playing days. The cards were kept in lacquered, wooden, compartmentalized boxes such as one finds in today's casinos. The Nine of Diamonds was the most powerful card called "the Pope." The rub was that Scotch Presbyterians hated the Roman Catholic papacy. The Nine of Diamonds playing card was thus known as Scotland's curse. Slater added a leaf to Scotland's card-playing history. It was at whatever card games he played: Pope Joan, faro, "muckie," poker, or *vingt et un*, that the dexterous Slater could fleece a player of his shilling. He was known as a card cheat.

He played Edward VII's favorite, baccarat. Baccarat for money was played surreptitiously at the clubs. In a court case, it had been adjudged a game of chance and not one of skill. Thus, it was illegal to play it for money. That discriminate opinion could only have aroused Slater's inclinations.

He was a master at pool and spent many evening hours at Glasgow's billiard halls. It was where he claimed he was playing, hoping to win, the late afternoon and early evening of December 21, 1908, after which his alibi took him home for dinner at 7 p.m. His mastery at pool required the skill and precision he had as a diamond cutter. That precision became instinctive. Playing "straight pool," as the game was known, honed his time-critical decisions. Slater was sharp, not sloppy—to a point.

Arthur Conan Doyle shooting "straight pool," the gentleman's game; his winning stroke, second round, the Billiard Association Amateur Championship, at Messrs. Ormis in Soho, 1913.

The Lure of Prostitution

With the Victorian era's twilight, the growth of industrialization, pauperized urban workers, and swarms of refugees escaping pogroms and poverty, rose a poor-woman's economy—prostitution. Not all working class women had a choice. Women who were guarded by their hustlers could make a small living. Their pimps gave them access to music halls and taverns. A cigarette, a drink, a dance, and then a tawdry twist. Ten shillings, sometimes more. Pimps were useful in warning the approach of a policeman, or looking after her room and possessions if the woman was arrested, and in helping her once released. For this, of course, the prostitute would have to pay up. Private lodgings, where affordable, improved the lot of a prostitute, particularly so far as privacy and cleanliness.

In 1901, when Oscar Slater and Mary Curtis Pryor left their London assignations and returned to Glasgow, Mary was arrested for prostitution and theft. Police were enforcing the 1892 Burgh Act that criminalized outdoor prostitution. The public had demanded a halt to the trafficking and streetwalking of unprotected young women. The spread of venereal disease was also an initiative. Included in the Act's prohibitions were public solicitation, brothel-keeping, and pimping. Those violations, had he been charged, would have landed Slater in prison. On a lighter note, leather-bound directories to the ladies of pleasure and their haunts were freely available to interested parties.

Slater and the Ladies

In Glasgow in 1901, on July 20, Slater and Mary Pryor married. With the benefit of marriage to a Scottish woman born in America, even though a working prostitute, Slater could declare American citizenship and also establish formal residency in Great Britain. Thereafter, he claimed he was American. Not once did he refer to British citizenship, though from 1895 until 1908, he lived in Britain. Why draw attention to the arrest record of Oscar Slater, fka Leschziner?

With the expansion of the railroads, Yorkshire, England also hosted high society with leisure activities that included fairs, circuses, music halls and park promenades. These events attracted the hustling class by which Slater and Mary earned an income. Too soon, their careers in Yorkshire came to a climactic end. In September of 1902, Mary was charged with two counts of theft from a customer. She was convicted and sentenced to two years in prison; Slater had not been charged though Mary stole for his purse and not her own. The man in charge, Oscar Slater, escaped arrest. He then took off for London.

In 1903, while Mary was still in prison, Slater was arrested for gambling in an illegal club. On the run again after Mary's release, they traveled to sunny, palm-tree-lined Monte Carlo. How graceless these two must have appeared in the glow of the inbred glitterati. They weren't there to dip into the cold, crystal blue Mediterranean Sea or stroll the pebbled beaches but for the legalized gambling, the ports, the casinos and the clientele.

Gauche in the environs of high-class tarts and high stakes gamblers, Mary and Slater frequented the port-side, black market hubs. Whether in Hamburg, Edinburgh or Marseilles, sailors who hadn't seen a woman's face in months went ashore in large numbers. Mary, unfamiliar with the French street scene would have been confined within unfamiliar doorways along Marseilles' steep, cobbled streets, taking whatever customers were willing. A sobered, pale Scottish chippy, out of her comfort zone in the south of France, couldn't fill Slater's purse. He was also hampered by his inability to speak either French or Italian. They returned to London.

Mary soon disappeared from his life, kept alive in name only with Slater's escape and alias excuses, saying these were meant to avoid her pleas for money. Her replacement was a much younger Jewish coquette to whom Slater became devoted even as he relied on her reliable income. Since it was illegal to operate a brothel, Slater solved that by living with a chosen mistress, as he then did for several years with the youthful Mademoiselle Andrée Hilaire Juno Antoine.

It was in Leicester Square, near the Empire Theatre, that Slater met 17-year-old Andrée. When she lived in Paris, frequenting its music halls, she would have been familiar with André Antoine (1859-1943), a modernist theater director and playwright who introduced progressive *nouveau* to theater productions. "Juno?" A beach front, pre-Normandy landing, within which lay marina towns, the Impressionists, and yea, monasteries.

Paris was also overwhelmed with thousands of refugees from eastern Europe and the consequent economy of prostitution. In 1883, a Directory for discerning gentlemen, "The Pretty Women of Paris," was published with the names, addresses and descriptions of the bodies, personalities, skills, and accoutrement of *les jeunes filles*. Mademoiselle Andrée acquired a *nom de guerre* to distinguish herself from competitors and because she worked with high-end clientele. Women who worked the lower-end streets, where the fleamarkets stood, chose more common names, such as "Nice Thighs," "Crucifix," or "Fake Bum."

In London, Slater and his lovely Andrée lived together in a flat where she hosted gentleman customers. Their maid was Katerina Schmaltz. As Andrée's boudoir assistant, Katerina attended with thread and needle to the pantalettes, chemise, corset, stockings, and garters removed carelessly late in the night. The three residents operated a relatively profitable brothel business seemingly under the radar. Slater arranged the household furnishings and purchases, and they shared nightly meals.

Leicester Square

Empire Theater

Empire Theater – Promenade room

Oscar Slater – *"I am not what I am."*

Oscar Slater had a reprehensible character flaw, and one tacitly ignored by his supporters. He was habitually violent. Some scoffed, saying this was unproven, and even were it admissible at trial, an isolated act of violence against a prostitute could hardly elevate to murder. There were suggestions that Slater had to have murdered in the past to show he was skilled or predisposed before the Gilchrist murder. Who knows?

When Slater operated brothels and living off his prostitutes' small earnings, he was repeatedly violent with his women. Among the abused was his wife-of-convenience, Mary Curtis Pryor. In Britain, where records were historically archived, Slater's record of criminal assaults grew. There were assaults and fist fights-- not murder-- but they were sufficiently violent that charges were filed by the police and he was taken into custody. Slater didn't fear a fight with men but was not generally a celebrated winner.

- March 1896, Edinburgh, Slater arrested for disorderly conduct stemming from a brawl in a gaming house. He was fined.

- April 10, 1896 in London, a charge of the malicious wounding of Isaac Levy over a bet. In the fight, Slater's nose was broken. There is no record of whether Levy appeared at trial. Slater was acquitted.

- Disorderly conduct in Edinburgh, 1899; convicted of fighting while drunk; fined. He was described by the arresting officer as a man who "had the reputation of being a low-class foreign bully."

- Annie Hansen, one of Slater's prostitutes, was arrested for "loitering with the purpose of prostitution" on March 24, 1900. "The woman, Hanson, often had bruises about her face," reported the policeman. She told the officer they "had been caused by Slater's ill usage."

- Again in Edinburgh, on May 15, 1900, he was charged with breach of the peace and assault of police constable James Stuart. When the officer visited him at his premises, Slater, angered by the police harassment, threatened to shoot him, "You bugger! I'll shoot you yet." The arresting officer wrote thus: "A notorious gambler and a drunken, dissolute fellow...*of a vicious disposition and was constantly quarreling and fighting with his associates over their gambling transactions. In these fights he used his feet more than his fists.*" (emphases added). He skipped court and Edinburgh.

- In London in 1903, Oscar was arrested in an illegal gambling house.

The fighting with his feet involved Oscar stomping on the victim with bone-breaking intent. This manner of fighting had come into widespread use, even in England where the Marquess of Queensbury's Rules were applied in gentlemen's sports. *Savate* (French, "old shoe") was a martial art become prominent in France among sailors and toughs with heavy shoes. In France, the closed fist was a legal weapon and subject to criminal prosecution. In England, kicking was considered unsportsmanlike; Edinburgh police expressed displeasure in regard to Oscar Slater's feet-fighting methods.

Conan Doyle seized on this form of martial arts. In 1903 (unintentionally coincident with Slater's arrest in London), he immortalized this form of combat in "The Adventure of the Empty House" during which Sherlock Holmes is described as an expert in Bartitsu (misspelled as "baritsu"). In 1898, it had been introduced by Edward Barton-Wright who named this form of martial self-defense by combining his name with that of Japanese Jujitsu.

Slater was a vain man with hypersensitivity about the condition of his face. He fought with his feet to avoid further facial injury. He'd suffered permanent disfigurement with the broken nose in London.

In Edinburgh, Oscar Slater's character darkened into that of a vile blackguard--a woman-beater. He was a pimp, greedy and aggressive. Slater's demands for money would have been a likely provocation for argument. Why not a prostitute's face rather than his own? The threat alone would frighten a woman expecting a fair appearance to attract customers. Prostitutes brought charges against Slater for his violent attacks. This was unusual given how the police would deride a prostitute's complaint.

Slater's character is easily drawn from his interactions. His violence was not an infrequent habit. It was repeated and relevant to the brutality committed upon the person and body of Marion Gilchrist. Because his past victims did not die, or because the charges were reduced to misdemeanor assaults because of the lowness of the characters involved, did not make Oscar Slater an unlikely guilty party. What woman would feel safe alone with him in a room?

Iago's singular utterance should have commenced in the introduction to books published by the naysayers. Iago—the villain and devil in *Othello*-- was not apologetic when he hinted of his hidden self: "I am not what I am..."

CHAPTER 8

Slater's Two Scottish Partners

2. Helen Lambie

Helen Lambie, age 22, was Miss Gilchrist's housemaid since late 1906, nearly two years prior to the murder. Lambie's position was comfortable. An average housemaid earned £50 annually. Thrifty Miss Gilchrist left Lambie £20 in her Will, a token of Scottish frugality. She had free room and board, free holidays and scant duties. She lived in a nice neighborhood, holidayed in Ayr, Scotland with Miss Gilchrist and her family, and took two days off a week.

A previous employer, Miss Agnes Guthrie, for whom "Lambie" worked the years 1903-1905, warned Marion Gilchrist that the young woman was "of rather low mentality, very cunning, and not at all trustworthy." These character traits made Lambie a likely partner with Patrick Nugent and Oscar Slater. Neither of the two men would have known about the jewelry collection had not Lambie disclosed this information and made accessibility a reality.

The police failed to delve into Lambie's employment with Miss Gilchrist. Most significantly, Glasgow police failed to investigate her unexpected visits to Agnes Guthrie after the murder.

Lambie's home before she went into service was in Holytown, a small, Protestant, mining town of Glasgow. Families lived in housing projects provided by the mining company, located close to the pits. About 15 miles from Holytown lay Roman Catholic Carfin, Patrick Nugent's home village. Long-standing religious rivalry strained relations between the

Roman Catholic and Protestant Glaswegians. Intermarriage was rare, Scottish Catholics, i.e. Irish families, were seen as a menace to Scotland's nationalism. To the Presbyters of Holytown and to Scotland, the Scottish kirk was its history and not the Roman Catholic Church and its pope.

During the murder inquiries, Lambie told police that she began to see a young man named Patrick Nugent, a bookie, at a New Year's party in January 1908. Though the two lived in separate communities, the mines brought interaction and it was there the two likely met. Lambie would have reached out to him, if she trusted him enough, to help her steal from a wealthy old lady. She didn't make that determination on a first meeting, New Year's Day 1908. They knew each other. Throughout the year 1908, they remained in touch.

She invited Nugent to the flat several times when Miss Gilchrist was running errands. She lied about Miss Gilchrist giving permission for male visitors when she was not home. Lambie was contradicted by Miss Gilchrist's prior maidservants. Lambie took her chances. Why? Companionship? He was engaged. He was a widowed father of three. He was a Roman Catholic. She carried on this acquaintance even though Nugent had November wedding plans with a Catholic girl in Carfin.

Lambie testified that she no longer saw Nugent after September but this was another lie. It was intended to show they had once been boyfriend and girlfriend and that the split occurred when she learned he was engaged to another woman. Lambie married a coal miner a month after Slater's trial.

Lambie and Nugent took preliminary steps in thefts from the flat but lacked the experience to fence jewelry. Lambie was given coins daily for errands. She would have known where coins were held and about the parlor safe and its contents. It was only a locked jewelry box in a spare bedroom that captured her interest. Miss Gilchrist kept the keys in her dress pocket, per the police investigation, and Lambie knew that.

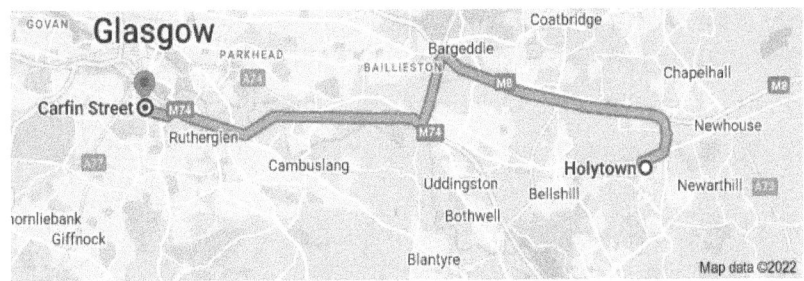

3. Patrick Nugent

Helen Lambie's friend was a 30-year-old bookie and gambler. It was small wonder that Patrick Nugent decided to forego the miner's struggle, choosing life as a bookie and mingling with toshers in the saloons and gambling halls of Glasgow's nightlife.

Nugent's community of Carfin was Scots-Irish…Irish immigrants established themselves in county Lanarkshire bringing Roman Catholicism to the Presbyters. Carfin, a mining community, was next door to the Protestant mining town of Holytown. Men of both religions worked in the mines. Sectarian prejudices and agitation were rife. Only the multiplicity of church steeples reaching the upper climes of Glasgow marked it as a peaceful, God-fearing city.

Nugent visited Miss Gilchrist's flat on many occasions. Lambie cooked dinner for him, he met Barney the barking terrier, and ambled around the flat and the spare bedroom with its jewelry collection and locked wooden box. Nugent would come to know that the downstairs tenants included a near-sighted, slightly built musician, his mother, and four adult sisters who gave music lessons. He would have heard their music streaming from downstairs.

As a bookie, Nugent ventured forth to his bettors, whether in the mining communities Holytown or Carfin. He had to be wary. He had his share of arrests for illegal bookmaking, fist fights, and assaults but he scraped by. Off-track betting was illegal and subject to imprisonment. Miners didn't have legal access to place their bets, so bookies went to the men at the mines, factories and tenements. Bets cost just a pence and rarely more than a shilling. Nugent would have been happily surprised if a wager reached half a crown; a bet of a sovereign would be serious gambling by a family man whose wages were but 30 shillings a week.

Bookies at the track, 1905

Nugent frequented the Sauchiehall streets and would have known of a certain bookie and jewel sharpie who could finesse his and Lambie's plan to burgle Marion Gilchrist. The man, Jewish, moved back and forth between Glasgow and London, but was last in Glasgow in 1905.

The idea of a Roman Catholic crook, of little if any education, partnering with a Jewish crook, was an incongruous lead. However, in later prison correspondence, Oscar Slater acknowledged that he knew Patrick

Nugent. After hearing his guilty verdict and sentence of death, Slater, shouting and bereft, confessed to a close acquaintance with Helen Lambie. He likely brooded about the two every day he spent in prison. The two Scottish natives had gone scot-free.

Was Patrick Nugent the murderer or was it Oscar Slater as Oscar supporters have heatedly argued? The murderer was described as clean-shaven. Clean-shaven Nugent was also in want of money. It was he who planned the scheme early on with Helen Lambie around January 1908. It was Nugent who visited the Gilchrist flat when the lady was not at home.

Following his luncheon with Lambie and Miss Gilchrist at Ayr in August 1908, and Nugent's disallowed visits to the flat, Barney the dog was poisoned. Lambie walked the Gilchrist dog when it was poisoned which eliminated its barking during Nugent's visits. These facts support his participation in the burglary and murder scheme, but he was not the murderer.

CHAPTER 9

Précis of the Plot

In the Sauchiehall world, distinct from respectability and legitimacy, Slater's and Nugent's acquaintances were fellow gamblers, heisters, bookies and bettors, fences, resetters of stolen gems, and racetrack habitués. Their livelihoods demanded they take chances. They cheated and they stole.

Slater was a fearsome, angry tough, a suitable fit for Lambie and Nugent who had been scheming for several months before Slater's eager return to Glasgow October 4, 1908. The draw of diamonds and financial stability was great. Slater laid out the scheme for robbing Marion Gilchrist's jewels. Unlike a winning card game, this final bet ended in tragedy.

Slater's discerning skill, whether card playing or shooting pool, was well-known. He was as canny in planning the December burglary. His objective led him to walk those cold streets. For several weeks during daylight hours and at night, he scouted the Gilchrist neighborhood and adjusted his outward aspect. He failed to figure delay as a factor and unanticipated witnesses on December 21.

The month between the November 18 pawning of Brooch #2 until the December 21 murder made it unlikely that Marion Gilchrist was murdered for the brooch or brooches. Both brooches had been pilfered by Lambie in October and November. There had to be another motive for the murder which was not explored by the police and not charged in the murder case; no author attempted to resolve the conundrum or threw in the distraction of a compromising Last Will and Testament.

First, Slater didn't want Marion Gilchrist reporting the brooches as stolen.

She hadn't to that point, which will be here explored.

Second, Oscar wanted no conflict as to his ownership of Brooch #2 at Liddell's Pawnbroker's.

Both Lambie and Nugent were familiar with the contents and the layout of the spare bedroom. They believed a valuable cache of gems was locked in a wooden box kept in that bedroom. At Slater's trial, Miss Gilchrist's prior maids testified that she kept jewelry locked in the box.

The trio planned for life after the burglary: Lambie would apply for another job. She had already applied for a job in November, a month before the murder. Slater would relocate to New York. Nugent wouldn't be going anywhere. He would quietly improve his family's home life in Carfin.

CHAPTER 10

THE PLACE: Marion Gilchrist Flat, 2d Floor, 15 Queens Terrace

Marion Gilchrist lived on the second floor of 15 Queens Terrace. She owned a beloved Irish terrier, Barney. She took him along on holidays. He could be counted on to bark, as terriers would, when strangers and visitors came to call, or if he were kept indoors for too long. It was after she had hired Helen Lambie that Miss Gilchrist's nephew, Dr. Francis Charteris, brought the Irish terrier. Dr. Charteris' medical practice was a few streets away, and he often stopped by.

Below the Gilchrist flat, on the first floor, lived a family of musical adults: Arthur Montague Adams, a gifted flutist with a Scottish orchestra, his mother and four of his five sisters—all of whom gave music lessons in piano, violin and flute in the home. A few months before the murder, the third-flood tenants above Marion's flat moved out because the building was too noisy. Their exit made the depraved December episode a surer one.

Doors Leading to the Gilchrist Flat

1. The outside door (L) opened into the entry lobby. Also referred to as the "close."

Front of houses, 15 and 14 Queen's Terrace
Showing close door of Miss Gilchrist's house (left); main door of Mr. Adams' house (right)
The windows of the dining-room are the two above the close door.

2. A second door within the entrance lobby. It led to the stairs to the Gilchrist flat.

3. The third door—entrance into Gilchrist flat.

Outer side of house door, 15 Queen's Terrace, showing portion of common stair.

The well-lit indoor stairs were wide and white.

Arthur Adams mustached, dressed for the symphony in Edwardian top hat and coat with velvet collar. He does not wear his eyeglasses.

Arthur Montague Adams.

In police reports and in his trial testimony, Mr. Adams said that he and the family rarely spoke with Miss Gilchrist in the 27 years they'd lived in the building. They were not friends even though Miss Gilchrist was close in age to the mother, Mrs. Adams. It is possible the music of some students was not always pleasing to the ear. It hadn't been with the third-story tenants who moved out.

Marion Gilchrist's outside door was at the left; the Adams' was to the right, at 14 Queens Terrace and led directly into the "close" or lobby entry. The indoor lobby was shared by the tenants.

Miss Gilchrist, the housemaid, visitors and shop people walked up the outside steps of 15 Queens Terrace, opened the outside door, walked into the shared entry and unlocked the entry door, or they rang the doorbell to be permitted access from the shared entry. If the doorbell rang for Miss Gilchrist, she used a lever in her flat to open the door. If the visitors were for the third floor, they would be let inside in similar fashion. To reach the third floor flat, one took the marble steps up towards Miss Gilchrist's, turned a slight left, and walked another flight.

On the night of the murder, it was apparent to the intruder that no one from the third floor would be interrupting the second-floor burglary and that the first-floor music practice during the Christmas season would be echoing up the stairwell.

A Curious Incident in the Nighttime

In October 1908, Miss Gilchrist heard footsteps in the flat during the night. The wooden floor creaked. There was no wee Barney to bark and to alert her. She became frightened—a late night visitor was creeping out of the flat. Miss Gilchrist walked downstairs and awakened the Adams' family. She said she'd heard an intruder. They agreed that in future, should she ever be in trouble, she would pound her floor (their ceiling) three times. Neither Miss Gilchrist nor the Adams contacted the police.

CHAPTER 11

A Case Old and Cold

In an effort to place guilt for Marion Gilchrist's murder squarely on Oscar Slater, the conclusions here reach further back in the crime's timeline to January 1908, about a year before the murder—the month of Nugent and Lambie's New Year's party. A series of burglaries from the Gilchrist jewelry collection unfolded after the New Year 1908. The Glasgow police investigation was limited to 30 days leading up to the murder. Oscar Slater's arrest in the New Year of 1909 brought the journey to a halt.

Indefensibly, the police dismissed the involvement of the maid, Helen Lambie and her friend, Patrick Nugent, in a routine of jewelry thefts from the flat. The two partners to Slater's crime were suspected by Conan Doyle who unflinchingly published their names. Lambie pilfered from Marion Gilchrist's jewelry collection presumably to be shared among the trio.

Nugent had been partnering alone with Lambie since January 1908 and all the way through September 1908. Nugent had been to the Ayr seaside in August—leaving him a recognizable person to Miss Gilchrist. Nugent had also visited Lambie at the flat in Glasgow. Neighbors may have recognized him. Lambie told her girlfriends about Nugent's visits and the tour she gave him of the jewelry room.

Fluttering through Nugent's mind at this time was his upcoming wedding November 25 in Carfin, and it was not to Helen Lambie. Nugent needed to shift the burden of fencing Miss Gilchrist's diamonds in order to turn a profit. He turned to a skilled diamond dealer and fence, Oscar Slater.

Slater was not living in Glasgow in the early months of 1908. What connection was there between him and Nugent, a Glasgow Catholic who was, like Slater, a bookie and hustler in the Sauchiehall haunts?

There was no testimony about these links in the chain of the trio's association:

1. Lambie's enduring contrivance in the plot.

2. The contents of the locked jewelry box.

3. Slater's plans to relocate to New York in January 1909, about a month after the planned heist.

4. Continuing searches by police of the flat, not so much for evidence of the murder, but for gems. The jewelry hadn't been in the locked box, as police discovered. The murderer left with one brooch which meant jewels were hidden somewhere in the flat.

5. Discovery by police and a leaked report to the newspapers, of a tray of uncut diamonds in a hidden corner of the Gilchrist flat, weeks after the murder. A "tray" of diamonds was the word imparted from information by a leaker to the newspaper.

6. Oscar Slater's acknowledgement of his acquaintance with Nugent and with Lambie.

What the Scottish prosecution did get right was that Oscar Slater's Atlantic voyage to New York was an escape arising from his consciousness of guilt. Once Slater read the December 25th Glasgow news and sensed the police were closing in on a swarthy fellow with a twisted nose, his immediate reaction was one borne of habit. He packed up and fled.

His swift exit from Glasgow fit the legal definition of a flight from justice. In other words, it was a flight to escape criminal charges for the murder he knew he'd committed. Not one of the Oscar Slater authors bought into this legal definition of flight. They interpreted Oscar's coincident, near-penniless departure across the Atlantic to America, with news swirling about the brutal Glasgow murder, as nothing more than a budget-conscious, long-planned relocation.

William Roughead's 1910 book, *The Trial of Oscar Slater,* was a collection of court stenographers' records and his conversations with the associated solicitors, barristers and the judge presiding. His compilation and introductory narrative about the case emerged as irrefutable fact.

It is a historical case. The conclusions cannot rest on solid foundation. The scene of the crime was not secured. People walked in and out: police, doctors, witnesses, and relatives. It had been raining outdoors. Coats, shoes and umbrellas brought further abasement to the mix.

Physical evidence or representative photographs were not produced at trial though they were included in Roughead's list of trial exhibits. There was no brooch with three rows of diamonds nor a sketch or its photograph produced at trial though Brooch #2 lay at Liddell's Pawnbrokers.

Nor did it appear that a particularly gripping piece of evidence was put on dramatic display for the jury-- the fawn waterproof coat with 25 brownish red/blood spots or tints left by use of a solvent.

The stained waterproof was first reported by the New York police who unpacked the luggage in Oscar Slater's presence. The police separately packaged the evidentiary items.

A waterproof coat was labeled as evidence in Roughead's trial list. The coat may have been lodged within the material evidence and rolled into a neat pile on the courtroom desk. No witness identified the coat and reviewed its particulars in the crime. No expert testified as to the splatter on the coat or the alignment, for example, with the splatter from the victim's body. Whether the fawn waterproof coat, with its telltale red/orange blood spots, received the attention it required at Slater's trial lies in the obscurity of William Roughead's annotations from the stenographers' trial transcripts.

The forensic doctors—the trial's expert witnesses—testified a solvent had dissolved the volume of blood in the stains on the coat and as a result the remnant was too insubstantial for conclusive testing. There was no DNA; it lay in the distant future.

Fingerprint analysis was not produced at trial. It was likely the killer wore gloves, commonplace in those days. Oscar Slater wore gloves even in retirement.

There were no diagrams of blood spatter. There were no lineup sketches nor photos, only arguably varying recollections.

Had a thorough investigation in Slater's case been renewed in 1910, or as soon as Conan Doyle and William Roughead took to promoting Oscar Slater's innocence, the evidence then available could have been tested.

There was the conspicuously stained waterproof coat. A match used by the killer to light the gas lamp had been found by the police in the spare bedroom. Slater was a hairy guy. A single hair—suggested by the Locard test-- removed from the scene and placed under a microscope would not have rendered a scientific match, but surely several of Slater's hairs would have found their way onto the body during the violent attack.

With this questionable inventory and an unready trial, a cynic might assert that there was and is only speculation, a hunch, as to Oscar Slater's guilt--- towards which Judge Charles Guthrie was strenuously inclined.

But this old and cold case had a sufficiency of facts and events, beginning with the Nugent and Lambie conspiracy in January 1908, that reinforce Oscar Slater's murder conviction. His guilt of the murder was not attributable to his ethnicity, lifestyle or choice of companions. The information was there all along—in the annotated trial transcripts, witnesses, police reports, leaks to newspapers, statements, itineraries, and correspondence--reassembled in a manner methodical.

The plotting among the three wretches, Lambie, Nugent and Slater, was easily discernible; one had only to step back several months.

👉 Slater supporters derided young Mary Barrowman's jarring identification of the man running from the Gilchrist flat *at the precise moment of the murder.* She stood, startled, as a man ran down the outside steps of the Gilchrist flat and paused beneath a shining street lamp, and then crossed the street and stood beneath another street lamp. Mary described the man that evening to her mother, then to a policeman neighbor, and then in a formal police interview the next day, on December 22. She was subjected to penetrating questions by police officers and didn't budge. The man seen by Mary Barrowman, facing her, was a man wearing a fawn waterproof coat and "with a crooked nose." It marked the denouement of Oscar Slater.

👉 The suspect, according to immediate, feverish police reports on December 21 and December 22, wore either a fawn waterproof coat or a grey coat, both of which were in Slater's possession when arrested on board the Lusitania in New York, January 2, 1909. The murderer wore the waterproof because it had been raining. Stains were easier to wipe clean.

Helen Lambie and Arthur Adams were in shock having viewed the mangled, still warm corpse of a lady they knew well enough. Lambie's obscure description of the murderer directly within her vision—and the police witless about her participation—was that he wore a fawn coat. That much she allowed herself to remember. Arthur Adams may have been near-sighted, but that had not affected his details of the man's clothing. The murderer exiting the flat, Arthur Adams said, wore a fawn coat, or grey. A wet waterproof would have a blending of colors.

Police updates included both fawn and grey. Understandably, they were on the lookout for a suspect wearing either colored coat...and had a crooked nose.

☞ Slater said the fawn waterproof coat, with 25 diluted reddish blood stains, found in his luggage by the police in New York, was his.

☞ Slater said the hammer, which the police found in his luggage, was his. There were flecks of blood discernible on the hammer. Slater bought it that November for "household repairs." Who takes a hammer while preparing for a journey by ship?

All the conjectures about greedy relatives, Detective Lieutenant John Trench's sainted service to the cause of Oscar Slater's innocence, and the conviction of a Jewish refugee upon freighted identification muddied the Record successively in each Oscar-was-Innocent book.

This instead was Slater's self: a liar, forger, a font of aliases, a violent pimp, a man who offered no civility nor respect towards women, a plotter, a cheat, a thief, a fence, and a murderer.

CHAPTER 12

Anti-Semitism

By the 17th century, anti-Semitism evolved into a popular ideology. Voltaire was among France's contributors. Great Britain was no less culpable in the spread of the disease and its endurance to the present day. Its own scholar of anti-Semitism was Houston Steward Chamberlain who, in 1899, wrote *The Foundation of the Nineteenth Century*, a treatise on the Jew as "mongrel," and that a Jew's morality was that of a "weed." British military losses—during the Boer War, for example—were attributed to the deterioration of Britons from the influx of foreign races.

With a decline in land values, aristocrats and estate holders blamed the downturn on wealthy Jews whose interests didn't align with Britain's. A persistent publishing of humbug about Jewish financiers began to arise from the pens of the alt conservatives and popular authors such as Anthony Trollope.

The endorsement of the neurotic science of physiognomy did no service to the perspective of Jews as ancient conspirators seeking to crush Christianity. This was the backdrop for allegations of anti-Semitism in the trial and conviction of Oscar Slater—a self-proclaiming German.

Sentiments of the Learned

Jewish, secular, faux-convert Benjamin Disraeli was Prime Minister under Victoria (1874-1880). What a benighted drubbing this statesman received from the pen of Anthony Trollope: "that flavor of hair-oil, that flavor of false jewels, that remembrance of tailors." Sherlock Holmes took on the disguise of a "Jew pedlar" (*Study in Scarlet*, 1887). In the *Adventure of Shoscombe Old Place* (1927), Sir Robert Norbertson was "deeply in the hands of the Jews." It was commonplace to refer pejoratively to a Jew, whether a diplomat, a customer, a salesman, or a gambler. Like Fagin in Charles Dickens' *Oliver Twist* (1839), Jews were malignant, stereotypical characters in fiction.

The fictional and poetic indulgence in anti-Semitism was rife in the late 19th century and into the 20$^{th.}$ Disraeli had no fear of the nativist aspersions of an Irish parliamentarian who had derided his ethnicity in public: "Yes, I am a Jew, and while the ancestors of the Right Honorable Gentleman were brutal savages in an unknown island, mine were priests in the Temple of Solomon."

Trollope's novels were riven with anti-Jewish invective. The strange, non-Christian, typically malevolent character attracted readership. Yet Trollope was prescient in his narratives, remarking that the changing world was no longer at odds with "the fair skin and bold eyes and uncertain words of an English gentleman or the swarthy colour and false grimace and glib tongue of some inferior Latin race" (*The Prime Minister* 1876). Rudyard Kipling's remarks about "Semites" in *From Sea to Sea: Letters of Travel* (1899) were so corrosive as to leave one to wonder whether his fingernails were as filthy as the corners of his mind.

One must read also John Buchan's Glaswegian spy novels (revolutionary Jews during the Great War: *The 39 Steps*, 1915, and *Greenmantle*, 1916). The stories and images impressed upon the reader the notion that a Jew was a wily foreigner who could never aspire to becoming a true Christian. The Holocaust finally put a stop to the repellent fetish, that is, until the latest iteration arose with the multicultural multitude in the United Kingdom and the Continent.

Ethnicity and Oscar Slater

Supporters were convinced that Slater's conviction was attributable to anti-Semitism and that he was a weak, maligned, stumbling refugee plucked from obscurity and trapped in the hell of a British trial. Author William Park, disputing the rationale behind Slater's conviction, used his own ethnic invective as proof: Marion Gilchrist wouldn't have opened her door to Oscar Slater, "an alien jew."

Slater voluntarily chose his livelihood. He was a heavy gambler and an itinerant gem dealer. He traveled. He owned nothing and lived off diamond sales, betting receipts, and the wages of his women. He pursued an illegitimate, portable livelihood as a matter of preference with none but dodgy acquaintances. It is not a hasty judgment to say he thrived in his role.

In prison, Slater swapped his truculent self and entertained a return to Judaism, all the while Rabbi Phillips persevered to free Slater from a wrongful conviction. While in prison, Slater informed his public: "Sorry to say I am not a great Jew, yet I am never ashamed of my Religion. At Peterhead I have shown it to them. I was the only Jew there for many years yet I have kept for 19 years the Jewish New year & Atonement day the 'Fast.'" Not before Peterhead, and not after release, did Slater tout his forebears and the ancient legacy Rabbi Phillips endeavored to cultivate in the insincere prodigal.

Glasgow had a sizeable Jewish working-class, tenement community called the Gorbals. Jewish immigrants weren't prevented from legitimate careers. Jeremy Morris was a Polish Jew who grew up so poor in 1910 Glasgow that he contracted rickets as a child. He became a renowned epidemiologist, earned the title "The Man Who Invented Exercise," and died at age 99 ½—swimming and bicycling into old age.

There were literary benefits with Scotland's Jews specially in matters of the mind and intellect. Poet Shaul Tschernichovsky translated to Hebrew Robbie Burns' Scottish lyrics of *"My heart's in the Highlands, my heart is not here, my heart's in the Highlands a-chasing the deer."* Slater's métier was captured by Burns' "To a Louse," "Moudiewort," and "The Mouse." Perhaps he read them when taking up literature studies at Peterhead Prison. They were a poetic reflection of his chosen pedigree, the character of which could not absolve him from the murder he committed.

CHAPTER 13

Oscar Slater and American Citizenship

The details of Oscar Slater's naturalization attempts were fuzzy. He may have been eligible for derivative American citizenship from his 1901 marriage to Mary Curtis Pryor, but she was no longer around once he met up with Mademoiselle Andrée. When Slater and Andrée shipped off to America December 26, 1908, Slater referred to himself at the hotel and on board ship as an American citizen. He'd been to New York often enough to pull that off with confidence.

Passing through Ellis Island was not complicated. He traveled second class and Port immigration allowed those passengers, and those in first class, to leave quickly so officials could interview the thousands of refugees (third-class, f/k/a "steerage") on board the newly arrived ships. In those years, the immigration service was primarily charged with excluding anarchists and political or labor activists.

At the Immigration Office, Slater would have learned that the process was not quite so simple. America had laws on its books that barred citizenship to the immoral, the mentally challenged, the physically handicapped, and the sexually disoriented. There was a loophole where a relative of an unfortunate could guarantee financial support. But as to criminal elements, there was shaky possibility. Slater's wife and natural-born American, Mary Curtis Pryor, was not there to plead his case. Mlle. Andrée's pretense, that it was she who wedded Slater in Glasgow, was doomed as fakery. An investigation and approval took between two to seven years, during which time, Oscar Slater's lengthy police record would have been cause for exclusion.

Not giving up, in 1907 Slater submitted a formal Declaration of American citizenship during a New York visit, this time using the alias "Adolf Anderson, dentist." He provided business documents as proof. During the interview, the Bureau inspector wrote down Slater's distinguishing features, including a "permanent nose disfigurement." That official description would be used at Slater's criminal trial by the Crown to complement Mary Barrowman's description of the suspect at the scene of the murder.

Slater's citizenship attempts were a measure of his audacity. He had no fear of authority. To his likely dismay, after the November 9th meeting with the immigration examiner, he learned of impediments that lay ahead.

With the alias, Slater had to prove his identity with supporting documents. An "A. Anderson" lease and business card were inadequate. The immigration process required authentic certificates: birth certificate, school records, transport records, financial records, family members, letters of support, etc. He would have had to prove uninterrupted residence of two years in America. Possibly, his extended stay in America in 1906 was intended for that purpose. All Slater had at that point was the A. Anderson business card he'd made while in London in 1905 at Robert Rogers' address. He was expected to provide proof of sound moral character. A sticky wicket. From 1895 on, his avocation was that of well-dressed gambler, bookie, pimp and thug.

In addition to his alias, Oscar may have submitted a false financial accounting to the Immigration Examiner. During his two or three trips to New York, he found temporary work in a music hall, a gun club and a gambling house, and he sold terriers (dogs like Barney). He had contacts—business partners who would act as sponsors for citizenship. But New York, gateway to global immigrants, was well on its way towards a regulatory bureaucracy. The immigration offices held ledgers containing the particulars of those who were admitted and those removed. There were departments which held birth, marriage and death certificates. Slater wouldn't find it easy to reestablish a new persona.

There was always the likelihood that a sizeable financial investment would overcome the impediments. Once Slater became a partner in the Marion Gilchrist jewelry collection, her brooch with three rows of diamonds and the additional haul from her flat, the sum could prove valuable enough for citizenship approval.

CHAPTER 14

Oscar Slater's Return to Glasgow

Authors ascribed Oscar Slater's traveling to (Jewish) wanderlust—a credulous assumption that Jews, like the nomadic Romani, wandered out of ancient habit. Slater traveled to escape the consequences of arrest. His departure from Glasgow the coming December 25 was part of a habitual pattern.

From 1901 to 1903, Oscar shuttled between Glasgow and London, working with fellow diamond dealers, Robert Rogers and David Jacobs. Midway in 1903, having to evade criminal charges lodged against him in three cities-- Edinburgh, Glasgow and London--Oscar and Mlle. Andrée made a brief hiatus to Brussels where she had family.

The two landed in the midst of the revolutionary Congress of Bolsheviks, Mensheviks and Jewish Bundists. Indifferent to the socialist diatribes but attuned to the commercial prospects of thousands of spectators and reporters, prostitution and the sex trade in Brussels bloomed. Oscar Slater and Mlle. Andrée were two stalwarts. Sex trafficking of English girls into Brussels raised the incomes of the seedier proletariat. Once the Congress was sent on its heels out of Brussels, Slater and Andrée set sail for New York, a city of prospering Jewish-immigrant entrepreneurs. They traveled as Mr. and Mrs. George.

In New York in 1904, Oscar operated a nickel-and-dime pool room. There were hundreds of them. His English fluency, a Scottish burr, and his assertive demeanor were suitable credentials, but the position required New York know-how such as greasing the palms of the Irish police. It required too much contact and parting with his own money…what little he had. The beguiling Mlle. Andrée's forays in an unfamiliar, rough culture were scant in collection. Though Slater was anxious for American citizenship, Mlle. Andrée was determined to return to the European orbit.

In November 1905, they returned to London. On November 24, he sent his watch for repairs to Messrs. Dent. Slater would not pay the bill until October 1908 when he was back in Glasgow, a participant in the Gilchrist plot. His watch would again require repair in December 1908, prior to the murder.

In the early months of 1908, Patrick Nugent and Helen Lambie were in the early stages of their scheme to rob Miss Gilchrist. During the same months, Oscar Slater was back in New York determined to acquire American citizenship. He made no such effort in Great Britain where his arrest records prevented approval.

This time, with the assistance of New York pals and an American partner, he prepared a financial background required by the Examiner at the Immigration Office. During this New York respite, Oscar had managed a gun club where his marksmanship—training from his school days—secured the employment. His jewelry business remained an out-of-pocket, come-what-may enterprise.

From October to December 1908, when Slater was back in Glasgow, he began to name-drop his American business contacts. One was at a State Street address in Chicago of a building of wholesale jewelry dealers. Another was a San Francisco partnership to which Oscar referred in a postcard he sent his Glasgow pal, Max Rattman, and about which Hugh Cameron testified at trial.

Oscar's Income in 1908

Some authors claimed Oscar's life was one of relative comfort. In fact, he survived on an irregular income from his girls, from thieving, and from sales of stolen jewels. Gambling was his demon; he lost as much as he won, according to Hugh Cameron.

At trial, the Crown introduced Slater's debts and his empty pockets as motive for theft and murder-- motive with absent proof of the bounty. A February 29, 1908 invoice revealed Slater had an open account (money owed in a prior gem deal) with fellow fence, David Jacobs of New York. At times, Slater received gems on a promise to resell for which he was bound to reimburse the dealer. Though he owed a large sum to Jacobs for the transaction, Slater left the debt unpaid and returned with Andrée to Paris and London in August 1908.

Oscar spoke of the August 1908 Paris diversion with Andrée as one required "for her health." They stopped at *Rue des Trois Fréres* in Montmartre presumably for its darker pleasures: the music halls, opium dens, jewelers, and chemists (including future PM Georges Clemenceau) who sold opium and cocaine.

In 1880, Paris was among the European cities where Jews by the thousands fled Russia's pogroms lured by Napoleon's *Emancipation.* Paris was also the home of Romanov aristocrats who escaped but with millions of rubles and precious gems, only to be later shadowed by Soviet cutthroats, Lenin and Trotsky. Gems were easily concealed in the course of escape. Whether from needy refugees or struggling Russian aristocrats in France, selling jewelry was necessary to survive.

Signs of Permanency in London

In early September 1908, Slater and Andrée were back in London. At that point, Slater could have informed his London friend, David Freedman, that he would be traveling temporarily to Glasgow but permanently relocating to America the coming January 1909. He did not do so. Instead, Slater's request that Freedman's girl sublet his Glasgow flat was by a hurried telegram only days before Slater's dizzying departure on December 25.

When Slater and Andrée arrived in London that September, it was at the conclusion of the summer Olympics. The Games were to have been held in Italy but a 1906 Mt. Vesuvius eruption led to Italy's withdrawal. London responded with panache, building the White City Stadium within 10 months. Opening ceremonies began in July, attended by Edward VII. Conan Doyle was in the stands writing for the *Daily Mail* about Dorando Pietri's marathon run. Competitions wouldn't be closed until October 31. Tourists, athletes, and residents held great promise for the street economy and Slater's keen eye—dancing halls, dancing girls, and gambling houses.

In London, Slater rented a large furnished flat in the name of Mr. O. Juno for three: himself, Mlle. Andrée, their maid, Katerina, and curtained space for Mlle. Andrée's gentlemen clients. For a working girl such as Mlle. Andrée, an address in a proper section of town lent a degree of prestige, a better level of customer, and security.

The Glasgow Diversion

September 5-- Slater ordered new business cards in the name of "A. Anderson, Dentist." They were delivered to the address of his friend, Robert Rogers, at 36 Albemarle St., in London. Slater's intention at the time was to live and work in London with an uncertain prospect of American citizenship.

The return to London was short-lived. From glorious Paris and the commercial hub that was London, Oscar Slater made a fateful decision to return to Glasgow, a parochial, coal-mining district which he'd last seen in 1905. The motivation must have been mesmerizing, drawing his attention from international travel and London's prospects.

 A conversation about Marion Gilchrist and her jewels...
likely occurred between Nugent and Slater on the latter's return to London. Here, one must speculate within reason. The acquaintance of the two men fits with other facts and with Slater's acknowledgement. It should be accorded credibility.

Presumably, it was Patrick Nugent who reached out to Oscar Slater in September 1908. Why? Nugent had the inside track from Helen Lambie, Miss Gilchrist's maid. Slater had been a bookie in Sauchiehall. Nugent may have remembered Slater as a chancer, willing to take risks. He wasn't afraid of a fight as proven by serial arrests. He was also a known resetter/fence, a skill beyond Nugent and Lambie's ability.

Nugent couldn't have asked Max Rattman of Slater's whereabouts because at the time Max was completing a stint in prison. If Nugent had in his possession a stolen piece of jewelry which he wished to sell, a resetter was a necessity. From the fence, Slater's skill was recalled but he had moved away to London. Nugent may have sent a telegram or taken the train to the Summer Olympics soon after his brief holiday in Ayr --so consequential was the intended fleecing of a rich old lady.

Hugh Cameron may also have known Slater was in London. Hugh had befriended Oscar upon his arrival in Glasgow in 1901 and through his departure in 1905. A native Scots, a bookie, a sometime jewelry dealer, and a Moudie with "cred" at Sauchiehall gambling clubs, Cameron testified he hadn't seen his good pal, Oscar Slater from 1905 until his return to Glasgow in 1908. When Slater returned in October 1908, Cameron saw him every day. No evidence indicated however that either Oscar Slater or Patrick Nugent shared the jewelry scheme with Cameron. It was their own private heist.

The Gilchrist jewelry scheme was so promising that Nugent took up the hunt for Oscar Slater with enthusiasm. How could Slater refuse? There was an old lady; Nugent had an insider; and there was a cache of valuable jewelry much of which Nugent had seen with his own eyes. Nugent would have goaded Slater into joining in the diamond theft because the duration and execution would be short term.

There was little correspondence produced. A remark was made at trial that all Slater's personal papers had been destroyed except those helpful to his defense. This was a creditable observation because no correspondence about or from family, police, immigration, brokers, creditor demands, nor about his ladies of pleasure were found at the Glasgow residence on St. George's Road nor in his luggage.

Slater, the bookie and jewelry broker, was a disreputable tenant in a low-rent community of gamblers. Nugent successfully enlisted Slater in the scheme. Like Scotland's bloody Macbeth, Oscar Slater was as "avaricious, false, deceitful, sudden, malicious, smacking of every sin that has a name." Here was the man for Lambie and Nugent.

CHAPTER 15

Timeline to Murder

JANUARY 1, 1908 TO DECEMBER 20, 1908

Some months listed below also include a specific day; these appear in the Record of evidence. The timeline begins January 1908. At Oscar Slater's trial, the timeline began in early December 1908.

Winsome Thoughts of Riches

Wed. January 1, 1908---On a cold and windy -4°F (-20°C) New Year's Day (or Eve--the night prior), two young people braved Scotland's wintry weather to attend a Hogmanay celebration—the Scottish equivalent of Catholic Christmas: Helen Lambie, age 21, and a 37-year-old widower and father, Patrick Nugent. They later claimed they met for the first time on this day—she from Holytown, a few miles from Nugent's home in Carfin. Fireworks were in the sky, while indoors there was food and alcohol aplenty, dancing, rousing songs and music. What an evocation of good will in the New Year to come.

The date was likely prearranged. They hadn't met by chance as Lambie told the authorities. The two attended together because a respectable woman was not allowed unescorted into a dance hall. That New Year's night, Nugent may have worn the same coat in which he would be seen running past Agnes Brown the night of the murder, December 21. At midnight, *Auld Lang Syne* would be sung as Glasgow's clocks chimed and its church bells pealed in unison.

Lambie admitted she told Nugent, as well as girlfriends, that she was maid to a wealthy old woman with a valuable jewelry collection. In the short time Lambie worked for Marion Gilchrist, it may have crossed her mind that with so many gems, Miss Gilchrist couldn't possibly notice the disappearance of a few.

Family livelihoods in Protestant Holytown and Catholic Carfin depended on men who worked long hours as bricklayers, in the quarries, and in the coal mines. These were not among Nugent's employment of choice even though he had children to support. Lambie, still a girl, chose Nugent as her partner because she trusted him. She saw he had a regular store of customers who trusted him as well. She was also attracted by his flashy dress. It was a sign of his success. He was a handsome Irish toughie who never let a robber get the best of him and the money he carried.

In the New Year, the two became confederates in a burglary plot, one in which Oscar Slater would eventually figure. Lambie had been Marion Gilchrist's housemaid for only two-and-a-half years but she had become familiar with her jewelry and her wealth. It was bewitching and exposed in her such a desire that Lambie could not catch a breath. The old lady was sure to die, leaving Lambie without a job and with little money.

By August 1908, Lambie's purpose became vile indeed, for she let into the elderly woman's life, a man who wanted her gems and who would kill to own them outright.

To a poor girl from Holytown, a bounty was within her grasp. She just didn't know how to convert it into currency nor how to avoid arrest and prison. In that regard, she sought out the services of a bounder whom she trusted. Her instinct about Nugent's character came from a long acquaintance with the Catholic from Carfin. Miss Gilchrist may have had no idea that a girl so young and inexperienced would have such a conniving mind and soul. In that, Lambie was quite the equal of Oscar Slater.

The Nugent and Oscar Savvy

Conan Doyle expressed his suspicions of Nugent and Lambie when examining the "Oscar Slater is Innocent" efforts following Oscar's conviction. Author William Roughead, in persuading Conan Doyle to add his pen to the struggle, falsely assured him that Patrick Nugent had been "fully exonerated" by the police. Detective Lieutenant John Trench was the officer who told him so. Conan Doyle committed himself in defense of Oscar Slater having put his trust in the ignoble John Trench.

If, on having read the police reports and transcripts, Conan Doyle's instinct led to his conclusion of a larger scheme than that heard at Oscar's trial, then Roughead must take posthumous blame for his rendition of the trial transcripts and the grotesque cry that Oscar Slater was innocent of the murder of Marion Gilchrist.

Nugent and Oscar Slater, two bookies in their mid-30s, were subjects of police interest in Glasgow as ne'er-do-wells. Both men nightly frequented the clubs around Sauchiehall Street. That didn't bother young Lambie, not for the entire year of 1908. She conspired in the plot to put an end to poverty and the uncertainty of her wages and employment.

At trial, the Crown impugned Slater's persona and livelihood in asking a loaded question of Oscar's friend, David Jacobs, the New York jewelry dealer:

> **CROWN:** "You told us he had no occupation, that he lost money at gambling, and that he was anxious to sell the pawn ticket; how did he

live, if he had no occupation and had lost money; what was he living on?

DAVID JACOBS: "On the gambling."

Unlike the aristocracy's gentlemen's clubs, Sauchiehall's were seedy, packed with men smelling of beer and cigarette smoke, the air dense with tension and phlegm. Some clubs and pubs were painted clover-leaf green for the Irish Paddy or the nationalist red and white of St. George's flag for the proud Scotsman.

These were the halls within which Nugent and Slater found their life's calling though craftier Oscar supplemented his earnings with under-the-table diamond brokering. The two toughs were of a kind--needy enough to plot the burglary of jewelry from a wealthy old lady who lived alone.

The police and prosecution focused on a one-man operation in the murder, misled from the outset by a hysterical young maid. With the capture of the suspect with a twisted nose, the investigation came to a full stop. In abbreviating the particulars of the crime and failure to pursue logical investigative leads, the authorities neglected to identify the profit motive and the participation of two other venal individuals.

February through June--- Nugent sent Lambie at least one letter about meeting him at a street corner near the Gilchrist flat. He visited when Miss Gilchrist was not at home. Ushered in by Lambie, Nugent set eyes on the diamonds and jewelry kept in the spare bedroom. How difficult could it be to steal from an old lady? Lambie cooked dinner for him. He kept up the acquaintance with Lambie through September (according to Lambie) or the end of November (according to Nugent).

Marion Gilchrist Carries On

March---Miss Gilchrist visited her jeweler, William Sorley, at his shop on Dumbarton Road, to have a diamond brooch (Brooch #1) cleaned. When Marion Gilchrist shopped in the area, she could still choose from a wide array of jewelers, stockbrokers, importers, solicitors, locksmiths and drapers slightly inland of the Firth of Clyde.

Dumbarton Road, trams, horses, carts and shops

Here by the wintry River, hardy Marion braved the cold as only a Scotswoman of a certain age could. She was conscientious about the condition of her jewelry which she kept in a spare bedroom. Special gems were kept in a locked box. She may have intended to wear this particular diamond brooch for an upcoming occasion.

At trial, Sorley produced a catalog illustration of a crescent-shaped brooch with one row of diamonds as being the same brooch brought in by Miss Gilchrist for cleaning the past March. Lambie had reported to the investigating police the morning of December 22 that it was *the* brooch that went missing the night of the murder. It was not found in Slater's possession.

Lambie would have assisted Miss Gilchrist with dressing that March morning. She knew how long Miss Gilchrist would be busy with her errands. She had a look at the brooch she was taking to be cleaned--a crescent-shaped brooch with one row of diamonds. Lambie had become attentive to the gems, yet she could hardly have known the difference between a brooch and a bangle, a diamond from a garnet. She was 21, had grown up in poverty, and went into service at age 15.

 MEANWHILE Oscar Slater in New York and London

May 1908---Oscar Slater was residing briefly in New York. There he entered an agreement with lessor Peter de Silvestri to operate a restaurant with a partner, John DeVoto. Neither of these New York business contacts appeared at Slater's extradition. They existed as names on a document for which, apparently, no money had been exchanged. Slater had unresolved plans for relocation to New York. Whether his Declaration of Citizenship as "Adolf Anderson" would be approved was undetermined.

That same month in London, a 16-year-old testified at a trial against a man who passed her on to a German-Jewish diamond dealer whose name was Oscar Shannock. She had met him at her parents' Bed and Breakfast in Brighton (where Oscar Slater would holiday after his release from prison in 1928). For several weeks, the young girl prostituted, giving all her money to Oscar Shannock. When she refused to rob customers or hadn't earned enough, he beat her. Here was the proclivity for violence against women. Oscar Shannock, fearful of what the girl would say, promised to give her a ring. He never did. The girl ran away, back to Brighton. A story of some coincidence. Oscar Shannock operated in London and made a swift retreat to New York when criminal charges were pressing

Back to Glasgow

Thursday, May 28--- Marion Gilchrist met with her solicitor to make changes to her Will. Her estate was valued at £15,758 (in today's dollars, $2.8 million), a healthy sum for a lady who had lived a long life. She made special bequests and held shares, stocks and bonds, rents, savings accounts, oil paintings, silver plate throughout the house, a jewelry collection, furs, and Victorian furnishings.

If Miss Gilchrist suspected thefts of her jewelry, she would have told her lawyer. No such conversation was reported. From this, one might assume that in May 1908 there were no missing gems or valuables. There were squabbles, however—over Lambie's manner with visitors, the supposedly secret visits by a boyfriend, and Miss Gilchrist's threats to fire Lambie without a reference.

Oscar was in New York with Mlle. Andrée and not yet a partner to the scheme.

Though there was much spin in the Slater books about the changing of the Gilchrist Will, the posthumous speculations signified nothing. Marion Gilchrist wanted to affirm the inheritance for her Ferguson grandchildren. Her connections to the Fergusons ran deep. Marion Galbraith had been her housemaid and left her employ when she married Alex Ferguson. She gave birth to three children whom Marion Gilchrist favored as her grandchildren.

Miss Gilchrist's relatives were also beneficiaries, including the Charteris brothers. Some authors proposed the killer was either or both of these professional, conservative gentlemen.

This book's timeline treads a steady path by Lambie, Nugent, and Oscar towards the December 21 murder. To discount their complicity by throwing in characters with vague motives and no *modus operandi* was a pointless effort that ignored the motives of three predatory individuals who in fact targeted Marion Gilchrist.

A Healthy Scotswoman

In the summertime, Marion holidayed on Scotland's northeast coast in tranquil, balmy Ayr but only after the annual National Hunt was held in April. She left before the second was held in September.

Ayr seaside

In the photograph below, a very tall Marion Gilchrist stands alongside the three grandchildren. David, Maggie, and Marion Gilchrist II. They were Marion Galbraith Ferguson's children. Lambie, wearing her uniform, arms akimbo for the photographer, stands to the right.

Miss Gilchrist's 'family' line-up on holiday at Ayr.

June 7---Unexpectedly, the third-floor tenants moved from Queen's Terrace. They found the building too noisy. Four Adams' siblings living on the first floor gave music lessons. And, when he wasn't on holiday in Ayr, there was Barney the barking terrier. The move of the third-floor tenants presented an opportunity that Lambie and Nugent wished to exploit.

August---Before Oscar Slater joined up, Lambie and Nugent plotted on their own. Nugent traveled to meet Miss Gilchrist at her country house in Ayr on a social visit with his girl, "Nellie" Lambie. Ayr lay on the western sea coast—37 miles from Glasgow. Away his train tore, as it did in Dickens' *Dombey and Son*, "...through the fields, through the woods, through the corn, through the hay..."

The two thought, mistakenly, that Miss Gilchrist would welcome Nugent...that he would charm her. He was a handsome, happy Irishman with a missing front tooth. It was a risky venture. She would be able to identify him in the future if ever a complaint were made.

When Detective Lieutenant John Trench interviewed Nugent after the murder, Nugent told him that it was a Saturday afternoon in August that he picnicked alone with Lambie. They planned the next day's tea with Miss Gilchrist.

Lambie testified that Nugent came to the Ayr country house for tea. Here was Conan Doyle's estimation: "...the very curious picture of the old lady, the bookmaker and the servant-maid all sitting at dinner together."

Miss Gilchrist had a look at the Irish Catholic fellow of no legitimate occupation, and Nugent got a look at the formidable Scots lady. She wasn't frightened of him but neither did she like him.

He pretended to be Lambie's intended, else why take the long train trip from Glasgow? The "boyfriend" was actually engaged to be married to a young, pregnant Carfin maidservant on November 25. After Nugent left Ayr, Miss Gilchrist sternly reminded Lambie that no men friends were allowed back home at the Queens Terrace flat.

Itching Palms and Jaundiced Eyes

According to the trial testimony of a prior maidservant--Jane Duff Walker, Miss Gilchrist left her jewels in the care of her jeweler, Mr. Sorley, for safekeeping while on holiday. Thus, Nugent and Lambie understood that a burglary could take place only while Miss Gilchrist was in residence, an extremely tricky undertaking.

The jewelry could not go missing while Lambie was alone in the flat. It would lead to suspicion and arrest. And, if Lambie were away on errands, leaving Miss Gilchrist alone at home, the burglary would have to be executed in such a way that would not incriminate Lambie—which could also lead to Nugent.

Previous to Lambie's employment, there were no burglaries while Miss Gilchrist was away, whether on summer holiday, visiting with the Fergusons, or while out on her own errands. There were no clashes with greedy relatives. No relatives broke in. No would-be robbers were observed staking out the building. Barney the dog lived and barked.

September--- Nugent connected with Oscar Slater who joined the two as salesman and as burglar. Nugent, one of four sons of a poor family, had no experience in gemology. Nor could he chance a burglary himself since Miss Gilchrist and others in the building would recognize him.

In police reports and at the trial, Patrick Nugent's participation was overlooked. His only connection so far as the police were concerned was that he'd been Lambie's unfaithful boyfriend. Lambie had been so taken with his attentions that she invited him to Miss Gilchrist's flat, against her employer's express command, and led him on a prideful, innocent tour into the spare bedroom and its jewelry collection.

Oscar Slater Acknowledges He Knew Patrick Nugent

In later prison correspondence, Slater acknowledged that he knew Patrick Nugent—and rather well. Bitter, of course, that he was the only one tried and convicted, but fortuitously having escaped the noose, he joined the chorus of "Oscar is Innocent." Though he had professed to the police and to the Court he knew "nothing of the affair," it seems he did. He had nothing to lose. He was serving a life term at Peterhead Prison.

Relieved of strenuous duty at the quarries, Slater had time to answer his correspondence. He grew confident in the pretense that he wasn't the murderer. After all, the public and a loyal rabbi proclaimed his innocence. The rabbi even arranged for ritual meals to be delivered to Slater on Jewish holidays.

In his Peterhead Prison records, and to his solicitors, Ewing Spiers and Alexander Shaughnessy, he accused "Nugent and a Nugent pal"--one of Slater's few references to his partners and the murder:

"My firm opinion is that the murder was one of Nugent's friends or a sweetheart of his."

As to Lambie, Slater wrote with transparent guile, she was **"...knowing so many boys..."**

How would Slater have known that bit of slanderous gossip?

Slater implicated Nugent from what source but himself? Trench hadn't disclosed the particulars of his December interview with Nugent nor did he interview Slater. Nugent hadn't appeared at the trial though his name was included on a list of witnesses for the Crown. Roughead's information that Nugent had no connection with the crime was the falsehood passed on to him by Detective John Trench.

Slater wrote that Nugent, with his pal, were plotters who got away but he was the one (wrongfully) caught. How well he must have known these two supposed strangers that he could defiantly mark them as murderers. He established that Nugent knew Helen Lambie, the tart, rather well, and suggested their motive. The motive, Slater speculated to a young lawyer and soon-to-be, frequent correspondent, Leslie Reade, was burglary. It was a two-person operation. For a man who exclaimed in fright at his death sentence, "I know nothing of *the affair*...," he knew positively that there had been a scheme involving those two miscreants who had not been charged. Doubtless Slater concluded their being gentile Scots caused the police to dump the plot into the lap of an innocent Jew.

With Arthur Conan Doyle in his corner, Slater felt confident enough of success that he thought he would try to get "Nugent and a pal" arrested as the murderers. Slater voluntarily chose not to testify at his extradition hearing or at trial. His post-trial crime solving came to nothing.

The Duo of Nugent and Lambie

Nugent and Lambie saw there were enough gems to sell and to share. Both he and Lambie, poor working-class people, could (separately) live in future comfort. There was also coin in the house. Miss Gilchrist paid the maid and her tradespeople with coin.

In mid-1908, Marion Gilchrist began to take precautionary measures by hiding jewelry in pockets and in underwear drawers. These were preventative measures. Lambie would turn to gossip and explain this conduct as that of a paranoid.

The jewelry wasn't strewn haphazardly, but secreted. There was a safe in the parlor. The keys to the locked box she kept in her pockets. On examining her corpse, the police found the keys to the jewelry box in her dress pocket.

Miss Gilchrist was a jewelry collector all her adult life. In January 1909, a month after her murder, a newspaper published information leaked to it about a tray of small diamonds found by police in a "hidden corner" at her flat and were "worth thousands." The leak corroborated the find with use of the word "tray." The tray of diamonds was the intended score. These diamonds answered the question of motive and the reason for Slater's frantic banging of the locked box the night of the murder with witnesses standing outside the door of the flat.

When Oscar Slater took the upper hand in the scheme, Nugent curtailed his visits to Lambie at the flat. He limited his contacts to meeting on the street during her errands as evidenced by the note he sent her and about which she testified at trial.

What can be assumed from Nugent's note to Lambie?

- She received mail at the house.

- She took care that Miss Gilchrist not know about her contacts with Nugent.

- Nugent knew that he was not allowed at the Gilchrist flat whether Miss Gilchrist was in the flat or not.

- Nugent's visits to the flat only when Miss Gilchrist was out on errands were highly secretive.

- He did not visit while Marion Gilchrist was home, notwithstanding the tea he'd shared with the lady and Lambie at Ayr in August.

- After August, Nugent wanted to keep his connection as secret as possible with no witnesses.

- Nugent needed to meet Lambie even though he was engaged to be married.

- Lambie met Nugent outside for reasons likely connected to Barney, to her pilfering of jewelry, and to the burglary.
- He knew Lambie had regular errands, and that she was routinely at the corner of St. George's Road and Princes Street outside the Gilchrist flat, 15 Queens Terrace.
- Their meetings coincided with Lambie's nightly errands and her off-days on Thursdays and Sundays.

Miss Gilchrist had cautioned Lambie about gentlemen callers when she was not at home. To have willfully ignored the rules of her employer did not flatter this maidservant. In spite of this duplicity, the police missed Lambie's lies.

Lambie's disclosures to Nugent about Miss Gilchrist's property, her errand schedules, the layout of the flat, and her steady pilfering of jewelry from the house, gave both Nugent and, later, Oscar Slater the entrée they needed to complete the planned heist successfully.

Sunday, September 7--- Barney the terrier barked during Nugent's visits and during his tea with Lambie and Miss Gilchrist in Ayr. Chillingly, Nugent knew Barney had to go.

When the Gilchrist party returned home to Glasgow, Lambie was back to her days-off schedule, Sunday being such a day. She took Barney for a walk outdoors from 1:30 to 6:16 p.m. The Irish terrier was dying when she returned with it to the flat. She told Miss Gilchrist she thought the dog took sick (and died) from something it had eaten in the street. Miss Gilchrist, no fool, told her maid she thought Barney had been poisoned, adding "what kind of a person would kill a little dog?" Dr. Perry, called by Miss Gilchrist to examine Barney, also concluded it had been poisoned...in a premeditated act.

These were two harsh souls whose first task was the killing of Miss Gilchrist's dog. A plan of breaking and entering had begun. Nugent could also return to the flat without fear of Barney's alert. He had time to familiarize himself with the lay of the house, the locks, the spare bedroom, the jewels, the secure places and a tray of small diamonds. Only a skilled gemologist like Slater would get them a good price on stolen jewels.

Miss Gilchrist had long experience with servants, tradesfolk, and merchants, as she had with her fellow congregants, relatives and friends. At her age, she acquired an estimation of character. It presented itself when she met Patrick Nugent at Ayr when she had eyed him ruefully. Lambie was described as "very cunning" by Agnes Guthrie, Lambie's former employer. If Marian Gilchrist had concerns about Lambie, no posthumous conversations were disclosed. Still, that November, Lambie applied for another job. Why was that? In December, she did so again.

Lambie knew Miss Gilchrist told the family Ferguson about the poisoning death of Barney, the terrier who had played with the children at Ayr. Mr. Ferguson, the children's father, visited Miss Gilchrist at the flat at least twice about finding another pup. Only four days before her murder, he had stopped by to report on his progress. Lambie was at the flat. There was enough time for the intended burglary before another dog came to disturb the peace.

---The retired maidservant, Jane Duff Walker, visited Miss Gilchrist in September, two weeks before Oscar Slater began pawning and selling gem stones and gold accessories in October. Barney was dead. Miss

Gilchrist told Miss Duff Walker that the upstairs tenants moved and their flat was still empty.

CHAPTER 16

Glasgow Donjon

October 1908—Oscar Slater resurfaced in Glasgow. He took a room at the Central Hotel, one of the several yellow stone buildings attached to the Central Railroad Station. He'd lived at the hotel in 1901 and 1905. The hotel and the train station were convenient to his frequent travels, and to Sauchiehall and the stretch of streets where stood the gambling clubs, snooker halls, and pubs. This was Slater's base of operation. Walking along St. George's Road, Central Hotel was about a half mile to the Gilchrist flat.

Postcard pleasant Sauchiehall, an electric tram driving past. To the rear stand the red sandstone Charing Cross Mansions, next to which was Slater's flat.

Shrewd Oscar took the upper hand in the plot.

Testimony of the Superintendent of the Southern Division of the Glasgow Police Force John Ord:

Q. Have you not met many cases of men like Slater taking a Scotch name?

A. No, not a man of his intelligence.

Nugent was too recognizable in the Gilchrist neighborhood. Miss Gilchrist, if confronted in the flat, would recognize Nugent but not the stranger, Oscar Slater.

On his return to Glasgow, Slater suddenly began to sell small, one-carat diamonds. These were from the brooch Miss Gilchrist had taken for cleaning to Sorley's Jewelry the previous March. Nugent and Lambie would have pilfered the brooch during Nugent's visits to the Gilchrist flat. It was the brooch Lambie declared was missing the day after the murder. Slater was selling the diamonds reset from the crescent-shaped brooch with one row of diamonds (Brooch #1). He began to pay his debts, make investments, and save money. The sales of these diamonds were as sudden as his return to Glasgow.

David Jacobs, Slater's fence/dealer/friend, testified at trial that he had seen Slater's wife, i.e. Mlle. Andrée, wearing a "half-moon with a row of diamonds." So, crescent-shaped Brooch #1 **had** come into the possession of Oscar Slater. He reset them--removing the diamonds to sell individually.

He also sold accessories: gold binoculars, a gold purse, pearl studs, a gold pencil case, and two gold rings. He kept a set of silver shaving accessories which he had engraved with the name "Anderson" and which he used when visiting his barber. With his diamond earnings, Slater paid his London watchmaker, Messrs. Dent, a debt he'd owed since 1905.

Oscar's enthusiasm was whetted with Lambie's incremental jewelry deliveries but a larger heist figured in the trio's scheme.

---In October, Miss Gilchrist's solicitor came to visit; reason unknown.

---Jane Duff Walker visited Miss Gilchrist, a regular routine. Miss Gilchrist told her she'd had to speak with Arthur Adams and alerted him that if she were in any trouble, she would knock with her cane on the floor of her flat. Miss Gilchrist was anxious about having been awakened in the middle of the night by the sound of footsteps from a person leaving the flat.

--- Lambie visited Agnes Guthrie—the employer who referred to Lambie as "very cunning." Lambie told her that Miss Gilchrist's solicitor had been to visit. Was she angling for information? After Barney's death in September, Miss Gilchrist began hiding her jewels.

Oscar's Arrangements in Glasgow

October 5---Robert Rogers, Oscar's London business pal at 36 Albermarle Place, sent a letter of reference on behalf of dentist A. Anderson to John Marr, broker for a Glasgow flat at 69 St. George's Road.

Why Slater decided on an alias in Glasgow was anyone's guess but from the habits of criminal types in those days, he couldn't be Oscar Slater in the scheme—a man with whom Glasgow police had familiarity. The "A. Anderson" name, which he'd used with U.S. Immigration, may have been familiar. A German grand chess master with that name, from Slater's homeland in Silesia, was so famous that on his death in 1879, a 19-page obituary was published.

Slater's motive in the scheme? No different than that of Nugent and Lambie. A fortune in diamonds. His portion could go towards a business in America and provide a financial background to qualify for citizenship where he'd applied in 1907. In the Sauchiehall locales, Slater began to drop hints that he planned to relocate to America the coming January.

October 15---Slater was back in London dealing with product and jewelers, including with "Carrey" about whom he wrote to David Jacobs on November 29.

October 21---Slater had money in his pocket. He paid Messrs. Dent for the watch repair debt owed since November 24, 1905. Lucky he did, for the watch would be sent back for expedited repairs in December.

October 29---In the evening, after several years' separation, he collided with "Moudie" Hugh Cameron. To Cameron, he was still Oscar Slater.

---During the diamond and accessories sales, fellow fence, David Jacobs, came to Glasgow to meet with Slater.

November---One bitter November, greed had sniffed out the homicidal Raskolnikov, a fictional, impoverished villain from semi-barbarous Russia, who took an ax to a Jewish old lady because she had money and he didn't (*"zhiden'kie volosy" [Jewish hair] ...she's wealthy like a* Jew." *Crime and Punishment* by Fyodor Dostoevsky, 1866). Oscar Slater was made of similar stuff, though dispassion ruled in the art of his steal rather than the psychosis that consumed Raskolnikov.

Samuel Reid was a Glasgow, Belfast, and London bookie of Slater's acquaintance of a dozen years. At trial, he testified he was surprised to see Slater back in Glasgow. He offered a modest alibi for Slater. In his thick foreign accent, Reid testified that he and his son ate dinner with Slater on December 20; witnesses who claimed they saw him loitering that night outside the Gilchrist flat were mistaken.

For three successive Sundays prior to Nugent's November 25th wedding date, wedding banns were read in the parish church. The couple was required to attend prior to the wedding.

November 3---At Bryce Pawnbrokers, Slater pawned two gold rings, 3 pearl studs, 1 gold pencil case, 1 gold purse, and 1 fountain pen, receiving a sizeable draw of £5 ($712 in today's money). He also sold a few individual gems and a diamond pin; price unknown.

Slater acquired these items to pawn or sell, even though Mlle. Andrée had not yet arrived in Glasgow to get her business up and running. He arranged Andrée and Katerina's move from London to Glasgow.

November 4—Andrée arrived in Glasgow. She and Katerina roomed with Slater at the Central Hotel. He decided that, instead of daily payment at the Central Hotel, to rent a flat for the ladies and himself for the two months he expected to remain in Glasgow. He found housing within the immediate vicinity, a few minutes from Marion Gilchrist's flat. In his rented flat, Slater could maintain privacy and the Mademoiselle could conduct business. He conserved cash by withholding rental payment on the flat until February, and made only partial payments on the furnishings.

St. George's Road. A busy commercial district

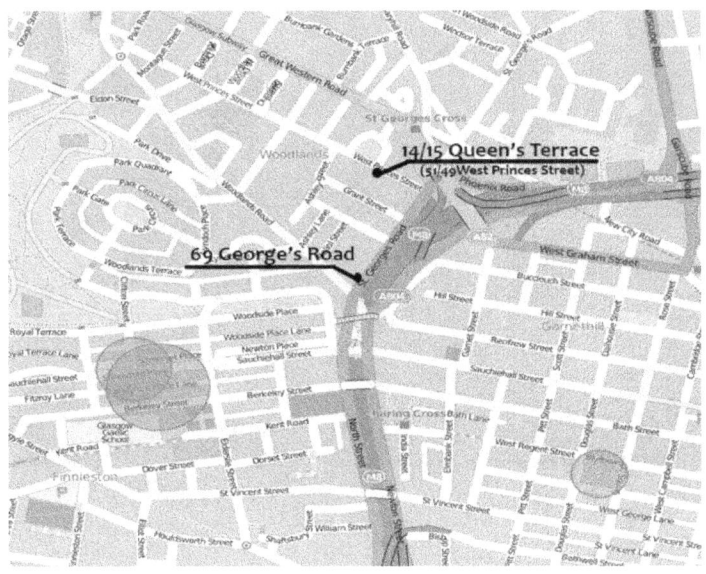

A recent map; Cumberland Street appears as Ashley Street to the right of Grant Street.

Slater rented the upstairs flat at 69 St. George's Road in a red sandstone building. Red and yellow sandstone were typical of Glasgow's architecture, the stone sourced from the local quarries where one day Oscar Slater would be consigned as working prisoner.

Kitchenette within a modest Glasgow flat located in the center of town where Slater lived.

Sleeping Quarters

Victorian Fireplace

November 5---Davenport Co. of London was among those who sent letters of reference on behalf of A. Andersen, dentist, formerly of 36 Albemarle Road, Piccadilly, London, to John Marr, the rental broker in Glasgow for the 69 St. George's flat. Slater's plaque, in the name of A. Anderson, Dentist, was hung outside. He couldn't use "Oscar Slater" on the plaque nor hold himself out as leaseholder. It was against the law to operate a house of ill repute and he had an arrest record with the Glasgow police. Customers seen coming upstairs could be mistaken for dental patients. The maid, Katerina, when questioned by police after the murder, believed that Slater used the Adolf Anderson alias to avoid an ex-wife chasing him for money.

November 6---Slater rented furniture from Isaac Paradise, whose shop was two doors down, with a down payment of £10. The furniture had to be paid before Andrée could begin work. He paid an additional £4 by December 10 because he didn't expect to leave Glasgow until January.

In the evenings, while Slater sallied forth to the gambling clubs, Andrée resumed her business. Walking a Glasgow street advantageously took practice. In certain areas, she might encounter competing streetwalkers holding up their skirts to lure a workingman. Young Andrée chose not to posture her perfumed self outdoors. She frequented dance halls where gentlemen might drunkenly admire her and have the coin to purchase a session. Slater made life safe for Mlle. Andrée as Katerina Schmaltz and Hugh Cameron would testify. Fellow bookie, Samuel Reid and his son visited Oscar Slater at the "A. Anderson" residence every Sunday for dinner. There was a familial glow to Slater's house of ill repute.

November 10---Slater tried to sell a 25-carat diamond ring to warehouseman, Jacob Jackson, who declined. Jackson would later testify that the ring looked to be worth only £15 ($73; today, $2000). Still, Slater had spendable cash. He paid several merchants with cash.

There was no proof that the merchandise Slater suddenly acquired and pawned in October and November were the property of Marion Gilchrist. It is important to remember that Slater's life from 1893 to 1908 was one of financial scrambling. He didn't have merchandise in his possession nor title nor deeds of ownership nor letters of credit on arriving in Glasgow. Mlle. Andrée didn't start business in Glasgow until about November 7, so Slater wasn't acquiring gold bric a brac through her. Yet, Slater had come into control and possession of jewelry and merchandise, frequented pawnshops for draws on pawned items, and also redeemed some during his occasional, pre-murder prosperity. He was also saving money. Presumably, the commodities were supplied by Lambie from the Gilchrist home.

A Hammer Was the Weapon

November 10---Slater bought a hammer along with a pail, brushes, and 24 coat hooks, the latter presumably for gentlemen callers. Yet, for his temporary, unpaid-for flat, Oscar claimed to author William Park, who visited him in prison in 1927, that the hammer was intended for minor fixups. The hammer held sentimental value since Slater packed it for his flight to America. He hadn't anticipated that the police and the forensic examiners would identify the apparent weapon as a hammer upon examination of the corpse.

In the 1820s in Scotland, two men made a living by providing corpses to the Medical College in Edinburgh. They soon followed with killing the future cadavers and. as a weapon, used a hammer. The trial was a sensation in the press. In Slater's heyday, newspapers routinely reported the killings of bookies with hammers. It was a weapon of choice. Silent and deadly.

Slater's was a claw head hammer with a steel head and a wooden handle. His plan was one of murder. The old lady had to die before he could scour the jewelry room for the diamonds worth thousands. The plan called for swift execution so that Slater would be gone before an investigation was underway.

The hammer he purchased was the one used to kill Marion Gilchrist. Having to explain its existence away, the Oscar-was-Innocent authors muddled the relevance of this crucial physical evidence. Some suggested the hammer he'd bought was tiny, like a toffee cracker, an unlikely weapon suitable only for pushing tacks.

The sole difference between the hammer Slater purchased and the one found in his luggage was that the hammer in his luggage had tiny red flecks...blood embedded in the wood handle and metal head when he was arrested at the New York port January 2, 1909. The forensic experts reported that it had also been scrubbed. The photo of Slater's hammer should disabuse anyone of its deficiency. For a man without a gun, it was a reliable weapon with which to attack a (choose: weak elderly startled defenseless) woman.

Slater's hammer--standard weight 448 grams; 24 cm. in length, wooden (birch) handle.

The photo below is that of a "toffee hammer," a gadget used to break up sheets of toffee for sale to candy lovers. The era's Suffragettes easily concealed toffee hammers in their clothing, using them in window-breaking campaigns to alert the public about women's unequal political status. Once women won the right to vote in the UK in 1928, the toffee hammers were limited to their original usage. Today, a patient might experience a physician's testing for the Babinski reflex from the foot to the heel using just such a tiny hammer—quite harmless.

Toffee hammer

There were improbable disputations about the hammer. Why? Because Slater "believably" wanted to make repairs to the rented flat at 69 St. George's Road. He'd lived in Great Britain since 1895 and never found the need to buy one. Suddenly, his purchase was likened to that of an industrious homeowner. Before his flight to New York after the murder, he packed that hammer in his luggage. He didn't leave it for the women who took over his flat. He didn't produce evidence of repairs made with the hammer. The evidence from the hammer were blood flecks stuck within it and that it had been scrubbed.

During his incarceration at Peterhead Prison, after having been found guilty of Marion Gilchrist's murder, warders wrote Slater up for assaults. Fellow inmates and warders at Peterhead remembered that he had great strength. In one incident, he attacked a guard with a hammer. Hammers were used by inmates in their daily enforced 12-hour hard labor at the quarries, pounding red and blonde sandstone to build up the Glasgow metropolis.

Oscar's Short-term Intentions

By all accounts, Slater made no secret of his plans to leave Glasgow in two months, whether to America, Australia, or Monte Carlo. These destinations all presupposed a generous store of cash. He did not reveal his plans to his close friend, Hugh Cameron-- not until December 21, some hours before the murder. On that afternoon, Slater wrote down his future, incorrect address: "Oscar Slater, c/o Caesar Cafe, 644 Broadway, San Francisco."

Other than Slater's circumlocution, there was no evidence that he was headed for San Francisco. What the evidence revealed was that Slater signed a restaurant lease with a New York friend. The lease was possibly intended to supplement his financials towards his Declaration of Citizenship. The brooch with three rows of diamonds wasn't claimed as an item of value in his financial statement for the U.S. citizenship examiner. This was because Slater did not possess Brooch #2 until he moved back to Glasgow. It refutes Andrée's testimony that he bought her this brooch a year or so prior to the murder.

Slater expected a successful outcome at the Immigration Service just so long as he had an appreciable sum of money and proof that he, Adolf Andersen, Dentist, was a reputable businessman.

Slater's barber, Frederick Nichols, testified on behalf of the Crown. He knew his customer as Mr. A. Anderson, a dentist from America. Chatty as people come to be with barbers and hair stylists, so too was Oscar Slater. He was shaved several times a week, often twice daily, for his heavy growth of beard. His hair grew fast. The day after he was arrested in New York, Slater requested permission to be given a shave, which was granted. Slater had a thick mustache which barber Nichols regularly trimmed. The barber testified that Slater's "nose seemed broken rather than twisted."

Slater provided his own silver shaving utensils, engraved recently in Glasgow, with the latest alias of "Anderson." In Miss Gilchrist's jewelry inventory there remained only a silver shaving brush holder – no longer part of a set. A coincidence? The police failed to investigate this clue.

November 12---Slater opened a Postal Office Savings Account in the name of Adolf Anderson, with a firm Glasgow address.

November 13---Still with ready cash, Slater redeemed items he had pledged with Bryce Pawnbrokers on November 3.

November 14---Slater pledged a woman's diamond scarf pin for a £5 draw in the name of A. Anderson with Liddell's Pawnbrokers. The clerk at Liddell's, Philip McLaren, would testify at trial that he first met Oscar Slater as a repeat customer in the month of November.

November 17---At Liddell's, Slater pawned a gold purse, a fountain pen, and the three pearl studs which he'd redeemed from Bryce Pawnbrokers on November 13. He also pawned a gold ring. He received a total draw of £6 (£797.07 today) and deposited £5 in his Postal savings account.

CHAPTER 17

A Tale of Two Diamond Brooches

A Red Herring and a Smoking Gun

There were two brooches in this whole sorry plot and BOTH were Marion Gilchrist's.

- **Brooch #1**: 1 crescent-shaped brooch with 1 row of diamonds
- **Brooch #2**: 1 round brooch with 3 rows of diamonds

☞ Oscar Slater, the diamond cutter and dealer, had been selling gems, jeweled accessories, and small diamonds upon his return to Glasgow in October.

Jozef Aumann testified that some time in November at Gall's Public House where they played billiards, Slater offered to sell him a 25-carat diamond ring. This was the ring Slater tried to sell to a warehouseman. Max Rattman had no interest nor the wherewithal to pay. Aumann offered to buy it for £30 or £35. The amount was a trifle and Slater refused.

The small diamonds Slater was selling, he'd separated from the brooch in which they had been encased. It was a crescent-shaped brooch with one row of diamonds—the one David Jacobs testified he had once seen Mlle. Andrée wearing. Each small diamond--assuming that Miss Gilchrist favored the one-carat-- would have had an approximate 1908 value of £1,000. The sales of the individual diamonds would have provided Slater (and presumably Nugent and Lambie) with pocket money, savings, and incentive for more.

November 18---On this day, Oscar received and then pawned at Liddell's, the *pièce de résistance*-- a brooch with three rows of diamonds for a draw of £30, and later, incrementally, draws for a sum total of £60. The brooch would be the red herring of the criminal investigation in the murder of Marion Gilchrist.

The term "red herring" arose from a metaphor attached to news reports. Often, journalists turn ambitious and become easily misled by false information or a false lead. A "red herring" is one that distracts from the real issue.

In the police investigation and Crown prosecution, it was alleged that Brooch #1 was stolen on the night of the murder and that it had been the motive for the murder. It was reported missing to police by Helen Lambie on December 22, the morning after the murder. The police and prosecution made an inexcusable error when they dispensed with the relevance of Brooch #2, the brooch pawned by Slater at Liddell's on November 18, a month before the murder.

In an instant, Brooch #2 was pronounced as Oscar Slater's property. The police and the Crown were fishing the wrong stream. Both brooches had been stolen by Lambie, Nugent, and Slater. This red herring diversion arose from Lambie's false identification—to the police in a murder investigation-- of a brooch that was supposedly missing the night of the murder.

Pawned Brooch #2 was not produced at trial. It was ignored, the Crown having yielded to the police determination that it was Slater's property. Missing Brooch #1, with one row of diamonds, remained the sole motive for murder. *But it was Brooch #2 that was existing proof of the crime committed by Oscar Slater.*

Brooch #2 was also stolen. Unlike Brooch #1, from which Slater extracted small diamonds for separate sales in early October, he pawned Brooch #2 for the substantial draws at Liddell's. Its three rows of diamonds were of a quality that prompted Oscar to hold on to the pawn ticket. He made no effort to sell until the frantic days following the murder.

Brooch #2 was the "smoking gun," another forensic idiom. Here we again associate Conan Doyle's contribution. In 1893, Sherlock Holmes introduced the term into the English language in his first professional case, "The Adventure of the Gloria Scott." In the story, mutineers confronted a chaplain holding a smoking pistol…the weapon! It was the strongest kind of circumstantial evidence.

There was no photo nor illustration of Brooch #2 at Slater's trial. After learning on December 25 from Allan McLean that Mr. Oscar had been desperately trying to sell a pawn ticket for a brooch, two police officers hastened to Liddell's with Helen Lambie to identify the brooch pawned by Slater. Was it the same one she claimed had been stolen? "No." Lambie said the brooch with three rows of diamonds at Liddell's was not Miss Gilchrist's. Here, statements of ownership from Mrs. Ferguson or Miss Duff Walker or a relative would have been productive, but in this too, the police and prosecution were remiss.

The pawn ticket was in Slater's pocket upon his arrest in New York on board ship. He told the officials that the brooch was his and the young Mademoiselle's. What fashionable young woman from Paris would be wont to wear a Victorian era brooch? In her photo, Andrée appeared the very modern model of a plucky Edwardian coquette. No jewelry appeared on her neck, blouse nor hat for a professional photograph. She never went to Liddell's to claim the brooch as her own. No one inquired about it when she was on the stand.

Mademoiselle Andrée

Slater held no certificate of ownership nor receipt. No initials were engraved within the brooch (as on his shaving accessories). He never mentioned the brooch to Hugh Cameron nor to Luise Freedman from whom he took money in order to flee to America.

Neither he nor Andrée had a collection of Victorian era jewelry. Slater had no furniture, no house, no pearls nor rubies of his own, and no generous store of investments—whereas Marion Gilchrist did. Furthermore, on searching the flat after the murder, police found a great number of Miss Gilchrist's receipts from large and respected jewelry shops in town, and the receipts were spread over the course of many years.

The police and the Crown failed to piece together the puzzle of the two diamond brooches, a remarkable misstep. Someone had reason to avoid Brooch #2's role in the trial. It wasn't just Oscar Slater.

Safekeeping of the Gilchrist Jewelry

A heavy safe sat in the house parlor. It would have required a locksmith with time on his hands to open it. It was reported to have held personal documents. The intruder wasn't after the safe. He knew there was nothing of value in the safe nor in the chest of drawers that stood in the dining room.

A wooden jewelry box in the spare bedroom was kept locked. It was large, strong and secure. On December 21, Lambie believed the wooden box held what they were seeking: diamonds. It would account for why Slater went mad in banging that box after he'd murdered Marion Gilchrist. He found nothing within but papers. No coins, no notes, and no single, unset diamonds worth thousands of pounds.

PHOTO: Victorian jewelry box with lock

November 20---Miss Gilchrist met with her solicitor, James MacDonald, coincident in time with the disappearance of a number of jewelry pieces. She requested a codicil to her Will. It would not eliminate her blood relatives but would assure her Ferguson grandchildren a generous portion of the estate. An exhibit of her jewelry list and chattel possessions were appended to the amended Will.

When Lambie visited Agnes Guthrie, she mentioned Miss Gilchrist's solicitor visits. Lambie was curious whether Miss Guthrie knew of the solicitor's visits or whether Miss Gilchrist may have voiced suspicions about Lambie.

 A Hidden Tray in a Hidden Corner

Included in a police report of January 1909 and provided to *Reynolds News* in London was a line of information that a tray of unset diamonds was found in a hidden corner at Miss Gilchrist's. The diamonds were worth "thousands." It had been hidden by Miss Gilchrist for a reason. The police report was not produced at trial and neither were the tray and diamonds though oblique reference to their existence was made in witness examinations.

David Dick's Inventory omitted the tray of diamonds. His testimony led to paths the police and prosecution failed to follow. In this excerpt, the highlights:

DAVID DICK, examined by the LORD ADVOCATE — I made an inventory and valuation of the household furniture, electro-plate, and jewellery at the late Miss Gilchrist's house. No. 22 of the productions is the inventory and valuation which I made. I found jewellery in the house to the value of £1382 12s. If bought in shops they would cost at least twice as much. **We found jewels scattered all over the wardrobe;** some were laid between dresses, and some were in an old, detachable pocket with a string on it for tying round the waist. I made a very careful examination for a brooch which I was told was missing. I am quite satisfied that it was not in the house. I was shown a sketch of that brooch. The brooch was shaped like a horse-shoe, crescent- shaped, with a double row of diamonds. Judging from the sketch the value would be between £40 and £50.

In Mr. Dick's testimony…

- There is no mention of single diamonds worth thousands in the Inventory.
- How it came to be that, after the murder, jewelry was scattered. On the night of the murder, police found that the murderer scattered only papers from the smashed jewelry box.
- He speaks of "We." There was no identification of the other party.
- No notes accompanied the Inventory.
- An old stringed pouch held some jewelry—was this the sort of pouch in which diamonds had been laid in the "hidden tray?"
- Superintendent Ord and Detective-Inspector Pyper testified about police searches which continued for several weeks after the murder.

Victorian tray and velvet compartments

Miss Duff Walker, who regularly visited Marion Gilchrist, testified that Miss Gilchrist was not a "resetter" of diamonds (as was Slater) nor had she ever seen uncut diamonds at the flat where she had worked eight years prior. They would have been newer purchases.

> "Have you heard that Miss Gilchrist was a resetter? — Yes.
> She was not? — No.
> Did she have unset stones in the house? — I never saw them.
> You have heard that rumour also? — Yes."

There were murmurs and rumors about diamonds. Police had even uttered a value: "worth thousands of pounds." This was published in the newspapers. The "rumor," about which Miss Duff Walker was questioned on the stand, appeared in the *Reynolds Newspaper* from information leaked by a police officer.

Marion Gilchrist was a woman of means left a comfortable estate by her father. Her neighbors, maids, fellow parishioners, relatives, and friends knew her to wear expensive but understated jewelry. She had been a collector for many years.

It was highly likely the tray of diamonds was what Slater sought and was the source of his desperation in reducing the locked box to splinters. He could only have learned of its existence from Lambie and Nugent.

The police, the Procurator Fiscal, and the Crown overlooked the tray of diamonds. It didn't appear on the List of Exhibits nor in Roughead's treatise on Oscar Slater's innocence. Lambie did not testify about them and neither did the officers who found a tray. The tray of small diamonds certainly approached the level of motive for the trio.

CHAPTER 18

November Pause

 The Trio's Breather After November 18

After November 18--- Slater was no longer selling nor pawning jewelry. Lambie had come to a pause in her pilfering. Nugent was not available as a go-between. He was getting ready for his wedding. Miss Gilchrist had begun hiding her jewelry and she'd met with her solicitor. Lambie was justifiably tentative about the thefts.

Why did Slater remain in town and not depart for America? He had accumulated some savings. Instead, he waited until early December, after the Nugent wedding and celebration, to begin reconnoitering West Princes Road and 15 Queen's Terrace.

Obviously, Brooch #2 was not the subject of the quest. Slater already held it at the pawn shop. There was something else the trio was after in the flat. It required an audacious break-and-entry and Slater was willing to chance it. Lambie could remove a piece of jewelry without drawing attention to herself, but what the thieves wanted was more valuable. Lambie believed it was contained in a locked jewelry box.

November 25--- Nugent's wedding. Oscar didn't begin reconnoitering

15 Queens Terrace in earnest until December 12. Witnesses took notice of a foreign-looking man walking the street in the late afternoon or evening. "Foreign-looking." It wasn't a description of Irish Nugent. It wasn't a native-looking Scot. It was dark-haired, dandily dressed, bowler-hatted Oscar Slater in the first stage of the break-in. With little to do in the afternoons, women peeked through the window curtains. Their separate observations may not have corresponded with exactitude but they were close enough.

According to Conan Doyle, Helen Lambie began looking for another position in November. This was odd. She was proud of her status as maidservant to a wealthy lady in a respectable neighborhood. She hadn't left by December 20 and Miss Gilchrist had given her the usual half-sovereign for errands on December 21. Conan Doyle remarked about heated remonstrances by Miss Gilchrist about Lambie's prying and that she threatened to terminate her services without a reference. Lambie may also have been taking stock of what was going to happen in late December. Taking another job was the wise thing to do if one's employer was either suspicious or dead. The police wouldn't suspect Lambie because looking for work meant she still needed a job and wages.

A plan for a date certain to enter and burgle the Gilchrist flat began November 20 after Miss Gilchrist met with her solicitor. The plot was stalled temporarily. For Patrick Nugent, the month of November wasn't convenient, He was getting married at the end of the month. December was good for Slater the bookie. The racetrack was closed all that month because Scotland's deep darkness fell by late afternoon. Slater took constitutionals around West Princes Street with time on his hands, free to observe the routine and the unexpected with less sunlight than in earlier months in Glasgow.

 *Lambie Muddies the Waters*

Continuing with events after November 20--- Marion Gilchrist was running an errand. Lambie took the opportunity to again visit Agnes Guthrie. Miss Guthrie's connection with Marion Gilchrist was minimal at best. She'd given her Lambie's reference two years' prior. Marion Gilchrist's friends, to whom she should have voiced her concerns, if real, were the Fergusons.

Lambie's intention was to plant doubt should Miss Gilchrist mention her missing jewelry. Lambie suggested to Agnes Guthrie that Miss Gilchrist's mind had become muddled. The word "paranoia" entered her limited vocabulary. It could only have been expanded by someone familiar with the English dictionary. That same someone directed Lambie to this visit with Miss Guthrie, a past employer who hadn't spoken well of her to Miss Gilchrist.

The instructions and the impromptu vocabulary lesson involved meetings among the three plotters. Lambie wouldn't have met Slater without Nugent beside her. It was during in-person meetings that Lambie noticed Slater's "peculiar gait" when walking. On the night of the murder, he'd come rushing out of the flat giving the eyewitnesses no opportunity to examine the manner of his walk.

Lambie feigned concern. Elderly Miss Gilchrist was imagining things—hearing footsteps, placing valuable jewelry midst clothing in drawers and in the wardrobe instead of in her jewelry box. With this subterfuge, notwithstanding Miss Guthrie's cynical opinion of her, Lambie looked to preempt suspicion about her conduct should police became involved. The trio would have discussed such grave consequences. Imprisonment was harsh—as Oscar Slater would soon learn.

Author William Roughead wrote that "constant dread" and "nervousness" was Marion Gilchrist's state. He took Lambie's tales for fact. Margalit Fox, in *Conan Doyle for the Defense,* wrote: "Marion Gilchrist was a remarkably frightened woman." The evidence rested on Lambie's ruse at Agnes Guthrie's. Authors believed that dangerous little fox without question.

Lambie worked for Miss Gilchrist for almost three years and it was during this time that these unsettling incidents occurred. Miss Gilchrist's prior maidservants met with no sordid accusations of gentlemen callers, disappearing jewelry, padlocks, poisoned dogs, and paranoia. Included in police reports was a statement that Miss Gilchrist wanted a replacement for Helen Lambie. The police failed to investigate Lambie's activities and made only minor inquiries into her relationship with Nugent.

What Lambie may not have discussed with Agnes Guthrie was that Marion Gilchrist continued to conduct her business affairs, amended her Will, dressed and wore her jewelry, went out to tea, shopped, ventured out in good or bad weather, rode trams, attended church where she was a prominent parishioner, holidayed, stored her jewels with Sorley's when she went away from the flat, arranged for a policeman to mind the building when she was away, nightly read newspapers and magazines, reviewed investments with her stockbrokers, entertained visitors for tea and visited them at their homes, and called for a vet when Barney was dying.

At trial, the solicitor should have testified that Miss Gilchrist was of sound mind. He wasn't asked. After all, he prepared the Will, special bequests and codicils that traditionally began with the words: "Being of sound mind..." There was no diminished competency when she added the last codicil to her Will in November.

How had Lambie come to believe that Miss Gilchrist was hiding her jewelry? Lambie's instincts would have been aroused when rifling through the drawers and wardrobe and finding jewelry the old lady had taken to secreting from the only other person living in that flat.

Lambie told Miss Guthrie about the oddity of Miss Gilchrist's complaint that Barney had been poisoned—even though a veterinarian had been called and agreed to the cause of Barney's death. She said she was driven by nameless fears and possible thieves and had installed three padlocks on the flat door. Thus, we learn the locks were installed during Lambie's service.

The padlocks were a common lock, a patent Chubb lock, and a bolt and chain. Miss Gilchrist was of a coherent mind in arranging for the locks. She had jewelry to protect and Barney was dead. A tradesman installed them.

Lambie would have informed Nugent and Slater. On the night of the murder, none of the locks had been secured when Lambie went out to buy the paper. It was a given that no dog would bark in the nighttime. The police reports were silent as to these clues.

Padlocks affixed at the left of the front door

Hall, 15 Queen's Terrace (looking east)
Showing inner side of outer door (left); dining-room (centre); door leading to kitchen (right)

Oscar Slater Takes Control

---In November and December, Slater peppered acquaintances with stories of business opportunities awaiting him outside Great Britain. He calendared his big score for December, awaiting a new future with his anticipated bounty, leagues from police scrutiny.

A few days before Christmas in Carfin, Nugent would be positioned as lookout on Grant Street. He was the second man observed by Agnes Brown the night of the murder.

Late November---In preparation for the plot and for his departure, Oscar asked his barber, Frederick Nichols, if he would buy his like-new furnishings—the furniture he'd rented from Isaac Paradise which had not been fully paid. He told the barber he was leaving for Queensland, Australia by December 30: "no money stirring in Glasgow."

November 23---Oscar offered to sell a 25-carat diamond ring—which Jacobson had declined—to Max Rattman while the two played cards at Gall's Public House. Max, like Oscar, had his share of arrests—four for fraud—and had just been released after two years in prison. Max also declined, suspicious that the ring was "hot" and overpriced.

November 25---This Wednesday morning, Patrick Nugent married a Roman Catholic girl, Martha Curran, 21.

To Detective Lieutenant Trench, Nugent explained away his abandoned friendship with Lambie and any connection to the Gilchrist murder. He said he'd decided against marrying Helen Lambie because she was a Protestant. Martha Curran was bearing another Nugent child. He related his wedding story to Trench when questioned at his home December 31, ten days after the murder. He told Trench his four brothers lived with them in the house.

November 28--- Miss Gilchrist met her solicitor at his offices where two individuals witnessed the signing of the codicil to her Will. This again disputed the paranoia about which Lambie had gossiped. The solicitor would have represented, along with the witnesses, that, in signing, Marion Gilchrist was of sound mind.

November 29---Oscar Slater wrote to David Jacobs in London to say he was relocating to New York "at the end of January." Slater's post-November 18 cash shortage prompted his message. Though both were Yiddish speakers, Slater wrote the letter entirely in English, concededly inexact. The correspondence was a convincing alibi should the need arise.

Slater had moved to Glasgow from London abruptly that October and he hadn't bothered to inform Jacobs. In his letter to Jacobs, Slater's excuse for an expected departure from Glasgow was that "Matters are here very bad. The New York bank affairs have done a lot to it" (the October 1907 bank panic in New York). The correspondence was necessary to Slater's scheme. It answered the question of why he'd gone to Glasgow for three months.

Having laid on the grease for Jacobs, Slater suggested that he could still broker deals with emerald gems, i.e. "pawn some of *your* emeralds." (emphasis added). Slater offered to divide the profits...an *in futuro* contractual obligation extended to Jacobs who was to allow Slater—residing in another city-- possession of emeralds without collateral. At the letter's conclusion, Slater contradicted his January destination, writing that in late January, he and Rogers were returning to London to resume doing business there. This was a subtle assurance to Jacobs that Slater was good to pay up in the future.

He let David Jacobs in on a big marketing secret. Slater heard from the grapevine that there was a market for emeralds in Glasgow *and* in Ireland-- of all places. It could have been borderline credible so far as Ireland where the color green was not only the symbol of Irish nationalism but made the wearer invisible to leprechauns. How would Slater pretend familiarity with a market for emeralds in Ireland? Doubtless invented hot air from Patrick Nugent, an Irish Scots, or Slater's having reset some of the Gilchrist emeralds.

Was Slater's cloying tone apparent to Jacobs? He compared a promising opportunity that he, Oscar, had had to reject, with an individual named "Carrey." He exaggerated his finances which he claimed were such that he could take a deal for 7,000 Russian stones, but regrettably would not ---because Robert Rogers cautioned him against it. *And you know me*, Slater wrote gratuitously. "I am not a correct judge."

Slater wrapped up with his opinion of Jacobs' "affair"-- his euphemism for legal problems and one he used when referring to the Marion Gilchrist murder. He advised Jacobs not to trust the friends he had in London. Instead, while he, Slater, was deceiving Jacobs about a gem deal, he was also promoting himself as a trusty friend and business partner on whom Jacobs could rely were he to require trial testimony. He told Jacobs he'd be back in London at the "end of January to start some business."

CORRESPONDENCE TO DAVID JACOBS, November 29, 1908

Dear Jacobs,

I have been coming too late to see your wife in London, and I hope that your wife and family are in good health. I expecting to be ready end of January to come over to New York myself. Matters are here very bad. The New York bank affairs have done a lot to it. Now I have found out here in Scotland it would be easy for me to pawn some of your emeralds not only in Glasgow; there are a lot of small towns around Glasgow, also in Ireland. If you scarf pins, and some loose emeralds; also send me the price list. Don't let me wait too long, because I have only two months time here. The profits I will divide with you. I am bringing the tickets over to you. I have been fourteen days ago in London, and have spoken to Carry. He made some good business. One lot I knowing of from Russia over 7000 pounds. I was offered to buy two lots of loose coloured stones, and only you know I am not a correct judge, and Rogers has advised me not to buy. Bravington in Kings X have spoken to me about your affair, and have told me you would be all right with your affair, only your friends there are the people is all could do the harm. Rogers and I have also seen Blytell, and he sends the best regards to you. I am coming over with Rogers end of January to start some business. Send the kind regards to the two Wrones (Henry Wrone, Gem Dealer, ed.). In case you don't like to send the stuff, please send answer. Best regards to you and your friends.

OSCAR SLATER.

Care of Anderson,
69 St. George's Road, Glasgow, Scotland.

November 30---Slater applied for membership in the Sloper Club. Owing to his dubious reputation —even among fellow gamblers—he was refused. Membership meant amenities, like a barber shop, but also more contacts. Slater could use the opportunity to restore his reputation. His request for membership in a local club supported an alibi—if he needed one—that he intended to live and work in Glasgow. He didn't contemplate a situation which would require him to hasten overseas.

CHAPTER 19

Oscar Slater's Nightly Strolls

The month of December---A stream of witnesses would report that a man—not the sort common in that quiet and respectable neighborhood-- strolled the streets, for two weeks prior to the murder, often between the hours of 5 p.m. and 7 p.m., by which time the Glasgow sky was pitch dark. According to eyewitnesses, including two street constables, he dressed like a commercial gent. Dr. John Adams, who lived across the way from Miss Gilchrist and who would eventually examine her corpse, reported that at least six times that month, around 11 p.m., upon returning from his medical office, he saw a strange man walking the street. He said he'd worn a fawn waterproof coat. Dr. Adams reported the loiterer to a constable who said he hadn't seen the man and did nothing more about it.

CONSTABLES

A Glasgow constable's primary role in the early days of the 20th century was to patrol an area with an eye towards suspicious people, fire, lit street lamps, and to arrest the unruly-- for which police work he received little training. The Sauchiehall area was the busiest police patrol. It was where "Sukie Tawdries" enticed their customers, where gamblers fought over bets, and where boisterous pub drinkers overstayed their welcome. The founder of London's police force, Sir Robert Peel, said of the police constable's mission, "The police are the public, and the public are the police." Yet, their wages were not much more than those of an unskilled menial worker.

December 1---Constable Christopher Walker (who denied having seen or spoken to Helen Lambie the night of December 21 as she reported) was on his evening shift. At 5:45 p.m., he observed a foreign-looking man whom he mistook for another Jewish man, Isaac Paradise (Slater's furniture broker). Constable Walker waved to the man where he stood-- near 15 Queens Terrace. It had not been Isaac Paradise. It was another man who looked very much like him: dark, foreign, Jewish. Oscar Slater was out walking his haunt.

December 4---Constable Walker saw the same man, at 5:45 p.m., walking leisurely down West Princes Street towards 15 Queens Terrace. The Constable recognized him as the man he'd seen three nights before. He gave Oscar Slater a friendly wave.

December 7---Slater's cash constraints unavailing, he pawned a pair of binoculars for £2 with Bryce.

December 9---Slater raised a further £9 with a draw on the brooch at Liddell's. He also sent his watch to Messrs. Dent, London watchmakers, to be fixed and returned no later than December 30. The watchmaker wrote that the watch looked as if it fell or suffered a heavy blow, and the back cover and pivots were badly bent. Slater did not have his watch the night of the murder.

In early December, Slater shaved off his mustache as his barber, Frederick Nichols, and his maid, Katerina Schmaltz, separately testified at trial. Slater's preparations to leave Glasgow were underway; the burglary was planned; he was conducting the preliminaries and walking the neighborhood. He was indicating for witnesses that he was not new to the neighborhood, or that he had regular business there so that he would not be an unusual sight if observed on December 21.

December 10---Oscar paid Isaac Paradise £4 on the furniture he'd rented. He was running short of cash but couldn't let on.

December 12 through December 18---A foreign-looking, dark-complexioned man resembling Slater was continually observed in the late afternoons and evenings, walking near 15 Queens Terrace, West Princes Street and St. George's Road. Observations differed in small respects so far as clothing.

In a community of pale Scots' faces, it was not unlikely that one's curiosity would be aroused to the Jewish man, seen consecutively at the same location, and fastening on his look and manner of dress. These neighborhood witnesses had not gathered in a collective conspiracy to convict an innocent man.

Constable Francis Brien's testimony:

"I knew him by sight. I saw him one night standing just a few yards from the corner of West Princes Street and St. George's Road. Roughly, that would be about 80 yards from Miss Gilchrist's house. I saw him on the occasion I am speaking to the week before the murder."

Constable Brien knew the prisoner by sight, having seen him several times in St. George's Road *over the course of seven weeks before the murder*. (emphasis added). One night, a week before the 21st of December, the Constable saw him at half-past nine.

December 14--- Mrs. Ferguson's husband stopped by to talk about another dog for Miss Gilchrist. It was a Monday. Lambie would have been in the flat during his visit. Miss Gilchrist hadn't had a dog since Barney's death in September. Was Mr. Ferguson there to persuade Miss Gilchrist, an independent but elderly woman, that she needed a dog for security? If she had expressed fears to the Fergusons, they were not disclosed at her death nor did they testify. Had Miss Gilchrist chosen not to confide in the Fergusons so they wouldn't worry, because she wasn't quite sure, or because Lambie was listening?

Between 1 p.m. and 2 p.m., Euphemia Cunningham, a photographer who worked on St. George's Road, was walking along that street on lunch break with her friend, William Campbell. They saw the same man, Oscar Slater, this day and also on the 16th and 17th. Campbell testified that these were very quiet streets with few walkers and for this reason, they both took notice of the gent they passed on the road.

December 15, 16, or 17, 5:45 p.m.---On one of these evenings, stockbroker Alexander Gillies of 46 West Princes Street, across from the Gilchrist flat, testified at trial as to his sightings of Oscar Slater:

> "As I was about to enter the close, I observed a man standing there, at the back of the close, at the foot of the stair. The close door was open at the time.
>
> ---Was the man standing in the middle of the passage, about half-way up to the first flight?
>
> He walked up there after I entered the close. He was a stranger to the close. I tried to get past him. When I did so he rather blocked my passage. He turned his back to me, and instead of allowing me to pass, he sort of blocked the passage, and the stair not being wide enough, I had to ask him to allow me to pass. His face was towards me. When I put my latch key in the door

and opened it he was still standing. I have not seen him again since that night, to my knowledge. He had a long fawn-coloured coat on, and a cap; otherwise I really cannot say anything about him. He was sallow, and had dark hair. He was about 5 feet 8 inches in height. He was clean shaven. On the 1st of March I went to Duke Street Prison and I saw the prisoner there. He resembled the man I saw on the stair, but I cannot say it was the same man."

December 15---Slater deposited £5 in his Postal Savings account. He was not yet considering an escape from Glasgow.

December 16---Slater again spotted walking by Euphemia Cunningham and William Campbell.

December 17---A Thursday. Lambie's day off. Mr. Ferguson stopped at Miss Gilchrist's about his progress in finding another dog. Besides Mr. Ferguson, Miss Gilchrist's solicitor, James MacDonald, also visited. It may have been about the codicil which she'd requested a month ago. Miss Gilchrist scheduled a visit with both men, Ferguson and MacDonald, on Lambie's day off. If she had something to discuss away from the maid, it was not revealed by the Fergusons nor the solicitor.

---Slater withdrew £5 from his Postal Savings account and was again spotted walking by Euphemia Cunningham and William Campbell.

December 18---Miss Gilchrist met with her stockbroker, John Stewart. The itemization of her copious shares, stocks, debentures, certificates, rents, and bank deposits was scrupulously drafted—so unlike the spare inventory of her jewelry collection by David Dick.

6:45 p.m.---Constable Walker testified that he saw the Slater standing at the foot of the chemist's shop on West Princes Street, across from 15 Queens Terrace near St. George's Road. In those days, a chemist sold commercial poisons. The chemist may have unwittingly supplied the poison intended for Barney the past September. The man seen by Constable Walker was a Jewish-looking man seen walking the area of Miss Gilchrist's for about two weeks before the murder. Sightings of Oscar Slater had also been reported to a constable by Dr. John Adams.

On cross examination, defense counsel McLure attempted to defeat the identifications. Constable Walker had identified a man he couldn't have seen on a dark December night, and that only during the interlude, from December until the May trial, did he become certain it was Oscar Slater and that his certainty arose from newspaper photos.

The Constable did mistake the man initially, but not fatally. He thought it was Isaac Paradise, a local Jewish merchant whom he knew and was friendly with. The man seen by the Constable was indeed a foreign-looking--Jewish-- gent. Subsequently and in court, he said he realized it was Oscar Slater.

Electric street lights were brand new in Glasgow, emitting much brighter lights along those dark winter streets. Gone were the dim street lamps lit by coal gas. Secondly, Constable Walker knew Isaac Paradise. He saw that after waving to the man across the street, it wasn't Isaac Paradise. He may have seen newspaper photos after the murder, but he'd had the opportunity, as a police constable, to observe the same man, in the same quiet neighborhood, who didn't live in one of the flats, looking up at 15 Queens Terrace for many days preceding the murder. After the murder, Slater didn't return for his nightly strolls.

In other words, several weeks before the murder, a strange man not of the neighborhood, clean-shaven, with a close resemblance to the defendant in the dock, Oscar Slater, piqued the curiosity of neighbors. His health-walking was described by some witnesses as a "rolling gait," his head jutting forward. Slater had a "hen toe," such that his left foot turned inward as he walked.

During cold, dark and damp December, Slater routinely took afternoon and evening constitutionals. He was there to make his own observations. He timed the infrequent rounds made by the Constables, important for the night of December 21.

The street along 15 Queens Terrace was narrow and quiet. He would have wanted to see what was visible from the Gilchrist dining room windows that faced the street. He was seen shaking the doorknob of the outside door. His interest didn't stretch further than 15 Queens Terrace. He turned around and returned to Sauchiehall Street, contemplating.

Witness Elizabeth Donaldson, a maid across the street from the Gilchrist flat, watched the stranger pass her flat on several occasions. She even waited for his routine, peeking out from behind the window curtains. He usually walked past after 5 p.m. A clean-shaven man who wore a fawn waterproof, he once stood at the foot of her building's stairs.

☞ What was there for Oscar to see?

No one lived above Miss Gilchrist. He knew that. The dining room which overlooked the street may have cast a dim light. Would an intruder be visible to someone outside? Oscar was also calculating the logistics: street traffic, the lighting, the evening weather, the police presence, the downstairs tenants. He was timing Lambie's errand run and her return to the flat, the approximate distance when fleeing the flat, and how quickly one could disappear.

December 19, 3 p.m.---A Saturday. Miss Gilchrist's niece, Margaret Birrell, who lived a few streets away at 14 Blythswood Drive, visited her for tea as she did every week.

---That evening, Slater was short of cash. He borrowed five shillings from George Sabin, secretary of the Sloper Club (where Slater was recently made a member). He also borrowed a small sum from another gambler. Slater was in such need of money that he asked Cameron to try selling the Liddell's pawn ticket for Brooch #2. This hadn't happened before. Slater's middle men were his landsmen and diamond dealers. In this case, with the intention of misrepresenting the ownership of the brooch, his request of Cameron served his purpose.

CHAPTER 20

The Trio Coordinates

December 20, 1 p.m.-3 p.m.---Slater was engaged in midday card games at the Sloper Club, observed by Allan McLean. That day, Slater was clean-shaven and wearing a fawn coat. McLean walked with a friend a few feet behind Slater and his friend as they all walked home. McLean saw Slater enter the close at St. George's Road. A close was private property. He saw where Slater lived and on December 25 would report his suspicions to the police.

> **a narrow alley was also referred to as a "close." Thomas Annan was a famous 19th century photographer of the closes, tenements and streets of Glasgow.**

It was a Sunday, the day before the murder, and Lambie's day off. She and Nugent met on the street. Lambie reported to police that she'd been talking to a constable in plain clothes. She may have been seen talking to a man (Nugent) the night before the murder. The police constable alibi was a perfect excuse. No constable corroborated her statement.

6 p.m. to 6:45 p.m.--- Not until she testified at the May 1909 trial did Lambie point a finger at Oscar Slater as having passed her on the street the same night before the murder that she met Nugent. She would recall that the man who looked like Oscar Slater was clean-shaven and had a peculiar walk. What Lambie was involved in at the time was a meeting with Nugent and Slater in preparation for the next night.

This put a halt to any ideas that she was connected to his crime. In her mind, she and Nugent did not agree to the murder but only to the burglary; thus, Slater acted on his own. She identified Slater because she knew he had killed Marion Gilchrist; she had seen him at the crime scene. Slater was part of the trio to rob her, but the murder was his doing. Sitting in the dock, he could not do her harm.

Later that evening, Slater again lost money gambling at the Sloper Club according to Hugh Cameron's testimony. He went to the Central Station kiosk to send a telegram to the Edinburgh Postal Account Service for the return of his Savings Account money "at once." Why did he choose to withdraw all his funds the day before the murder? He was short of cash. He may also have been preparing for his anticipated January departure.

Among William Roughead's claims about Oscar Slater's innocence was that he was not in Glasgow on the night of the murder. Slater's telegrams flatly contradict him.

At this point, Slater was anxious that his affairs were orderly so that his January departure from Glasgow would be without suspicion. He did not anticipate the struggle with Marion Gilchrist.

7:40 p.m.---A commercial-looking gent was observed by Mr. and Mrs. Robert Bryson waiting for a cab on West Princes Street, six paces from 15 Queens Terrace. "It was a very clear, decent night—not a wet night. Not another living soul on the street." Mr. Bryson was a cabinetmaker who'd done work for Miss Gilchrist 10 years prior. He was familiar with the area and the building. The street lamp at the corner was very bright...incandescent. That evening, he saw a man standing on the Gilchrist steps outside the door which appeared locked. After attempting unsuccessfully to open it and seeing the couple, the man walked back down the steps, passing them. Mr. Bryson stared at him. He was "small looking" and "peculiar looking." That night, Slater had "a small droopy black mustache" and wore a black bowler hat. Bryson thought the man may have been waiting for someone… "a ladylove."

Why would Oscar have been jimmying with the lock the night before the murder? Was he making a last-minute foray to remind Lambie about keeping the doors unlocked?

9:15 p.m.--- Andrew Nairn, a produce merchant, was standing outside his residence at 46 West Princes Street, waiting for his wife and children. Across the street, he saw a black-haired, broad-shouldered man looking up at the Gilchrist flat. Oscar Slater again. There were two lampposts and both cast a very bright light—the same two street lights which illuminated Oscar Slater's face for Mary Barrowman minutes after the murder the following night. Nairn continued watching the man because in the past weeks, there had been instances of housebreaking in the neighborhood.

9:30 p.m.---Constable Francis Brien, whose beat was 6 p,m. to 2 a.m., observed the man he would identify as Oscar Slater walking about 80 yards from the Gilchrist flat.

Here was a man, whose physical features were described by numerous reliable witnesses who saw this same person walking their neighborhood, daily for over three weeks in cold December. Such witness evidence laid a foundation towards the proof that the defendant in the dock, Oscar Slater, was the man accused of the murder. After December 21, the neighborhood witnesses no longer saw the walker from their windows or along the street.

CHAPTER 21

DECEMBER 21, 1908 – The Day of the Murder

Monday, December 21--- As usual, Miss Gilchrist rose at noon. After a late breakfast, she dressed in her furs and left to run an errand. She routinely wore three gold rings on her fingers—one with her name inscribed and two of family members. They were not found on her corpse.

Lambie's girlfriend stopped by while Miss Gilchrist was out. Was a friendly chat what Lambie needed to steady her nerves? Was the girlfriend intended to be a suspect in the event questions were asked about the burglary?

Miss Gilchrist returned at 4:30, cold, wet, but in time for tea.

 Glimpses of Nugent

1. Lambie's admitted to police and in trial testimony that Patrick Nugent was her friend since January 1908; that he had visited Marion Gilchrist's holiday home in Ayr as well as the Glasgow flat when Miss Gilchrist was out; and that he was shown the spare bedroom and the jewelry collection by Lambie.

2. Witness Agnes Brown observed two men running up Cumberland Street minutes after the murder;

3. Detective-Lieutenant Trench's visited Nugent at his home in Carfin on December 31.

Not one witness identified or described the loiterer as a tall young Irish-Scot. Oscar Slater was not misidentified because of the lineups. Trench testified that when Slater was placed with 11 other men, though they were native Scots, some were as dark-complexioned as he was.

12:30 p.m.---In advance of the murder, Slater took a £30 draw on Brooch #2 held at Liddell's. He redeemed other items he had pawned.

Slater asked Katerina to pick up his expensive shirt from the laundry. He also gave Katerina notice that her job was at an end because he and Mlle. Andrée were leaving town, either for San Francisco or Monte Carlo. They had not yet packed.

He recouped his personal shaving items from Frederick Nichols, the barber. Nichols would testify that his customer, Oscar Slater, was a hirsute fellow, with thick, black hair, usually a mustache, and a heavy stubble of beard that needed a twice-daily shave. He did not have a mustache on visiting the barber December 21, which, according to witness Robert Bryson had been slight and drooping the night before.

3 p.m.--- John Clunes, 26, lived not far from the Gilchrist flat. Walking down the street, he saw a man he recognized as a habitué of the racetrack and described him later to the police. The description fit the suspect being sought by police after the murder. Clunes hadn't seen him before in the neighborhood. He didn't know his name.

Slater stopped at the laundry to pick up a shirt that hadn't been returned to the A. Anderson home with the wash. He told the clerk, Miss Mary Cooper, that he wouldn't need laundry services after the Holidays. She described A. Anderson as having a crooked nose, that he was "abrupt" and "dominant," characteristics that fit the trio's Schemer-in-Chief.

4:30 p.m.---Slater tried selling his pawn ticket for Brooch #2 to Aumann and Rattman at the billiards club (seeing them earlier than his alibi of 5 p.m. to 7 p.m.) with no success, he turned to a man named Anderson, a friend of Allan McLean. Anderson would tell McLean about Oscar's pawn ticket.

These were fraught moments for Oscar Slater. The burglary was to begin in less than two hours. He saw Hugh Cameron and in his nervous state told him he was moving to America...to San Francisco. He wrote down an address for him.

CHAPTER 22

Slater Prepares for Murder Night

December 21, 1908 5 p.m.--- Slater sent a telegram to London's Post Office Saving Center as "Adolf Anderson" requesting that all his savings be wired immediately.

Unproven alibi, 5 p.m. or 6:20 p.m.---Slater claimed he played billiards in these hours with Max Rattman and Jozef Aumann at Johnson's Billiard Hall. Neither of the men recalled a conversation or even about his departure for New York in a few days. Their recollections were unsure whether he played billiards with them on the night of December 21.

6:12 p.m.--- Slater sent a telegraph to Messrs. Dent, his London watchmaker, saying he needed his watch repaired and returned asap. He could not wait until December 30 as originally instructed. The telegram was sent from the Central Station office at Renfrew Street, about a mile and a half from 15 Queens Terrace. This was another intended alibi.

Slater did not return home from the Central Station office. The crime began in earnest. In the cold rain, wearing his fawn waterproof coat, he walked at a fast clip having practiced for over a fortnight. He would have arrived at the front of the flat by 6:35 p.m. for the night's bloody business.

Slater might have been concerned that he was not wearing his watch. The crime was to start and finish within a prescribed time. He had to rely on being fleet of foot and as attentive to detail as he would playing cards or perusing a diamond.

Helen Lambie's claim that she left for her errand at 7 p.m. was intended to align with Slater's alibi that he was at his home eating dinner at 7 p.m.

with Mlle. Andrée and Katerina.

The group's intention may have been that Slater knock the old spinster unconscious and then wrench open the locked box of diamonds while her head lay on the dining room table, stirring to consciousness. It would take mere minutes.

CHAPTER 23

Oscar Slater Enters 15 Queens Terrace

Three Doors For Entry to 15 Queens Terrace

With a plan, a schedule, motive, and an appointed hour, Slater walked briskly to 15 Queens Terrace. He walked swiftly and without the inconvenience of an umbrella. He wore gloves.

Ahead stood the black iron railings at the outdoor perimeter of Queens Terrace. The regal naming expressed taste and comfortable security. Stone steps led to a stolid front door. An ornate Victorian knocker was substituted by door bells once the building tenanted three separate flats.

Times were changing in 1908. Slater's fortnight of walking was a mark of a steady shift from Victorian life to urban 20th century Edwardian. Pavements were swept and clean. Urban leisure walking was not out of the ordinary, though darkness, rain and cold temperatures cast doubt on an individual's judgment. That hour of night, either a household's tea time or suppertime, Slater walked to Miss Gilchrist's, unobserved.

Marion Gilchrist was alone. Helen Lambie stepped out, as she did routinely, to buy the *Evening Chronicle*. The MacReady News Shop was across the way, around the corner on St. George's Road. No sooner did

Lambie walk out of the building that the intruder entered through the unlocked doors.

Three doors with ease of access fit the predetermined timing of his mission. Three doors for entry, each normally requiring a key, and each requiring a minute to unlock, open, and close shut.

He did as follows: opened the outside door to the building, entered the lobby and then either let himself in through the second, unlocked entry door leading to the second floor, or he rang the lobby bell for Miss Gilchrist to open the door. In the lobby were two doors: one to #14 and one to #15. The door to #15 had been left ajar as Arthur Adams would report and testify.

To enter #15, one rang the doorbell. The Adams' family could normally hear a visitor in the lobby, or the door opening and closing, or the doorbell ringing. On the night of December 21, no one heard these sounds. This meant that Marion Gilchrist was not alerted to the intruder's entry. He entered through the lobby door which had been left ajar. The lights along the stairs had been extinguished.

At trial the following May, Lambie preempted any questioning of the door having been left ajar. She interjected, in a long narrative, that she too noticed the entry door was ajar but only when she returned from buying the paper. It hadn't been how she left it.

The time of entry was disputed because Lambie reported to police that she'd left the flat at 7 p.m. to buy a newspaper. The intruder, Oscar Slater, was at the front door by 6:35 p.m.

Helen Lambie's Intrigues

One might posit on the side of the devil, that the man surveilling Marion Gilchrist's neighborhood for the past several weeks watched a housemaid leaving the flat, and from which he could instinctively deduce: that she was the Gilchrist maid, that she left, daily, at that unchangeable hour, on an errand, and that some days she would go off on further errands.

Would Lambie's return to the flat also have been routine? Her in-and-out of the flat was not the same each night. On Thursdays, for example, Lambie had the half day off. She wouldn't have been available. The doors would not have been left unlocked on her day off. Was Lambie's errand routine a reliable construct for a lone intruder's planned entry, theft and murder? No.

Helen Lambie told the police she'd been out to fetch the paper and was gone at 7 p.m. for about five minutes...maybe 15. During those five minutes, she told police that she'd chatted, in the rain, with two plain-clothes constables, separately. Neither officer recalled speaking to her. Her lie was bold. It showed a damning lack of conscience for a person, just age 22, and particularly on having witnessed the bloody cruelty visited upon her helpless, 82-year-old employer.

The Adams family did not hear Lambie leave the flat nor lock the doors, sounds which usually could be heard at #14. They did not know whether she left the flat at 7 p.m. They did know that Arthur Adams, having heard ominous thuds from above, ran up to the flat at 6:50 p.m. and reported "the girl was not inside." Lambie was out of the flat much before 7 p.m.

Lambie told police that she left a half sovereign on the dining room table where Miss Gilchrist was sitting and reading a magazine. The coin was for additional errands later that night. She might just have kept on going that night and completed the errands in one run. Instead, the plan was that she return to the flat and to say she had done so to pick up the coin. The surprise appearance of the downstairs tenant, Mr. Adams, outside the door, was an unanticipated complication.

Edward VII gold half-sovereign

Lambie expected to return to the flat, ostensibly to retrieve the half sovereign, and by which time, the intruder would have exited unobserved. She would have shut the doors on the way up, lit the lamplight, entered the flat, surveyed the scene and helped Miss Gilchrist recover from the blow. Then, Lambie would call for the police.

6:50 p.m.--- Constable Francis Brien, on duty, reported that he walked past the Gilchrist flat. He saw no one including not seeing Helen Lambie. Oscar Slater was already inside.

6:55 p.m.--- Mrs. Rowena Adams Liddell (no relation to Slater's pawnbroker), a married Adams daughter who did not live at 14 Queens Terrace, walked east along Princes Street with her mother towards the flat. Neither saw Lambie coming or going. Arthur Adams was already knocking at Marion Gilchrist's door.

Mrs. Liddell said she saw a man outside their building--dark-haired, clean-shaven and leaning over the rails. He had a long nose with a curious dip to it. It was later described by witnesses as broken, twisted, or turned. Mrs. Liddell assumed the man was waiting for a music pupil.

She and her mother exchanged no greeting with him. Was this man actually standing at the iron rails waiting to burgle the Gilchrist flat? It was believed that her sighting was imagined in the confusion of the murder scene she and her mother would soon encounter upstairs from the Adams flat.

Lambie had walked out of the flat without asking Miss Gilchrist to secure the padlocks. The intruder entered *sub silentio*.

The lights along the inside stairs were extinguished, either by Lambie or by the intruder. When he ascended the indoor steps to the Gilchrist flat, he left behind a puddle of water. The door to the residence at #15 beckoned.

During these minutes at the point of Slater's entry, Lambie did not return to the flat.

Marion Gilchrist stood waiting by the fire in the dining room for Lambie and the newspaper. She may have been chilled from her own errands that day. The amber glow of the candelabra shone above the table where the magazines lay in a neat pile. There was no sign of tea things, nor of any chair out of place left by a visitor.

She stood warming herself. A hearth rug lay at her feet. It had once been a bedsit for Marion's dog, the late Barney. An eight-foot tall grandfather clock stood outside the dining room. Its chimes generally tolled a melody of bells on the hour, a sound sonorous and startling.

Grandfather Clock

Hall, 15 Queen's Terrace (looking east)
Showing inner side of outer door (left); dining-room (centre); door leading to kitchen (right)

Though it was either 6:35 p.m. or 7 p.m., no one reported that the grandfather clock had ticked or chimed. There was no evidence that it hadn't been working. Slater needed to know the time to keep to the schedule. His watch was still out for repairs. Had Lambie wound the clock the night before? This was an unfortunate omission from the police reports and all the Oscar Slater books.

The Victorian Grandfather Clock

Edwardian era clocks struck with quarter-hour chimes. The Gilchrist grandfather clock was a 19th century product. Its Westminster chimes would have struck on the hour while the pendulum beat every second. It required winding either every 8 days or 30 days, with a silent strike option to allow for an uninterrupted night's sleep. We will never know whether footfalls, aberrant night noise, or the clock woke Miss Gilchrist from her sleep causing her to walk down in her nightclothes to alert the Adams family about an intruder she'd heard in the house weeks before.

I am a Very Villain

On the Gilchrist door were affixed three padlocks. They were not secured on the night of the murder. The intruder opened the flat door and quietly locked it from the inside; later, when Arthur Adams started banging on the door, he found it locked.

If the grandfather clock hadn't been wound, which was likely, since no one mentioned its chimes, there was the kitchen clock. We know the kitchen clock was working because Lambie was emphatic in stating she looked at it on leaving the flat and that it read 7 p.m.

Slater walked towards the kitchen. In his coat pocket, he held the claw hammer. Was he planning to clobber her lightly, leaving her unconscious, or had he planned to bludgeon her to death? The question is merely rhetorical for his victim was bludgeoned and murdered. Her final few moments on this earth would be unspeakably hellish.

Slater had knowledge that the only other tenants in the building lived downstairs-- a family with whom she'd had little contact in 27 years. He was aware that no new tenants had moved in above the Gilchrist flat and he knew that no little dog would bark. He also knew exactly how much time he had to stun Miss Gilchrist and to burgle the locked box.

This night, there was an absence of music from downstairs. Slater may have expected the building to be thrumming with musical interludes which would muffle sounds from above. Alas, Arthur and his sister, Laura, were wrapping Christmas presents. Arthur testified that his married sister, Rowena, was also in the house. She could not have seen a man standing outdoors, a man with a peculiar dip to his nose. Was the nose already being discussed upstairs at the murder scene while Rowena stood about with other onlookers?

☞ It is a convincing circumstance of identification that every witness described the man loitering in the neighborhood over more than a December fortnight as different or foreign-looking, with dark black hair beneath his hat. Witnesses observed him, again and again, as they peered through their windows or passed him on the street. He was clean shaven and had a "rolling gait." He dressed well, like a commercial gent. He was not an ordinary, native Scotsman.

Of the trio here involved, Slater's physical or facial characteristics were described by numerous, unrelated witnesses. Most times, the man appeared to be clean-shaven. We know from both his maid, Katerina Schmaltz, and barber, Frederick Nichols, that for the past two weeks, Slater had been shaving off his mustache. He was doing so to alter his appearance for his walks in the Gilchrist neighborhood. It is clear that Slater was scouting the neighborhood.

No witness described a tall, handsome, Irish-looking, black-haired sort as the neighborhood walker. None of the descriptions matched that of the Irish Scotsman, Patrick Nugent. He was not the man loitering the streets near 15 Queens Terrace. The man who had a dark undergrowth of beard, a foreign look to him, not so tall but broad-shouldered was Oscar Slater.

Facts in police reports, witness statements, and in testimony identified a dark-haired, dark-complexioned, foreign-looking, peculiar walking, commercial gent seen in December weather, night after night, watching and examining the 15 Queens Terrace building.

It is indisputable that both Nugent and Slater were involved in the plot for reasons explained above. Witness Agnes Brown introduced the likelihood of two men being involved. Concededly, she could not solidly identify them because she did not observe them frontally. The police did not follow this lead though Detective-Lieutenant took hold of the baton and met privately with Nugent.

Miss Brown reported what was minutes after the murder, that as she walked west on Cumberland Street, two men raced past; one of them almost knocking her down on the narrow pavement heedless of the woman. It brought her to a stop. It was such uncivil conduct.

She watched them but saw only their sides and backs. Her observation was unobstructed because there was no one else on the street. Both men were in their 30s, fit enough and frantic enough to race madly up Cumberland with hell on their tails. The second man, fleet of foot, had been Slater's accomplice, Patrick Nugent. Helen Lambie, the prosecution's star witness, absolved Nugent as the murderer or participant as did the police via Detective Lieutenant John Trench and later, author William Roughead.

Helen Lambie at the Extradition Hearing

Q by Slater's counsel. Have your suspicions in this case ever turned towards that gambler (Nugent)?

A. Never

Q. Do you know any other man who would be as familiar with those premises, the wealth of the old lady, her jewellery, and the way to get into those premises as that man?

A. No, sir.

Q. by hearing Commissioner. Was the man you met in that hallway, when you came in from buying the paper, this gambler he speaks of?

A. No, sir.

Here Slater's counsel, presumably from Slater's accusation, pointed the finger at Patrick Nugent. Slater's lawyer inserted Nugent as an alternative suspect...a gambler (known by Slater), someone who had the opportunity for an exacting search of the Gilchrist jewelry collection, and, most importantly, a taut connection between Nugent and Lambie. The Crown ignored or missed the larger plot and three participants.

Lambie stated she had neither seen nor heard anything of Nugent since the beginning of September. Author William Roughead described her as having been "browbeaten" by the lawyers. He supplemented her defense of Nugent with his own pronouncement: "No suspicion whatever now attaches to Nugent in regard to the case." Roughead improvidently expressed this opinion in his book and, with that ill-advised premise, persuaded Arthur Conan Doyle to take on the case of Oscar Slater's innocence.

In other words...those of Roughead and all the Oscar Slater supporters... none of the trio was involved in the murder of Marion Gilchrist. A fly-by-night entered an unlocked flat-- in the few minutes Lambie had innocently absented herself for 10 minutes to fetch the paper-- murdered the old lady, created havoc in the spare bedroom, and, scrunching his body down so the blood stains on the front of his fawn waterproof coat would not be seen, face partially covered by a soft cap and lowered down towards his collar, sidled towards two eyewitnesses—Arthur Adams and Helen Lambie-- who stood open-mouthed at the flat's doorway, and escaped.

The burglary had been planned during the hour Miss Gilchrist would be alone. The intruder would know there were no visitors with her. It was daring. By law, burglarizing with a resident in the home brought a heftier criminal sentence. Murder brought the criminal to the scaffold.

Nugent on the Murder Periphery

Slater was the murderer and Lambie and Nugent were co-conspirators. He was not wrongfully convicted. Patrick Nugent was not the murderer. Lambie testified she hadn't seen Nugent since September, yet Miss Gilchrist had been awakened in the middle of an October night having heard footsteps leaving the flat. Nugent *was* still in the picture, but come November, Nugent would be otherwise occupied.

Nugent was entering a busy and expensive time in his life. He was engaged to marry a 21-year-old Catholic girl. The wedding was set for November 25. Before that date, the duo would be expected to fulfill the Catholic marriage requisites: pastoral instructions—especially since young, pregnant Martha Curran was committing herself to a 37-year-old widower with three children; announcements and banns; sacraments for a period of months; classes; and music selection. There was also the planning of a wedding party, guest list, liquor, food and a November honeymoon. Nugent took his Catholic faith seriously from the appearance of three priests in his wedding photo.

Some authors, including Conan Doyle, explored the possibility that the murderer was Patrick Nugent and not Oscar Slater. However, witness descriptions were all, without exception, of a foreign-looking or dark-complexioned fellow with a peculiar manner of walking. Never was there a description of a native Scot or Anglo-Saxon or Celt or Dane or Swede.

Those are simply the facts, unpleasant though is the troubling scar of ethnic profiling. The man had a twisted nose. It had been broken in a fistfight. The nose was described minutes after the murder. It was corroborated by Slater's barber, who shaved him twice daily, and documented by the U.S. Immigration Service.

Recently, upon hearing an account of Oscar Slater's guilt, two stubborn mainstays of Oscar Slater's antique legacy pointed the *je t'accuse* finger at Patrick Nugent. Both legal *amici* were steaming from their nostrils at the Slater accusation. One maintained, with steadfast delusion, that poor Oscar was but an immigrant *schlub* who barely spoke English. "The police targeted him."

Was newly married Patrick Nugent taking nightly excursions, leaving his young wife and the children each dinnertime to stroll the dark streets around 15 Queens Terrace? Unlikely. What was likely, and criminal, was that Nugent stood in a close of Grant Street the night of the murder, waiting for Slater to flee with a haul of diamonds and coins.

Slater had been in charge of the plot and the plotters and he wanted first dibs at the Gilchrist jewelry box. To his discreditable credit, under his direction, the trio suffered no repercussions from October through December 21.

Was it Nugent who was caught in the flat? No. Arthur Adams was a witness who stood beside Lambie at the flat door. He admitted to being slightly nearsighted but he could identify the man who skulked out. The suspect was only as tall as Arthur Adams, about 5'6. He was wearing a fawn waterproof coat, though a year later, at trial, Arthur was no longer certain of the coat.

What did Patrick Nugent look like? None of the witnesses observed features similar to his.

November 25, 1908 Patrick Nugent wedding to Martha Curran, with three priests in attendance.

Here is a photo of Patrick Nugent. He is at the rear, the second to the right. Quite noticeable is the missing front tooth at the top left of his smiling mouth. His nose wasn't broken. He was not the man described as the neighborhood loiterer, nor the man with the twisted nose, nor the man caught at the scene of the murder at 15 Queens Terrace.

Witnesses who saw his face would spot that missing tooth.

PATRICK NUGENT

When Slater walked past Euphemia Cunningham and William Campbell on an early afternoon along St. George's Road, had it been Nugent, his greeting would have inclined a smile.

Or, if Oscar Slater was *not* the man with the twisted nose whom Mary Barrowman witnessed minutes after the murder, but Patrick Nugent, midst his heavy breathing from the exhausting dynamics of the murder, his mouth would have been drawn open. Mary didn't witness a missing tooth. She saw a man with a twisted nose. That was Oscar Slater.

CHAPTER 24

Tricks about the Time

Helen Lambie's Deceits

Lambie stepped out on her nightly errand across the street to MacReady's News Agents, 190a St. George's Road, to buy the *Evening Chronicle* for Miss Gilchrist who waited indoors for her return.

The time of Lambie leaving the premises on her nightly errand varied:

- According to Lambie, she looked at the kitchen clock upon leaving and it read 7 o'clock. She did not mention the chiming of the grandfather clock which stood near the entry door and which Lambie would have passed as she left. She did not have a watch. She also omitted having walked through the laundry and its pulleys hanging in the kitchen.

- 7 p.m. according to author William Roughead because that's what Lambie said.

- 7 p.m. according to author Steven Hines.

- 7 p.m. Author Whittington-Egan inserted imagined evidence to corroborate Lambie's estimation of the time: "The seventh and last chime of a nearby clock was just fading on the damp air as Nellie Lambie set off through the rain and darkness to MacReady's, the news agent. It was less than three minutes away."

- Had Lambie left at 7 p.m., she would have encountered witness Mary Barrowman. Mary witnessed Slater as he raced down the stairs, away from the murder scene, a few minutes after 7 p.m.

- Arthur did not report having heard the grandfather clock's chimes when he went upstairs.

- Lambie said she'd only been gone 10 minutes.

- Dr. John Adams (no relation to Arthur) was called to the scene by Arthur Adams and arrived at 7:25 p.m. He lived across the street.

The family Adams did not hear Lambie leaving the flat nor her opening and closing (or not closing) the downstairs doors. Helen Lambie said she was gone "only 10 minutes." No one corroborated this but later authors repeated it as fact.

Lambie reported the 7 p.m. time with steady accuracy to the police, though she was in a hysterical state. She repeated it at trial. She was described by Superintendent Ord as having a "want of confidence to speak straight." She was also described as "hesitating" or "stupid." In retrospect, her hesitation in speaking straight was the mark of a guilty mind.

In the 10 minutes outdoors in the rain, Lambie said she'd chatted separately with two plain-clothes constables, one of whom was Constable John Harrison to whom she spoke for three to five minutes. No constable corroborated Lambie's conversation nor the time. No constable reported that he was familiar with her errands at that time, every night, on St. George's Road. Lambie used the chat diversion in order to explain the time which allowed the assailant's entry and activity.

No constable was in the vicinity when Mr. Adams went rushing out of the building at 7:15 - 7:20 p.m. looking for a policeman after discovering Miss Gilchrist's body.

Lambie testified, without a penetrating cross examination, that Miss Gilchrist's back was to the fireplace as she sat reading a magazine and that she was wearing her gold spectacles. Slater expected her in this position--Miss Gilchrist's back to the fireplace-- because he came in the rear door where he could get at her from behind. He knew which door to use. Miss Gilchrist was alone. This was known to the intruder.

Nugent was within a close on Grant Street. If Slater was burglarizing for the purpose of stealing diamonds and coins, Nugent would have wanted to be there, upon Slater's exit, for a division of proceeds. They had planned a quiet and unseen exit by Slater after the break-in.

Oscar Slater's Alibis

Prior to the time of the murder, which conceivably began at about 6:35 p.m., Slater said he was at Johnston's Billiard Hall on Renfield Street with two fellow gamblers, Jozef Aumann and Max Rattmann, and with a third unnamed man, until he went home for his dinner at 7 p.m. At trial, neither man could confirm that Slater played billiards that early evening between 5:30 p.m. to 7 p.m. and they did not remember details of Slater's dress or conversation. Slater did not stroll home for dinner from Johnston's Billiard Hall in anyone's company on Monday night, December 21.

He was at Central Station sending a telegram at 6:12 p.m. From that time until 8 p.m., no one offered creditable testimony that Slater was within the confines of his home with Mlle. Andrée and Katerina the maid. At some point during his New York detention, Slater would have reminded his devoted Andrée of the timing of his dinner while dispelling in the young woman the nonsense of his having murdered an elderly lady.

At trial, Slater's dinner alibi sagged. Katerina testified she couldn't recall if it was 7 p.m. or 8 p.m. on December 21 that they ate. Neither could Mlle. Andrée. Neither loyal lady recalled what it was they ate that night.

CHAPTER 25

Oscar Slater, the Killer

6:30 p.m. until 7:30 p.m. ---This was the prosecution's expansive estimate of the time of the murder. It aligned somewhat with Helen Lambie's false account—that she looked at the kitchen clock when she left to buy the paper and that it was 7 p.m. She omitted reference to the grandfather clock which should have been chiming at 7 p.m. Then, according to her testimony, Lambie made a circuitous turn from the kitchen to the front of the dining room, looked in, and saw Miss Gilchrist sitting and reading.

6:35 p.m. to 6:40 p.m. ---This was the probable time of Oscar's entry into the building. He had awaited Lambie's fixed departure which was at least a half-hour earlier than the 7 p.m. she reported to police.

Oscar's intention was to be silently *out* of the Gilchrist flat a few minutes *before* 7 p.m. in order to be home for dinner--his alibi-- just a few streets away on St. George's Road. The swift entry, the clubbing of the spinster, and an optimal yank of the jewelry box would take no more than 20 minutes.

The words of Scottish poet, Robert "Rabbie" Burns (coincidentally, the poet hailed from Ayr) should have been echoing in Slater's ear:

> *"The best laid schemes o' Mice an' Men,*
> *Gang aft agley,*
> *An' lea'e us nought but grief an' pain..."*
> THE MOUSE

Time Was On His Side

6:40 p.m.---At the outset of the crime, Oscar didn't waste a minute of his earmarked 20 minutes. He had no need to break the door locks. Arthur Adams, the downstairs tenant, noticed, when he left his flat to see about the noise upstairs, that the lobby entrance door which opened to the stairs leading to the Gilchrist flat, had been left ajar. That was unusual. Also, he hadn't heard the doorbell ring at the entry though it was usually heard. The door was left ajar. There had been no need to ring the doorbell to go up the steps to Miss Gilchrist's. Arthur also hadn't heard Helen Lambie leaving the flat and locking the doors.

Slater entered, soaking wet from the rain, but perspiring. He had raced over from Central Station. It took about 10 to 15 minutes from the time, 6:12 p.m., that he sent a telegram to Messrs. Dent.

The flat door was unlocked. Someone gave Slater access. He would not have rung the doorbell. He didn't have duplicate keys. Witness Robert Bryson said he saw the man jiggling the outside locked door the night before.

There were two glass panels on either side of the door which, had it been locked, Slater could have smashed. That would have alerted Miss Gilchrist. Had she heard the doorbell, Miss Gilchrist would have left her seat in the dining room and walked to answer it. Slater had been made aware that she sat alone by the fireside, reading, her back to the fire. There were no visitors. The dining room was where the crime occurred.

The intruder was familiar with the layout of the residence. As Slater entered, the door to the flat did not open silently. The old wood would have creaked. Affixed to the inside of the door were three padlocks: a lock and chain, a bolt and two patent locks. The much-publicized padlocks were not secured, but even so, they would have rattled as the door opened.

A Victorian kitchen with laundry pulleys

"The Hours of Folly are Measured by a Clock"

The sounds of time. Were Slater's movements muffled by the steady pendulum ticking of the grandfather clock? It stood to the immediate left of the entrance. Had Lambie intentionally failed to wind it? Otherwise, its Westminster chimes would have sounded a melody at each quarter of the hour. No report was made of this inanimate but striking witness.

Lambie told police that she knew it was 7 p.m. when she first left on her errand because she had looked at the kitchen clock. She may not have expected her Mistress to be murdered. She may have said to Miss Gilchrist: "It's 7 o'clock and I'm leaving for the paper." The grandfather clock couldn't have been wound because its chimes would have kept Miss Gilchrist on her toes about the time.

With the statement she later made to police about the time of her exit, one would conclude that Lambie walked through the kitchen, its pulleys and hanging laundry just to see the clock... rather than looking at the grandfather clock and hearing its 7 p.m. chimes on her way out the door.

Her reference to the kitchen clock was necessary to avoid drawing attention to the grandfather clock. There was no evidence that the clock did not work. Clocks were diligently maintained in that era. A grandfather clock was a venerated piece of furniture, often bequeathed from generation to generation. Possibly, Lambie failed to wind it the night before and its chimes were not working on December 21.

Slater walked towards the kitchen. He didn't approach the dining room from its front entrance. He crept into the kitchen, with its hanging laundry and pulleys, and circled about the kitchen utensils as he made his way to the back entry of the dining room. He would approach Miss Gilchrist from her rear.

6:50 p.m.--- Police Constable Francis Brien walked past the Gilchrist residence but saw nothing out of the ordinary.

Marion Gilchrist in her Final Moments

Surely Miss Gilchrist would have heard someone entering the flat in that dead silence yet she had no reason to fear. Lambie may have returned with the paper and gone into the kitchen first to shake off her wet shoes and coat. Barney was no longer there. Only the fire lent a comforting crackle. The sound of a swishing raincoat wouldn't have put her off.

It was apparent that Lambie left on her errand without reminding Miss Gilchrist to lock up. She testified that she spoke to her Mistress as she was leaving, saying she'd be back with the paper and would then take the half-sovereign for her errands.

Slater had allotted the minutes during which he would stun the old lady and then head for the locked box in the spare bedroom. Thus, the attack that did ensue was committed with hysterical rapidity. He wasn't prepared for the sight of the tall woman standing, staring at him in fright as he opened the dining room door. The speed of the murder arose from his own shock and stony heart as by his fixation on the spare bedroom, its wooden box of promised treasure, and the time constraints.

As Chapter 1 (above) unfolded, Marion Gilchrist suffered a brutal death, pitiless and grippingly painful. In the struggle, the irons and tongs beside the fireplace may have clanged an echo-- like orphans addressing an empty table.

Female frailty did not inhibit Oscar Slater. Let us recall that, among his arrests for fist fights (with men who fought back), there were those of his ladies who complained to police about his violence. He beat them. He punched their faces—on which their trade relied-- with his fists. One of the complainants was Slater's first wife, Mary Curtis Pryor. These scarlet women, though constrained by public and police opinion, were so unmercifully abused by Slater that they took their chances and made attempts to file charges against him, their dandily costumed pimp with a vicious streak.

Having beaten the elderly Marion to death, Slater, panting and perspiring, removed the chair from her body and placed it upright. He covered her with a skin rug and a hearth rug. The ghastly sight of Marion Gilchrist's face was beyond even his iciness. In subsequent ambivalent denials, he would say he had nothing to do with "the affair," unable to speak the unspeakable, to confront the crime or to utter the victim's name.

Arthur Adams, who had been wrapping presents with his sister, Laurie, ran up the stairs to check on Miss Gilchrist because he and the family heard loud thuds upstairs.

Detective-Inspector Pyper's Testimony About the Blood in the Flat

Q. There are signs on it of blood having run down the whole length of the coal scuttle? — Yes.

Q. There were bits of the woman's brain found on the rug? — Yes.

Q. And a great deal of blood on the carpet? — Yes.

Q. There was a rug over the top of her? — Yes.

Q. Had not that rug blood on both sides? — Yes.

Q. Did it bear the appearance of having been put over her to cover her after she was dead? — Yes.

Q. There was blood on the top side of the rug as it lay over her. I show you label No. 17, the second rug. Was not the hairy side of that rug covered with blood — was there not a lot of blood on it? — Yes. That may have been caused by the constable who lifted it before I went there. He lifted it and saw the body.

Q. Was she lying upon this rug to any extent? — No, she was not on it at all. She was lying on the other rug.

Q. This second rug was on top of her? — Yes.

Q. With the hairy side on the top of her body? — Yes.

Q. If that be so, how would the blood which appears on the other side have come there? — The place was smeared with blood, and throwing it off and throwing it down blood may have gone on to the other side in that way.

Both sides of the rugs were filled with blood. On the rug upon which Barney once napped, Slater methodically wiped his boots, the hammer, his face, and his hands. He wiped wet blood from himself and his clothing. If he hadn't worn his gloves for the deed, he now slid them over his bruised hands. No one would see his hands because he routinely wore gloves.

Having wiped the hammer, no blood would stain the inside pocket of his fawn waterproof. The exchange of hair and clothing fibers, fur and rug fibers, hand prints and bloody footprints surely were in condition to have been dutifully examined. But they were not.

6:55 p.m.---Shaken from the murder, breathing heavily, Slater didn't have Marion Gilchrist's keys for the box. They were in her dress pocket. A search of her corpse was too grisly a task and he was pressed for time. He was sure to have heard a frantic male voice, knocking at the flat door. Finally, the man had given up and left.

Slater spent no time opening drawers in the dining room. He went swiftly to the spare bedroom and the locked box with the anticipated— presumably-- diamonds and coins.

No one examined Lambie, nor the prior maidservants, as to where Miss Gilchrist kept her weekly money—a small cache reserved for expenses. There was a safe in the parlor, but it was a room with which Slater didn't bother.

At the door, short-sighted, Arthur Adams wasn't wearing his spectacles. In his formal photo, he did not wear them. At the Gilchrist flat-- which he had not visited in 27 years--he peered through the curtained glass on either side of the door. He saw lights within yet no one answered his frantic calls. He had heard sounds "like the chopping of firewood" and assumed the maid at her work, or perhaps Marian Gilchrist. Miss Gilchrist was unable to respond. The force of the blows into her skull had spewed out brain matter and knocked out her false teeth. Her left hand lay on her breast.

It was Slater in the spare bedroom banging on that locked wooden box.

The box was locked for security's sake and not from paranoia. According to Jane Duff Walker, a former housemaid, Miss Gilchrist kept jewels in the box. Yet, there were no jewels in the box. Lambie said Miss Gilchrist was so paranoid that she hid gems in secret places in her wardrobe and among her clothing.

Prior to Lambie's employment, Miss Gilchrist had no difficulties with her maids. There had been no strange footfalls in the middle of the night. This was another path of the plot left unexamined by the police and the prosecution.

Lambie said she was gone between five and ten minutes. She would continue to lie to the police and to the Court about that kitchen clock and her 7 p.m. departure. In fact, she would have left a half hour earlier, about 6:30 p.m.—before Slater entered the flat at 6:35. It was up to him to steal whatever it was the trio wanted from the locked box within the time allotted. Nugent and Lambie waited outside, near St. George's Road and Grant Street.

Lambie joins Arthur Adams at the Door

7 p.m.---Lambie was unprepared for the appearance of a witness, Arthur Adams, standing upstairs at the door. He was banging and calling out. Then, to mutual surprise, he saw Lambie enter the building. He thought she'd been inside cracking wood for the fire, but here she was. Her mind must have been racing when she saw the agitated Arthur. The well-thought-out plan was being upended and that was just the start.

Lambie was returning at 7 p.m. and not exiting. She had no idea of the dire noises that put the Adams family on alert. He hadn't heard Lambie leave the building at 7 p.m., as she said, since it was 7 p.m. as the two of them stood there. Who could have predicted that the family, with whom Miss Gilchrist had had minimal contact in the 27 years they lived below, would show such concern?

There was no mention by Arthur Adams nor the police that she brought with her a wet *Evening Chronicle*. She said she'd been gone five to ten minutes. From the time of Slater's entry to the flat, nearer to 20 minutes elapsed.

Once she walked up the stairs, she paused before unlocking the door. She heard noise within. She and Arthur stood there for at least two minutes. This was Mr. Adams' second time at the door. He went back up to the Gilchrist flat because his sisters were still concerned about the unresolved noise and the thuds. Lambie, disoriented by his unexpected presence, instinctively lied. She had an idea of what the noise was inside the flat. She wanted to allay his fears so that he would go back to his flat. She would have been consumed with fright. Not for Miss Gilchrist but for herself.

Lambie told Arthur that the sounds he heard must have been the kitchen pulleys on which the laundry was hanging to dry. She was suggesting that 82-year-old Marion Gilchrist was up and about, doing laundry.

Mr. Adams wasn't going anywhere. His sister, Laura, had urged him to find out what was going on. They were concerned about their elderly neighbor who had not once responded. The classical flutist and Miss Gilchrist's housemaid would express differing recollections.

Bedroom, 15 Queen's Terrace, showing toilet table and gas bracket.

Slater, the Witnesses and the Locked Box in the Spare Bedroom

Inside the flat, Slater may have expected the voices by the door to depart. Or, he thought the voices were those of Nugent and Lambie.

Marion Gilchrist was dead and Slater was in the spare bedroom. The bedroom had been dark. The police found that the intruder used his Runaway matches to light the bedroom's gas lamp. A spent match was left behind. An apt brand name, to be sure.

With the room lit, Slater adjusted his clothing in the full-length mirror. He saw the blood evidence.

Lambie said the Runaway brand was not from the household. Was the box Slater's? He was a smoker. The match was not examined and no connection was made to Slater. No cigarette was left behind. He waited for his smoke until 8:15 that night when he was spotted by a grocery boy who knew him. Slater stood outside his residence, in the bitter cold and rain, not wearing a coat, puffing away.

Following his release from prison, Slater was photographed on many occasions. In one, outside his garden in Ayr, he appeared holding a cigar in his gloved right hand.

Oscar Slater in his garden at Ayr

Why didn't he simply pick the jewelry box up and flee? After the murder, he wasn't thinking clearly. It would have been tricky running out, past the alerted Adams' family, carrying a box. It would also impede his speed. The box could not be hidden in a deep coat pocket…as could the gems within.

Had Slater, with a life's experience in working with young, unschooled girls and women, leapt to an irresponsible conclusion about the contents of that box? Were the contents so seductive that, for weeks, the conspiratorial covetousness overwhelmed common sense?

Neither diamonds nor money were in the box, and yet the box had been locked. Papers—only papers-- from within the box went flying as he banged at it. Lambie would testify that "papers and accounts" were kept in the box. This statement kept her safely away from motive. She'd seen the contents of the box on the floor and heard the police say only papers and the broken pieces of the box lay strewn about.

Previous maids testified that Miss Gilchrist kept jewelry in the box. Had Miss Gilchrist shifted the contents? Her papers would normally be kept in the parlor safe; she didn't need to get at them regularly. The originals of her official papers, such as the Will, were held at the solicitors.

Arthur Adams and Helen Lambie Enter the Flat

Mr. Adams said Lambie unlocked the door. He must have known the door was locked. It was unlikely that he hadn't tried to open it himself when calling out for Miss Gilchrist. Slater locked the door from the inside when he entered.

While in that spare bedroom, exhausted from the killing and the splintering, frantic Slater was confronted with witnesses. The scheme had brought him nothing. It was time to go. The lights were on. His only way of escape was through the front door, where the witnesses stood, and it lay several feet ahead.

> *"Considerate*: 'Take care...your head bowed low
> **By such a weight...lest head o'er heels you go!'"**
> **Cyrano de Bergerac suggesting that one with a large nose be careful of imbalance**

Arthur Adams saw the man emerge from the bedroom. He wasn't bolt upright, but skulking and crunched-down as he slid along the lower edge of the lobby wall. The crouch helped hide Slater's bloodstained coat.

Lambie, like Arthur, had no idea Marion Gilchrist was murdered minutes before.

Instead of calling out to Miss Gilchrist, Arthur said Lambie turned left "past the clock to go into the kitchen." Her conduct became cunning. She knew the intruder. It was Oscar Slater. Not Patrick Nugent. Not a stranger. Not a Gilchrist relative.

Murder wasn't part of the burglary plot in which Lambie and Nugent were involved with Slater. Did the lack of knowledge limit a conspirator's guilt? Not then and not now.

CHAPTER 26

Motive: Diamonds Worth Thousands

"The most highly valued of human possessions, let alone gemstones, is the diamond." **PLINY**

Slater was without money. That was apparent from his pawnbroker draws. He wasn't paying his rent. He had gambling losses. He had no more gems to sell. He had liquidated his Post Office accounts. The sums weren't enough for his planned January relocation to America.

On December 21, the plan had been to steal diamonds. What had motivated Oscar Slater, fence and diamond broker, to attack that locked box with such vigor, given that two witnesses were banging at the door?

This motive may appear as surmise, but its phrasing in a police report, and in a January 1909 account in *Reynold's News* from London, and in a reference during questioning at trial, and in regard to Slater's livelihood lend firm credibility to Marion Gilchrist's diamonds "worth thousands."

The report of police discovering a tray of diamonds was used to tar Miss Gilchrist as having herself been a resetter and fence for stolen diamonds. On the contrary, for all her adult life she had been a jewelry collector. She particularly favored diamonds—and this Slater well knew, as did Nugent and Lambie.

Detective Lieutenant Trench learned something about the late-discovered tray and its diamonds at the police department. The police had continued searching through the flat and, unlike unlucky Slater, found a tray of them in a "hidden corner" of the flat. These exact words were reported, and in the second week of January, the newspapers repeated them including the value of the diamonds at £5000.

Trench had not been selected to be among the investigators searching the Gilchrist flat. Police investigators continued to rummage. They weren't immune from pocketing a small bit of prosperity. No one, truthfully, was immune from the pull of a diamond's glitter.

In 1912 (after the May 1909 trial and conviction of Oscar Slater), when Conan Doyle took a look at the case, he was convinced the breaking of the wooden box was a "blind"-- meant to suggest to police that the motive was theft rather than murder. He believed otherwise-- that murder alone was intended and that Helen Lambie and her friend, Patrick Nugent were the perpetrators.

Conan Doyle was correct in focusing on Lambie and Nugent but his conclusions about the motive were incorrect. The murder of the elderly woman served no purpose. Furthermore, Conan Doyle was conflicted about the motive and accusing Slater because William Roughead and John Trench had enlisted his assistance in the campaign to release Oscar Slater.

It was Slater who murdered the elderly woman. His bashing of that wooden box, despite the noise at the front door, was for a burning reason. He was desperate for what he believed was kept within the box. He could have saved himself had he escaped as soon as Arthur Adams went back to his flat the first time. Slater could have exited though empty-handed. He chose not to. He wanted the contents of the box. He had to believe it held diamonds. That was the motive.

Felony Murder

Would a "constructive murder" concept apply to Nugent and to Lambie? Lambie and Nugent were guilty of felony murder, a crime in Great Britain since at least 1716 and which declared that all participants in a felony were equally culpable regardless of intent. Scotland did not have this rule, but instead, its euphemistic equivalent: "Art and Part" with similar outcome...death by hanging within days of the sentence. In 1883, the felony murder rule was applied with less severity...not as a capital crime but reduced to manslaughter. It was brought where an individual's intention had been to do an act which could probably kill or do great bodily harm-- regardless of whether the actor (Nugent and Lambie) knew that such a result would occur. A Scottish jury would consider the heinous nature of the murder, the various burglaries, the months-long scheme, the bookie/diamond-dealing foreigner who did the actual killing vs. distinctions between the states of mind, emotion, and intellect in deciding a reduced fate for Patrick Nugent and Helen Lambie.

Slater was guilty of murder, and Nugent and Lambie were guilty of felony murder. They committed a felony: breaking and entering while a resident was in the home; Slater had no legal right to enter the premises without Miss Gilchrist's consent. Helen Lambie had no legal right to allow entry to a stranger. In the course of which criminal act, Marion Gilchrist was murdered.

Was their actual knowledge of the dangerous character of the intended burglary a necessary factor? Lambie took great precautions in making the entry and theft as manageable as possible. The burglary involved the likelihood of physical violence to an elderly lady in her home. Lambie and Nugent might have expected her to be stunned from behind; that in itself was a contemplated physical assault. Additionally, a thorough police investigation would have uncovered prior thefts by Lambie and sales by Slater which would have led to the motivation of stealing a larger cache…separate diamonds hidden somewhere in the flat, most likely in the locked jewelry box.

CHAPTER 27

Oscar Slater's Inglorious Escape

7:03 p.m.-7:08 p.m.---Arthur said he saw the man crouching towards them, but he "had no reason to suspect" him. Lambie said nothing. She stared in mute shock. For 18 feet, the man sidled along the wall! This was no "fleeting observation" by Lambie as William Roughead wrote. Lambie would testify implausibly at trial that she didn't get a good look at his face.

7:10 p.m.-- Mr. Adams assumed the man, dressed as a commercial gent, was someone known to Miss Gilchrist. Arthur was so civil an Edwardian, and disconcertedly timid, that he didn't look directly into the man's face.

Lambie did not greet the man. Still, Arthur was unsure whether or not he was a visitor. Lambie watched as he crept along the wall, stood up straight, and walked out the door. She said she was unable to see the man's face because it was face down into his coat collar. When one looks at the photo of Oscar Slater led down the Lusitania gangplank (below), his head is cast downward but his facial characteristics are clearly visible.

Slater walked swiftly towards Arthur Adams-- as if he were going to greet him "quite pleasantly." Only when he glided past, saying nothing at all, did Arthur realize something was wrong. Wordlessly, Slater walked out between the two witnesses, with a contrived nonchalance, and ran, Arthur said, "like greased lightning." Neither Lambie nor Arthur saw anything in his hands. They said he was wearing a fawn coat. They were uncertain if his hands were in his pockets. They didn't see blood on his person. The police testified at trial that the lighting was very good in the outside hall--the lights had been extinguished at the time of Slater's entrance but Mr. Adams turned them on.

Mr. Adams' and Lambie's observations were so anemic in detail that, as to Lambie, her hesitation was meant to avoid connection with what she believed was supposed to have been a burglary. As to Arthur, his near-sightedness and his reticence proved him a dismal eyewitness. He could see well enough. He just didn't want to be pressed.

Arthur observed that Lambie scooted inside in the direction of the kitchen "and called out that it was all right, meaning her pulleys." Arthur testified that he had to demand that Lambie look for her Mistress. In the minutes at the door, and watching the intruder leave the spare bedroom, and Lambie calling out from the kitchen, there hadn't been a sound from Miss Gilchrist. Worse was to follow.

Lambie realized Arthur wasn't going anywhere unless she complied. This was a challenge that would have immediate effects on the young woman. She was in danger of being caught up in the plot. Standing in the kitchen, her body shaking and heart pounding, Lambie would have been struck with terror. She was completely on her own in a scheme that had fallen apart because Slater was seen and his fawn waterproof appeared bloody. In much later statements, Lambie remembered that the murderer was indeed Oscar Slater. He was the man she saw earlier in the street, and he was a liar if he claimed he didn't kill Miss Gilchrist.

CHAPTER 28

"That's When Your Heartaches Begin"

Electric street lamps: Queens Terrace at West Princes Street and the corner of St. George's Road

Oscar Slater's Escape From the Murder Scene

7:05 p.m.--- By sheer unlucky coincidence for Slater, that evening, 15-year-old Mary Barrowman was on an errand from the High Street for her employer/brother.

Scotland's youngsters completed school at age 12 and Mary was healthy, alert, and employed. Slater's Mademoiselle Andrée was but 17 when he met her working a street corner. Mary's parents kept her in more respectable circumstances. She continued to attend religious services and revival meetings but a new day was dawning for Edwardian women of which Mary would have been aware. Newspaper headlines and shop talk raised the profiles of Glasgow's Suffragettes and their protests, shouts, "unladylike behavior," and militant mischief.

This night, she walked down West Princes Street and paused at 15 Queens Terrace just as a man ran out of the flat towards the street lamp. He stared at her and then crossed the narrow, cobbled road to St. George's Road where he stood underneath another street lamp. Mary was quite obviously fearless.

***

Street Lights in Glasgow

The ghostly gas lamps fail at twenty feet
"221B" by Vincent Starrett

Gaslight, which relied on coal gas, was replaced on Glasgow's streets with electric lighting in 1893. Arc lamps within the glass took the place of filaments. They greatly illuminated the streets. Constable Christopher Walker testified that at St. George's Road, "there was an electric street lamp that threw a very bright light." The Constable recalled his sightings of Oscar Slater at around 7 p.m. in that vicinity on three separate occasions prior to the night of the murder..."a foreign-looking man."

The Crown went further in examining the Constable about the lighting in that neighborhood, preempting an argument as to Mary's' ability to see a man's face beneath one. She recalled a consequential detail that foretold the apprehension of Oscar Slater: the man had a twisted nose.

Q. Are the lights in West Princes Street incandescent?

A. Yes.

Q. And is it electric light that you have in St. George's Road?

A. Yes.

Q. Was there an electric light in St. George's Road near the corner, near No. 6?

A. Immediately opposite, on the St. George's Road, right in the centre of West Princes Street.

Q. It throws a powerful light on that corner where you see No. 6?

A. Yes.

Mary Barrowman's testimony for the Crown

"I was just at the lamp-post near the close when this happened. I saw him coming out of the close. I saw him coming down the steps. He was coming very fast. When he came down to the foot of the steps, he turned towards me...the man knocked up against me."

The sequence of Mary Barrowman's sighting of Oscar Slater:

- Slater ran out of the lobby entrance. Mary saw him.

- Slater ran down the steps. Mary saw him.

- Slater got to the last step and turned towards her at the street light. Mary saw his face.

- Slater knocked into her in his hurry. He was right next to her. Mary got a good look.

- Slater crossed the cobblestone street, at St. George's Road, stopping under another streetlight. He turned around and gaped in Mary's direction.

He was looking for Nugent. Or wondering what harm this young girl could cause him. Mary Barrowman continued to stare, transfixed. She thought Slater might have been waiting for a tram.

In that lighting, with just the two of them on that quiet street, Slater was well-illuminated. Mary had a good look at his face. No mustache and…a twisted nose. He was wearing a fawn coat. He had dark hair. Mary did not know Oscar Slater but described a man with those features and clothing.

When she went home that evening, December 21, she immediately told her mother what she had seen and the strange man. Her mother, who had already heard news of something having happened to an old lady on West Princes Street, that very night informed a policeman neighbor.

With Mary's description of the twisted nose and of a man who had just bolted from the Gilchrist flat, the bell tolled for Oscar Slater.

Peter Hunt wrote indefinably: "Slater, let it be said, was not possessed of a twisted nose." In fact, Slater's nose had been broken in a fist fight. His barber, who daily shaved his beard, said Slater had a broken nose. Its description was included by the examiner in the 1907 U.S. Citizenship interview document in New York of applicant "Adolf Anderson, Dentist," an Oscar Slater alias. It was 1951 when Peter Hunt wrote his book, *Oscar Slater: the Great Suspect*, referring to him repeatedly as "the German Jew."

At trial, a reporter for London's *Reynolds News,* wrote: "...his distorted nose gave him a distinctive appearance." In New York, where Slater was bound over for extradition, his own lawyer referred to his broken nose and that the British government's sole piece of evidence was that the absconder from the murder scene "coincidentally" also had a broken nose.

In a Peterhead Prison photo taken in 1909, Slater's nose in profile is crooked and a marked contrast to his formal portrait taken prior to the fist fight that broke his nose. Thomas Toughill idyllically misdescribed Slater's nose as "aquiline" from his side profile...perforce that of an ancient Greek or Roman. One look at the front of the Peterhead photo and an observer sees what Mary Barrowman saw: "a solid lump of flesh and bone." (the "Pedant," *Cyrano de Bergerac*). Upon release from prison, Oscar had surgery to straighten the nose. Cyrano be damned.

Oscar Slater on entry to Peterhead Prison, September 7, 1909; the nose is lumpy and twisted.

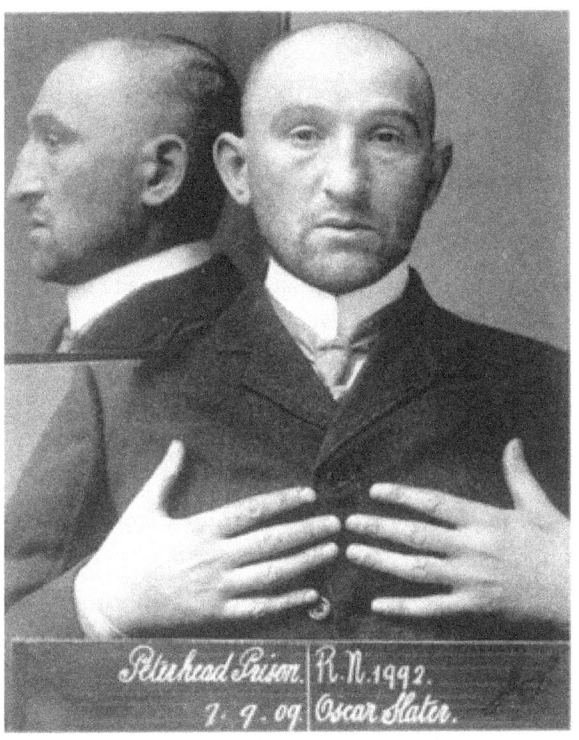

Make Haste, Make Haste

Slater fled from the Gilchrist flat a little after 7 p.m. It took longer than anticipated, first, because of the time it took to murder his victim, and second, because he couldn't find the diamonds which were the target of the burglary. He scored nothing and had killed an old woman in the process.

Nugent was not outside 15 Queens Terrace. Mary Barrowman saw only one man and he had a twisted nose. She was curious and followed Slater a short distance on St. George's Road. Instead of going straight to his home down St. George's, Mary saw Slater make a right at Grant Street. As fate would have it, witness Agnes Brown had emerged from her home on Grant Street just minutes before.

7:08 p.m.---We know Slater was assisted by a second man from Agnes Brown's recollections. Many an author scoffed at this likelihood, saying the second-man theory was imagined by police stymied from descriptions of two different coat colors: fawn or grey.

Slater took a circuitous route down Grant to meet up with a partner hidden within a close. This was Patrick Nugent. He was Slater's partner. He made the 37-mile journey to Ayr from Glasgow to meet Marion Gilchrist. He visited the flat to see Lambie when Miss Gilchrist was not at home. It was undisputed that Lambie had shown him Miss Gilchrist's jewelry collection.

This night, the two, in a panic, raced Grant Street a few yards west to Cumberland and made a right turn. As they ran on Cumberland, they were seen by witness, Agnes Brown, walking that rainy night to teach a class. She walked from her home on Grant Street and turned right at Cumberland, minutes ahead of the two.

Nugent may have held an extra coat for Slater as part of the getaway plan for the burglary. The happenstance of two men was likely since Slater could just have gone running on West Princes Street towards Kelvinbridge train station rather than making a circuitous diversion to Grant Street, then Cumberland, and then the Kelvinbridge train station. Or, he could have just raced home for dinner down St. George's Road in plenty of time for his 7 p.m. dinnertime alibi.

The police version was that the suspect skipped out of the crime area to avoid being seen walking or strolling home and having to clean himself up and dispose of bloodied items. Had he not been caught at the scene of a murder, Slater would not have been in such a race against time.

It is doubtful that Slater had a moment to reveal to Nugent that he murdered the old lady. Nor would he have had the inclination to confess. The two ran because Slater would have blurted out that there were witnesses at the scene. Slater knew that Lambie and a gentleman had by now discovered the murdered body of Marion Gilchrist. Once Nugent learned of the catastrophe, he erased himself from the entire incident.

As Miss Brown walked up Cumberland, the two men who were in their vigorous 30s, pushed past her on the pavement. These were quiet streets with quiet closes and such incidents were unusual. A woman, walking on her own, on a routine path, would have taken careful notice of the two helter-skelterers.

The man nearest to Agnes Brown flew past so close that he almost knocked her over. No attention nor pause by him; no "pardon me," "are you hurt?" "may I help you in any way?" The men were running as if hunted. They ran without stopping. They were not old men.

Still, Miss Brown had a direct look at the side of the man's face closest to her. He had black hair, glossy, and his ears stuck out. Nugent. Both hands were kept in his pockets as he ran. She believed he wore a large, grey overcoat.

The man further from her was shaped "squarer" than the other. Oscar Slater. She said he was of medium build, clean-shaven, and with jet-black hair. He wore a navy-blue Melton coat with a velvet collar, unbuttoned and blowing in the air and rain. He held something in his right hand which she could not see.

Agnes Brown introduced to the suspect's clothing list a heavy, navy-blue Melton coat with a velvet collar—a tightly woven wool, also wind-and-rain resistant. Miss Brown's description of their coats differed from the color worn by the murder suspect at the door of Miss Gilchrist's flat-- "the fawn waterproof." The police reported a fawn or a grey coat because near-sighted Arthur Adams, in the immediate aftermath of having confronted a murderer, found the colors indistinguishable. Slater owned a grey coat, a fawn waterproof, and a navy-blue Melton coat with a velvet collar. He wore the grey coming off the Lusitania and the Melton when attending his Edinburgh trial. When he ran up Cumberland, Slater's Melton was unbuttoned because Miss Brown saw it blowing in the wind.

As Miss Brown walked behind, watching them race ahead, she looked at a clock in a nearby shop which read 7:12 p.m. The squarer-shaped man turned right at Rupert Street, up to Great Western Road, going west to the Kelvinbridge station on the River Kelvin.

Edwardian Era Men's Coats

7:30 p.m.-8 p.m.---At Kelvinbridge station, train clerk Annie Armour said a man came rushing for the train, dropped his penny at her window, and flew through the turnstyle.

Kelvinbridge station, now abandoned, ran beside the River Kelvin. It is doubtful that Slater tossed clothing into the River or on the riverbank. Police made thorough searches of the river bank's bare and icy thickets and boggy footpaths. They found nothing.

The ticket agent did not describe a second man, so our Patrick Nugent, on hearing Slater's breathless account of no diamonds nor coin as they raced up Cumberland Street, veered off and took a turn back home to Carfin.

Slater's heated appearance at the train station fit smoothly within the minutes after the murder. Annie Armour described him as clean shaven, dark-complexioned, and wearing a light waterproof. It had been such an attentuated event that she took stock only of the rushing man's face. The "dark-complexioned" and "clean shaven" descriptions were also formed by witnesses from different sightings.

At 10 p.m. when Miss Brown returned home from class, she told her two sisters about the encounter because it had been so unusual. The ladies hadn't read the evening paper nor ventured outdoors near the murder scene. They had no idea of the coming sensationalism.

CHAPTER 29

"That Man Has Done Something to Miss Gilchrist"

Once the intruder ran out, Arthur Adams described Lambie's walking in and to her left. She then walked from the kitchen to the spare bedroom. Unthinkably, she went to the spare bedroom to see about that locked box without first calling out for Miss Gilchrist. She became distracted by the condition of the room, with papers strewn about and the box splintered apart. It looked as if Slater may have grabbed the jewelry from the box.

Hearing nothing from scampering Lambie, Arthur spoke bluntly from the door, telling her to find her Mistress. No sooner did Lambie tentatively venture into the dining room than she was confronted with a hellish sight. Covered with bloody rugs was the corpse of Miss Gilchrist lying prostrate on the floor. Lambie screamed hysterically, calling out to Arthur:

"That man has done something to Miss Gilchrist."

The horror of the moment didn't enrage her enough to identify the man--whom she later accused as Oscar Slater. Was it fear? Self-preservation? Lambie ran out the door, handing off to Laura Adams downstairs the household keys. She went wailing down West Princes Street to the home of Marion Gilchrist's niece, Margaret Birrell, a few streets away. The neighborhood window watchers were on alert as both women, weeping and in shock, walked back to the flat supported by Miss Birrell's lodger, Charles Cowan.

7:15 p.m.--- As Lambie ran off, Arthur raced to the home of his own doctor, John Adams (no relation), who lived across the way. Dr. Adams and Police Constable William Neill went upstairs with him. Arthur again ran out and found Police Constable Francis Brien. The police then sent Arthur back downstairs to his home, in full sweat, shock, and exhaustion. While home with his family, he telephoned the police station and reported all that he had seen and experienced that evening. Within the next half hour or so, the neighbors and newspapers were alerted.

Arthur's actions were propitious in providing clues to the murder, but his and his family's descriptions were hardly luminous. It was unfortunate that, because of their 27-year estrangement, the Adams family could shed little light on the affairs and entanglements of Miss Gilchrist or her maidservant Helen Lambie.

A Physician's On-Scene Examination

Leave it to Scotland's medical practitioners, of which Arthur Conan Doyle was one, to pinpoint the execution of Marion Gilchrist in a way the police could not.

Medical study in Scotland was available to all students, no matter their religion or ethnicity. The curriculum was as illustrious as the university's teachers and researchers--studies in anesthesia, use of the microscope in medical research, epidemiology, surgery, amputations, cell development, and a whole horizon of anatomy.

Dr. John Adams was first on the scene at the Gilchrist flat. He examined the body not 15 minutes after the murder in the immediate condition seen by Lambie and Mr. Adams. Marion Gilchrist's ravaged face and body lay in a soup of blood. He could not have avoided kneeling in it. He lifted the rug from the victim's head and determined the victim was deceased.

Dr. Adams described the injuries to the skull and the manner of striking and gouging through the eyes and mouth *as caused by the claw end of a hammer...the pointed end.* This (accurate) conclusion was made at the scene, immediately following the murder, and without a weapon in evidence. This would not be good news for Oscar Slater.

Dr. Adams rose to examine the room, the blood splatter, the rugs, and the position of the victim's body. He looked for a weapon, including the fireplace tongs, and the heavy wooden chair beside the body. Blood dripped from the chair legs, particularly on the left back leg farthest from the body.

The doctor determined that when Marion Gilchrist first saw the stranger at the dining room door, she held onto the heavy mahogany chair in front of her with her right hand. The chair seat would have faced Slater and as he pounced on her, it partially obstructed his approach and his hammer thrusts. Clambering upon the chair seat as she fell, he also used it to crush her and stomped her with his feet. This the doctor concluded from his examination. Recall Oscar Slater's ruthless foot work when street fighting.

The chair seat offered Slater some protection from blood spurts. His coat did not escape the splatter entirely; that was how 25 red/orange stains appeared on the front of his fawn waterproof coat and right sleeve. A bloody hand print was left on the wooden chair but it was not produced for the jury. No impress had been taken.

7:40 p.m.---Dr. Adams, having completed the examination, informed Detective- Inspector John Pyper of the results.

CHAPTER 30

The Investigatory Team of Police

7:55 p.m.---The police constables were joined at the flat by John Pyper, Detective-Inspector, the Western District of the Glasgow Police; Superintendent William Douglas, the Western District; and John Ord, Superintendent and Chief of the Criminal Investigation Department.

At the crime scene, police were in no less shock at Marion Gilchrist's brutalized corpse than was her hysterical maid. The frozen horror on the old woman's face was unspeakable. The photo still arouses today a visceral hatred of the killer's inhumanity. Superintendent Douglas reported "part of the deceased's brains were on the rug between the body and the fender of the fireplace." The victim's hair was drenched in blood.

On the dining room table lay Miss Gilchrist's magazines and her gold spectacles. She had not been reading. It was likely she'd been standing by the fire. Detective-Inspector Pyper said he'd found the half-sovereign beside her dead hand and that Constable Neill placed it on the mantelpiece. If that were the case, she believed it was Lambie at the door and she had been holding the coin for her.

On the senior officer's instruction, the body was removed to be examined by medical coroners, Doctors John Glaister and Hugh Galt. It would be their testimony, not Dr. Adams', that would introduce the weapon—the hammer. The weapon had not been found in the flat but taken by the murderer after the killing.

9:40 p.m.--- The police issued a report of the murder. It took place between 7 p.m. and 7:30 p.m. The suspect was between ages 25 to 30, 5'7" to 5'8" in height, clean-shaven, and wore a grey overcoat…or fawn.

CHAPTER 31

A Dogged Investigation

Police Procedure at the Gilchrist Flat

At least 30 minutes elapsed before Helen Lambie returned to the scene of the crime, accompanied by Margaret Birrell and Margaret's tenant, Charles Cowan. Upon their arrival, the rooms were filled with police, relatives, acquaintances, a doctor, and witnesses including Arthur Adams, Laura Adams, and Rowena Adams. The police brought in Miss Gilchrist's nephew, Dr. Francis Charteris, from his medical office on Great Western Road a few minutes away. He was exonerated at the scene. He was the nephew who bought Barney the dog for his aunt.

A police hierarchy examining the premises:

From Glasgow's Western District:

- Superintendent William Miller Douglas
- Detective Inspector John Pyper
- Detective Constable Duncan MacVicar

From Glasgow Central District:

- The Procurator-Fiscal James Neil Hart
- Superintendent John Ord
- Detective Lieutenant William Gordon

Police and forensic investigations were as yet unpolished in their early evolution. There were treatises and guides, including one by Sir Howard Vincent, head of CID at Scotland Yard, published in 1881, with instructions for police investigations in *The Police Code and Manual of Criminal Law*.

A theme in Sir Howard's book was that a distinct class of professional criminals had arisen in British society and that they lived entirely on the proceeds of crime. Such a criminal did not act in haste. There was motive and strategy to be considered. In the murder of Marion Gilchrist, the police were confronted with just such a professional. Though police recognized the type once Oscar Slater was identified, their short-sighted investigation failed to reinforce the case for the Crown.

It had been raining outdoors. On entry to the Gilchrist flat, Slater left behind water stains from his boots on the steps, on the carpeting and floors, and on the rugs with which he covered the corpse and presumably wiped his boots. Sir Howard's Manual included a section on the examination and preservation of "footmarks." Sherlock Holmes was expert but the Glasgow police oblivious.

> "There were no footmarks.'
> 'Meaning that you saw none?'
> 'I assure you, sir, that there were none.'
> 'My good Hopkins, I have investigated many crimes, but I have never yet seen one which was committed by a flying creature. As long as the criminal remains upon two legs so long must there be some indentation, some abrasion, some trifling displacement which can be detected by the scientific searcher."
> ***The Adventure of Black Peter* (1905)**

The Manual recommended making an impression of a footmark using plaster of Paris and comparing it with a suspect's footwear. It warned of the damaging effect of weather, such as rain, and advised covering and preserving the footprint. A wet footprint appeared on the stairs to Miss Gilchrist's. It goes without saying that there were wet prints in the close and bloody footprints in the flat, along with wet leaves, mud, and pebbles.

What did they do to preserve the crime scene? Their care and custody of the dead victim were inadequate. Police and civilians rummaged through the flat; access to the victim's valuables was not precluded; there was no cataloging of the condition of the flat from corner to corner. The spare bedroom floor was littered with splinters from the broken jewelry box, with papers strewn about–none of it was stored. Sir Howard Vincent's maxim was to *show...don't just tell*.

Further formal techniques were in practice in 1908: mugshots, fingerprinting, and crime scene photography. Here, there was no crime scene photography: no photos of the scattered jewelry, the bloody rugs, the blood spatter, the kitchen pulleys, the door knobs, the match, the wooden chair legs (nor was the actual chair produced), the condition of the spare bedroom and dining room, wooden slats and hidden corners of the floor, the safe and its contents, the grandfather clock, the hall wall along which Oscar slid, and, worst of all...no photos of the jewelry and gems where they had been placed or hidden.

Fingerprints. Yes or No?

A fingerprint was evaluated in the same manner as today, of its arches, loops and whorls as illustrated by Sir Francis Galton in his 1892 book, *Finger Prints*. Fingerprints had been in routine use by Scotland Yard and in British courts since 1901. Fingerprinting was an expertise developed in British India in 1858 to identify "natives, often with the intent to frighten the malfeasor out of his wits." In Sherlock Holmes' *Sign of Four* (1890), a partial print was concluded to be the suspect's: " 'There's the print of Wooden-leg's hand,' he remarked as I mounted up beside him. 'You see the slight smudge of blood upon the white plaster.'"

No bloody fingerprints from the Gilchrist flat were produced at trial—not from the kitchen, not from the wooden box, not from the weaponized chair, nor even from the matchstick used to light the gas in the spare bedroom. Police found that the assailant fingered various papers from the locked box but thrown them aside. Reportedly, a bloody hand print appeared on the back of the wooden chair used to crush Marion Gilchrist.

Glasgow, Edinburgh, and London police had Oscar Slater's fingerprints on file from prior charges. In fact, on February 25, 1909, police compared Slater's fingerprints with a set found on a door handle from "the Whiteinch (Glasgow) Murder. In that case, a prosperous middle-aged woman shop owner was bound, gagged, her head smashed with a hammer, and then robbed. That 1904 case remained unsolved.

No fingerprint impressions were shown to the jury in the Oscar Slater case. A skeptic is left to wonder why. Detective-Inspector Andrew Keith of the Glasgow Police didn't clarify whether police lifted fingerprints at the flat. He did explain that in 1909, fingerprints weren't admissible at trial. Fingerprint evidence was a new concept and still an untrustworthy methodology among which issues were whether a single fingerprint should be evidence of guilt rather than the fingerprints of an entire hand.

Between 1912 and 1914, Detective-Lieutenant Trench secretly removed the police department's Slater case files. He unlawfully shared them with authors, newspapers and Slater's new attorney, David Cook—Trench's acquaintance. No fingerprints survived the disclosed contents. A 1914 court review of the Slater case barred an examination of police conduct.

Exchange of Fibers

In 1909, the same year as Oscar Slater's trial, Edmond Locard, in his Lyons, France laboratory, determined that traces of human interaction invariably adhered to a surface or object and that these provided clues in a criminal investigation: "Locard's Principle of Forensic Exchange."

Traces of Oscar Slater would have been left on his victim and her traces on him. Every contact leaves behind fibers, fluids or hair. Did the fibers of Marion Gilchrist's clothing, or the rugs used by the killer to cover her body, drift to his coat? And vice-versa? Of course.

Shock and chaos interrupted the scrutiny of procedure demanded at a murder scene. Still, it was inexcusable. Securing the scene and marking exhibits was common practice.

CHAPTER 32

A Puzzling Motive

Police and prosecution missed the participation of three plotters in the murder and missed the months' long planning. Little incisive thought was given the motive. Burglary? Of what? Why a murder for the theft of a single brooch? And what reason for the brutality? The lack of a "bricks and mortar" foundation required of a proper criminal investigation and trial misled trial watchers, investigators, authors, and independent sleuths.

The motive lay in a detail included in a police report several weeks after the murder. It was about Marion Gilchrist's loose diamonds. The report was leaked to the *Reynolds News* of London, the description given was a "tray of diamonds" "discovered by police" in "a hidden corner" and valued at £5000.

A Clutch of Diamond Poachers

Oscar Slater and his two partners, lured by an old woman's diamonds, murdered her. Corruption, unconnected to the crime, prevented a clear-eyed view of the motive and of the co-conspirators, Lambie and Nugent. Not only was an old woman left dead but the murder scene was not secured and neither was her jewelry collection.

Prior to the murder, Lambie, alone or with Nugent, rifled Miss Gilchrist's dresser drawers and wardrobe. Amongst the linens, sleepwear, and underthings, jewelry had been hidden away. The two suspected Miss Gilchrist's intention --to keep the gems out of reach. So, they and Slater invented a ploy...and it worked. Lambie followed up with a visit to her former employer, Agnes Guthrie, who had once described the girl as having "a low mentality."

Lambie had gone there to gossip. She said Miss Gilchrist was becoming worrisomely paranoid, chief among which signs was her fear of robbers especially after the death of her dog.

Instead of speaking with Dr. Charteris, Miss Gilchrist's nephew and medical doctor, or her long-time friend, Maggie Ferguson, Lambie chose to express her concerns about Miss Gilchrist's psyche with Agnes Guthrie. This mean-spirited gossip was echoed thereafter by the Oscar Slater apologists in their books. So consumed was Miss Gilchrist with an irrational fear of robbers, related Lambie, that she had begun to hide jewelry in her wardrobe and among her clothing. "Hiding" was the operable word. The only other resident in the flat was Helen Lambie. So, from whom was Miss Gilchrist hiding her jewelry?

There was a wooden jewelry box in the spare bedroom. Miss Gilchrist kept it locked and the keys on her person. If Slater and Nugent believed there was a cache of unset diamonds at the flat, they would have come by that information only from Lambie. Lambie believed valuable jewels were kept locked in the box, and she would have informed her partners.

In 1905, Miss Gilchrist's Last Will and Testament contained words that jewelry had been "specifically bequeathed," that is, it was not gifted during her lifetime, but identified as was the beneficiary. The solicitors and trustees had power to distribute but their power on administration of the Will was limited to the inventory of jewels assembled by David Dick.

After her death, disturbing rumors arose that Marion Gilchrist was herself a fence and "resetter." This notion came about from a reported discovery of a tray of diamonds "in a hidden corner of the flat." Private citizens as well as the police searched inside and outside the flat...a queue of would-be jewelry collectors. There were no police reports about unauthorized persons in the flat though talk about it was rife.

What Marion Gilchrist had been all her Victorian life was a collector of diamonds. Diamonds were a trend among wealthy and middle-class women—not machine-made but unique, hand-crafted jewelry. The inventory of her jewels revealed a number of diamond brooches. In her formal photographs, she always displayed one.

The hidden and later-discovered diamonds were not included in David Dick's Inventory List. Nor was a valuable diamond necklace which Miss Gilchrist's niece described. Detective-Inspector Pyper testified that a great deal of jewelry had been found by police between December 22 and January 4. It was after those dates that David Dick conducted his inventory of the jewelry. He did his work within the flat and testified that jewelry was found scattered in the spare bedroom. From this, one must assume that jewelry had been picked over and left unguarded. When police first entered the spare bedroom on the night of the murder, they found only paper and the splintered box on the floor.

With the murder's publicity, newspapers touting discoveries in South Africa mines, and the jeweled displays by gentlemen and their ladies, diamonds represented wealth so remarkable that common sense lost its aspect in solving this crime. Diamonds were the motive in the murder. For Oscar Slater, they conjured a fatal vision.

CHAPTER 33

A Murderer's Ensemble

The police internally circulated a tentative description of either one or two men, wearing either a fawn waterproof or a grey coat. Both may have been 5'7" or 5'8", clean shaven, and wore soft caps. There was a great deal of mummery in the Slater books about a Donegal ("something of that shape;" "split in two."), soft, flat, green, brown, and tweed caps.

When police arrived at Hugh Cameron's residence on December 26, he believed Slater had worn a soft cap with ear flaps. The dithering descriptions came about because people sized up a fellow's face but paid less attention to the type of cap he wore.

Whatever Slater's cap, it sat on top of a head of dark black hair. He wouldn't have worn a bowler on the night of the murder because that would have easily toppled off his head...not a hat in which one would engage in dangerous business.

Newsboy caps

Edwardian soft cap

Arthur Conan Doyle, cap and pipe

Downcast defendants wearing soft caps: hair, eyebrows, mustaches are all visible.

Fawn Waterproof Coat

Male models in waterproof coats, 1910

The waterproof, or "mack," a rubberized fabric, was developed in Glasgow in 1846, and quickly became ubiquitous in that damp...*oorlich* Scottish weather. It rose to the status of trench coat in the Great War and a fashion statement in hard-boiled detective thrillers. Its fabric made it easily identifiable from the wool of a great coat.

Helen Lambie and Arthur Adams described a fawn coat. Mary Barrowman saw that the man fleeing the Gilchrist flat wore a fawn waterproof. Though Slater owned two wool coats, if soaked, they would be difficult to dry in front of the coal stove or fireplace. He bought the waterproof as a necessity. When he was arrested and led off the Lusitania, he was wearing his wool great coat. The fawn waterproof, with 25 reddish/orange stains, was packed away in his luggage.

Waterproof coats came in grey or fawn cloth. "Fawn" was a pale tan, similar to a deer, with a soft, pinkish hue. They were made waterproof by using beeswax within the cloth. Once Slater returned to Glasgow the past October, and making money, he bought the coat from heisters--"off a truck"-- according to a gambling friend and witness.

It was not difficult to remove blood stains from a waterproof using water, vinegar, or kerosene. The forensics established at trial that the coat's stains had been diluted.

Slater's clothing was professionally laundered but his stained coat was not. Kerosene, a common household product for fuel and for lamps, would have been in his Glasgow residence. Kerosene was likely to remove 90% of a blood stain. But a tint would remain. That is why tints remained on Slater's coat.

Presumably, he began the stain-removing process December 21, the evening after the murder when he stood outdoors, coatless, for a smoke.

Two days after the murder, Slater hopped a tram. He wore the fawn waterproof with its diluted stains. This must astonish the modern fussbudget. Why not toss the coat in the waste or even in the stove? Slater saw the stains as diminished. They looked like ordinary wear and tear in the Scottish winter. The coat was new. His friends knew him to wear it. Was it better to be rid of it, or better to keep it and dilute the stains? It would show he wore such a coat and if any stains remained, they were the stains of ordinary street splashes.

His frugality was commendable; his parents would have been proud. He'd left Silesia as a poor young man. He lived by his wits and his women. He couldn't dispense with a coat that may have cost him several pounds.

By December 25, having been out in the rain and snow, and following up with more kerosene, treatment was finished as much as could be expected. Once a description of a "twisted nose" became known, he packed up the coat in his luggage. He couldn't risk Luise, Elsa, Katerina, Andrée, or the police finding a blood-stained, fawn waterproof coat.

Slater's Attachment to the Fawn Waterproof Coat

Clearly there was remnant blood on the murder items when Slater hurriedly packed his luggage. Skeptics scoffed: If he were guilty, he would have immediately disposed of a blood-spotted fawn coat and a bloody hammer.

Why didn't he? It's probable he thought a few days of dilution would fix the waterproof with its washable outer fabric and having to avoid suspicious friends asking about the whereabouts of his new coat. He scrubbed the hammer. He didn't consider how swiftly the police would be on to him—once that damning observation was made by Mary Barrowman.

♣ Why Didn't Oscar Burn or Bury the Coat?

As he removed the waterproof the night of December 21, breathless and overwrought from his escape, he saw its numerous blood stains. He didn't take the stained coat to his laundress.

Katerina, the maid, was always home. Mlle. Andrée may already have been out for the night. He was not yet aware that a fawn waterproof had been described to the police by Lambie, Arthur Adams, and Mary Barrowman.

Was there anything the laundress could have done for 25 recent blood stains on a waterproof coat? The use of kerosene, turpentine or petroleum was in wide use at launderers as a solvent for fabrics. The Slater residence held not only a hammer but kerosene as well. Kerosene lamps were ubiquitous in many homes. The blood stains were fresh and wet from the rain. A waterproof coat would be more adaptable to removing stains than would a cloth coat. Slater acted quickly, soaking the stains-- in cold water and/or kerosene.

Because Katerina or Andrée could be questioned by police about the coat the night of the murder, Slater told them nothing. Either they were unaware of his coat's stains, or they knew but would not incriminate him. Five months after the murder, at Slater's trial, both women were firm in support of his alibi: they were all having dinner.

ST. GEORGE'S CROSS

A 1905 photo of St. Georges Cross where Oscar rented his flat at 69 St. Georges Road. A rag picker stands at attention at the left, his cart empty. There are no bins. They are located in the closes. The streets, swept clean, are filled with pedestrians, workmen, and traffic.

✿ Possibilities for Disposal of the Coat

TOILET: Oscar couldn't very well send the coat down the toilet. Indoor toilets were shared with other tenants. A coat would cause a massive clog.

THE FIREPLACE: Slater could have burned the coat slowly in the small fireplace. That choice would involve smell, fumes and a long time to just char the coat. Katerina would have been a witness as would tenants in the building. The coat would have been burning all night and the coal bucket would have had to be replenished. The scorched coat would have been noticed if disposed in the collective ash bin outside the close.

GUTTER: The "wynds," long, narrow lanes in the closes at the rear of buildings, made conditions for a stealthy burning improbable. There were sewage drains and gutters but these were too narrow down which to stuff a coat. Slater/Dr. A. Anderson would draw the attention of neighbors or the odd urchin if seen anxiously wrestling a coat down into a gutter. Nor would the coat dissolve, clogging the gutter sitting at its mouth, and lead to discovery.

SANITARY AUTHORITIES: In 1900, the bubonic plague arrived via Glasgow's river fronts. Town officials took extreme measures to end it and prevent recurrence. Disinfection was ordered of every item a person owned or operated and in all means of transport. Rats were exterminated by an army of rat catchers. Sanitation controls became meticulous. Government-paid scavengers daily swept the streets and hauled away trash from ash bins to refuse dumps. Police regulations were enacted in order that residents disposed of waste at scheduled times. Prosecutions of errant filth disposal were serious charges and fines were imposed.

RUBBISH HEAPS: Refuse was twice daily collected to prevent the rise of odors or disease. Ragpickers and their carts were stationed in great lines along the city streets. Rubbish was sorted or dumped into large heaps at dump sites where it would be picked through by the poor for rags, boots, paper, etc. The dust yards also employed poor women to plod through the heaps for saleable items.

TO DIG OR NOT TO DIG: Oscar might have dug into an available garden or park space—the green space wasn't available in the center of town where he lived and if it did, it wasn't isolated. He also hadn't purchased a spade along with that hammer.

THE RIVERS—CLYDE AND KELVIN: The Clyde lay almost 15 miles from Slater's flat. The river Kelvin, in the direction of the Gilchrist flat, was about 10 miles from his home. The waterproof coat was rather light to toss off a pier or bridge and remain at bottom even if tied to a brick. The hammer would have fallen like a brick to the river bottom. Industrial and shipping debris in the river would have proved useful cover. Not so for mudlarks and scavenger hunters who were always on the lookout for the rivers' detritus, even in wintertime when the low river brought sewage and town discards packed within its snow.

Numbers of policemen searched along the River Kelvin's miles of muddy and snow-fringed trails for evidence tossed by Slater. The trees and bushes stood bare for six miles along the icy river. It being winter, it was easier to spot discards. There were none of Oscar Slater's.

Children along a low bank of the Kelvin, 1910

CHAPTER 34

From Plans to Panic

Oscar Slater prepared for a police investigation. Well in advance, he'd instructed Helen Lambie with a tactic intended to divert the police about a missing brooch.

When the evening's burglary did not go according to plan, chaos unfolded. A large crowd gathered outside the Gilchrist home. The outcry over the brutal death grew with rumor, witness sightings, police statements and newspaper reports. Slater would react with slowly rising panic as police relentlessly pursued an as yet unknown suspect.

December 21, 8:15 p.m.--- Grocery clerk, Duncan MacBrayne, saw Oscar Slater that rainy December night, standing outside his house, coatless, and having a smoke. Duncan recognized him because the two often passed one other as Duncan pushed his delivery cart along the street. Slater waited outside, smoking, as his coat's stains were being treated.

If Slater's numbed fingers shook while holding his cigarette, it wasn't from the cold. He needed to flee the consequences of what an investigation might uncover. He had some savings. He had a pawn ticket for a brooch with three rows of diamonds. So caught up in the believability of his career falsehoods, Slater had not prepared for the frenzy that was about to follow.

9:45 p.m.--- Among Slater's alibis was that the night of the murder, he was at the gaming clubs, a routine after dinner at home. Now, his desperation grew for he was cash-poor. His savings from a Postal

Savings account hadn't arrived. He left his flat for the Motor Club where he met up with Gordon Henderson. Henderson knew him as "Anderson" but knew his acquaintances knew him as "Slater". Oscar Slater asked Henderson for money, offering a check in exchange, but Henderson wouldn't do it. Henderson thought Slater appeared very anxious. He may have lost money gambling. That night, Henderson heard—from Slater's associates—that Slater tried to sell a pawn ticket for a diamond brooch. Henderson would tell police that talk began that very night, even among Slater's friends and fellow gamblers, that he was the murderer.

CHAPTER 35

Hunting a Killer

Oscar Slater emerged as the murder suspect from early witness statements—not by name, not from Helen Lambie's lying eyes nor Arthur's limpid details. At the outset, the suspect was unnamed. Then came the Gilchrist neighbors telling of having watched a male stranger taking daily strolls in mid-December.

Descriptions came incrementally: gentleman's garb, a peculiar walk, very black hair, clean-shaven, not too tall, and in his 30s. Then, the nose. No one called it a Jewish nose. It was said to be twisted, broken, or with a peculiar dip. On the morning of December 22, police suspected one assailant because only one man raced out of the flat in the presence of two eyewitnesses.

Detective-Inspector Pyper issued a report from which fevered news reporters published a description of the man's waterproof coat color: "fawn or grey." The dual colors were not confounding given the hysteria of the witnesses at the crime scene. Arthur Adams thought the coat was fawn *or* grey. His sister, Mrs. Rowena Adams Liddell (no relation to the pawnbroker), thought the man she saw outside the flat at 7 p.m., leaning over the iron railings that dark, rainy night had *a peculiar dip to his nose*. She said he wore a brown tweed. Her sighting was given short shrift. It was presumed Rowena was repeating what she'd heard said by the family and the police at the murder scene upstairs. Still, there was early discussion about the assailant's nose.

The word was out in the neighborhoods, in Glasgow, and in all of Scotland about the murder of a wealthy, elderly spinster. The *Scotsman News* and the *Glasgow Herald* reported an "Old Lady Battered to Death."

When she got home that evening, flushed from the incident with the strange man on the street, Mary told her mother. Mary's details were remarkably specific. She had looked into his face. He was a stranger to her but she wasn't timid. She also had a curious mind. No crowd had yet gathered when Mary Barrowman looked at Oscar Slater's face. There were just the two of them on that quiet street. Mary was given a start. She stood her ground and watched him. Slater looked at her, stunned from encountering another witness. She was lucky he didn't take it into his head to lend the girl a hammer blow.

Her description, particularly of his twisted nose, remained unchanging when recalling the incident to police, the New York extradition attorneys, and, finally in testimony for the Crown at Oscar Slater's trial.

Mary's mother alerted her neighbor, Detective John McGimpsey, what Mary had seen outside the Gilchrist flat the night before. She repeated for him her daughter's description: "You'll know him by his crooked nose."

Some authors conjectured that (like Rowena Liddell) she had heard accounts from the crowd standing outside the flat. Conjecture is defeated by the factual incident. Mary was propitiously at the scene--just as Slater ran down the steps of 15 Queens Terrace.

Mary Barrowman with her parents at the trial of Oscar Slater, May 1909

Police and Perpetrator Activity December 22

December 22--- In the morning, Lambie returned to the flat where she was questioned by two physicians and the police. She was led into the bedroom where the splintered box and its paper contents were still strewn about the floor. Lambie told them, in precise detail, that just two days ago, on Sunday, her day off, she happened to see in the spare bedroom a diamond crescent brooch, "about the size of half a crown," lying in a little ornamental dish. It had one row of diamonds. Lambie recalled the brooch was gold and the diamonds set in silver. She saw now that it was missing. It was taken, presumably, by the murderer. There were no bloody fingerprints.

A gold and diamond ring remained untouched in the dish. Detective-Inspector Pyper testified that a gold bracelet in a case and a gold watch and chain also lay on the table.

Lambie made her false claim even though the night before she had stepped into the blood of her murdered mistress. She put the police on a hunt for a crescent-shaped brooch with one set of diamonds. That brooch (Brooch #1) was stolen two months before, in October, and its diamonds sold separately. Though Lambie was traumatized in having viewed Marion Gilchrist's mutilated corpse the night before, she was still of a mind calculated to keep the police sidetracked. Who put an unschooled housemaid on to a professional swindler's shell game?

The recollection about the crescent-shaped brooch was made by a young woman who said she did not get a good look at the murderer's face as he crawled along the wall, face forward some 18 feet until he reached her, Arthur Adams, and the door. The incongruity should have alerted the police.

Police questioned Lambie about her boyfriends and came to learn about Patrick Nugent—a bookie with a police record. Lambie denied to police that Nugent was the man who'd come out of Miss Gilchrist's flat. She said she hadn't seen him since November. The inaction of the police and prosecution in ignoring Lambie's contrivances was the ruination of a provable case of a plot and murder involving three greedy serpents: Lambie, Nugent, and Slater.

The police continued to limit their search to one man. Lambie's information led police on the hunt for a Glasgow jewel thief. The locale of many a swindler and jewel thief was in the Sauchiehall district.

Only one man was seen at the flat and that was by an educated, reputable Scotsman, Arthur Adams. Dr. John Adams, when examining the body, told police that he had himself reported sighting, six or seven times and late at night, a strange man walking in the immediate vicinity of West Princes Street and Queens Terrace (where the doctor also lived). Dr. Adams described him to a constable as wearing a fawn waterproof, between 5'8 and 5'9, with dark hair.

While Lambie was misleading the police, that same morning Agnes Brown was reading the newspaper. The *Scotsman,* the *Glasgow Herald,* and the *Evening Chronicle* published some details about the murder. Neighbors and witnesses were reporting a man seen loitering West Princes Street for over a fortnight.

Agnes Brown believed that one of the men she saw running past—wearing the unbuttoned navy-blue Melton with a black velvet collar--might have been the suspect. That it was two men, not one, whom she saw streaming past, did not disengage her from her suspicions.

Before Christmas Day, Agnes Brown spoke with two detectives, Superintendent William Douglas and Glasgow Chief Constable James V. Stevenson, and to James Neil Hart, the Procurator-Fiscal. She added that the man's Melton coat was large enough and flapping open that it may have been worn over another coat. He had been holding something in his right hand which she did not see. The police were guardedly now on the trail of two male suspects.

That same day, December 22, Helen Lambie went back to see Agnes Guthrie. The intent of the young woman, still in shock, was presumably to give her version of the murder. It was Oscar Slater, Lambie knew but she did not say. What she did not know was whether he'd left with the diamonds.

The visit did not go well. Miss Guthrie was anxious to learn the horrific details. About Helen Lambie, she was no fool. Lambie was cunning when she had been in her employ and cunning when in service for Marion Gilchrist. It was a character trait Agnes Guthrie did not overlook.

Lambie told Miss Guthrie that she wasn't sure about the intruder's identity, yet she could imitate the way the man walked, almost as if she knew him. When he was in the hall, she recounted, he had slid along the wall from the bedroom, keeping his head down into his collar because

Lambie and Mr. Adams were standing at the door. "Well, if that were so," Miss Guthrie countered ominously to the girl, "Why would Miss Gilchrist have opened the door to such a perfect stranger? You yourself told me she would never do so." To this remark, Lambie flew into a huff and left without saying another word.

 Miss Guthrie concluded:

"The impression I had was that she knew all about it and knew the man." (from interviews quoted by William Park and Richard Whittington-Egan--neither of whom weighed in on this remarkable account.).

Oscar Slater the Day After the Murder

On December 22, Slater was faced with an exit from Glasgow with empty pockets for his intended January departure for New York. He had initially expected two weeks in December to collect money, pay for transport, redeem the brooch at Liddell's, and arrange his affairs in Glasgow. Instead, an escape was made urgent because of the murder and the police fast on the heels of a suspect. Fate had been cruel to Marion Gilchrist and extended its perversity to the murderer.

Slater began to marshal his resources: £30 draw on the brooch (Brooch #2) held at Liddell's Pawnshop; £39 18s.3d. from his Post Office savings; and a yield of about £50 on his stock for a total sum of £120. He could sail but the brooch would have to be redeemed at a future time.

12:01 p.m. ---Slater sent an urgent telegram to Messrs. Dent in London for the immediate return of his watch because he was leaving December 24 for Europe.

4 p.m.---Slater redeemed binoculars from Bryce Pawnshop which he hadn't picked up December 7 with his other items. The assistant, William Kempton, observed that Slater had a "slight, stubbly mustache. It was quite noticeable." He was wearing a dark overcoat and a "hard" hat, i.e., his bowler.

---Slater had a shave. He told his barber, Fred Nichols, he was headed for Australia or San Francisco on December 30. Perhaps Slater was considering these destinations or simply seeking Fred's suggestions. Or, he was leaving false clues in the event police came knocking for information at the barber's door. He told Fred that his wife wouldn't be joining him; she was too ill to travel. Slater sensed that trouble was at his doorstep and planned on leaving Andrée behind.

9:40 p.m.--- Detective-Inspector Pyper issued an updated alert from Helen Lambie's account of the missing brooch: a crescent-shaped, gold brooch with one row of diamonds "graduating towards the points" of the brooch. Such expertise! The diamonds were separately set in silver. Burglary was the motive. The murderer had stolen one piece of jewelry. It was not yet released to the newspapers.

---The *Evening Citizen* reported the overkill of Marion Gilchrist which had been leaked to the paper by an unnamed police office present at the murder scene:

"Her body was more fearful to look at than that of a man run down on the railway. One tenth of the battering would have been sufficient to kill the old woman."

There was also information published from the mouths of neighbors: "A lady from the neighborhood and her maid had watched a man loitering about in the same area and time for several days prior to the murder. They believed he'd worn a grey coat."

10 p.m.---Slater met up with Cameron, Rattman, Aumann, Johnson and Gibb at Johnston's billiard room. He borrowed £4 from Hugh Cameron. Had the men talked among themselves about the murder? Without a shadow of a doubt. During the billiard shoot, Slater muttered a crafty reference to having played billiards with the boys the night before—the murder night. Rattman and Aumann ignored the subliminal message. Neither could recall being with him that night. Slater had raised suspicions among the men.

Slater asked Cameron to try and sell the Liddell pawn ticket for him. He told Cameron--laying a shaky foundation for ownership—that the pawn ticket was for a diamond brooch that belonged to him and Mlle. Andrée. Slater explained that he'd pawned it in November to defray the costs of resettling in Glasgow. He said he no longer wanted the brooch having collected sizeable draws. He made no mention of relocating to New York in several days.

How deluded was Slater that, in the heat of the news, police and public attention about the murder and talk of a missing jeweled brooch, Cameron wouldn't entertain a suspicion about Slater's request to sell a pawn ticket for a brooch that was suddenly—so far as Cameron knew—in his possession? Slater didn't want a prospective buyer making a connection of the Liddell brooch to the murder and to him as the murderer. Cameron could step up as the putative owner/seller.

Slater's livelihood was built on prevarication—selling stolen gems, welching on bettor scores, schemes to rent premises, padding of official immigration documents, assuming aliases, fudging as to his intended travels. Gaming clubs denied him membership not because he was Jewish but because his reputation was that of an unscrupulous gambler, bookie, heister, and gem dealer. There was a vestige of Edwardian honor expected of gamblers even among the lower classes.

Slater gave no thought as to whether his lies were apparent. With Hugh Cameron, he took for granted that the man believed his froth about the brooch at Liddell's. His deceptive persona continued during his incarceration in future exchanges with the unswervingly loyal Rabbi Eleazar Phillips of the Garnethill Synagogue and with Arthur Conan Doyle.

The crescent-shaped brooch with one row of diamonds (Brooch #1), missing at the murder scene, had not yet been reported in the newspapers. By December 24, police would hear of yet another brooch (Brooch #2) pawned at Liddell's by Oscar Slater, gambler and diamond dealer with a broken nose.

Slater's desperation—whether he would be fingered as the murderer, or whether he could dispose of his pawn ticket for a good price-- had not yet hit a frantic state. That would come December 25.

Superintendent Ord, proceeding on a communique sent him by an overseas ship captain who'd read of the Glasgow murder, added to the suspect's description as being a "foreigner." According to the ship captain, the heinous murder in Glasgow was characteristic of the frequent brutalities now familiar in New York. New York's thieves were in the habit of beating in a victim's head so there would be no witness. Ruefully speaking, Slater read the crime sections of the New York papers during his several visits to that city or heard lurid accounts during his employment in the seedier districts.

December 23 Headlines and Descriptions

The newspapers were scoring readers with grisly headlines. Rewards were offered. Mary Barrowman and her mother were further interviewed at the police station that day. The papers added descriptions of the suspect that included "twisted nose," a clean-shaven look and well-dressed. Slater's facial imperfection was not going away. He was seen before, at, and immediately upon fleeing the crime scene. Oscar Slater was hardly "oblivious of the crime" (*Conan Doyle for the Defense*).

6 p.m.--- Tram Conductor William Sancroft would testify at trial that a dark-complexioned man, such as the man who sat in the dock, Oscar Slater, boarded his tram on this evening. The Crown produced the tram ticket found in Slater's luggage by the U.S. Marshals on January 2.

Slater sat in the upper level of the tram wearing the stained fawn waterproof coat. In a nearby seat, a boy was reading the news of the Gilchrist murder. The Conductor, interest piqued, asked the boy whether he thought the killer would be caught. During this short conversation which must have proved dispiriting, Slater got up and hurriedly climbed down the steps to get off.

The stop was sooner than the fare for which he'd paid and the Conductor tried to tell him so. All day long, the Conductor took notice of his passengers. This one held his attention. Slater fled. The Conductor watched him "running full speed across to Garscadden Street." Not earth-shattering testimony but revealing of Slater's rising panic.

Calm Before the Storm

December 24---Slater's photo had not yet figured in newspaper accounts. Headlines read "Still Unsolved." From internal police accounts, it was known that the man wore a fawn or grey overcoat, had a crooked nose, and was between 28 and 30 years old. The police were now convinced that it was not Marion Gilchrist's jewelry that the thief was after. This, they reasoned, was because jewelry was left in the ornamental dish in the spare bedroom and Lambie reported only one missing brooch. The police were baffled as to motive.

10 a.m.--- Police returned to the Barrowman home, and later, to Mary's workplace. Her recollections did not vary; that meant trouble for Slater. He was not yet named in the newspapers, but a preliminary description of a suspect in the *Evening Citizen* was ominous.

Slater ran into Max Rattman and effusively invited him for Christmas dinner at his home the next evening. He didn't tell his friend of plans to leave Glasgow the next day. The hasty decision to leave Glasgow hadn't been made--not even by the morning of December 25.

5 p.m.--- Hugh Cameron, walking with his wife, encountered Slater on the street. Hugh told his wife he'd be home for tea in an hour and accompanied Slater on errands. His mustache was now "very stubbly." Cameron testified that Slater had shaved it in mid-December. Cameron was among the witnesses who testified that Slater was "clean-shaven" in December. Those were the days when he was loitering the Gilchrist neighborhood and on the night of the murder.

Cameron returned Oscar's pawn ticket to him saying he had approached two prospects but both declined. Slater told Cameron that he planned to leave Glasgow. He did not say when that would be. With the murder news consuming conversations, Oscar couldn't give the appearance of guilt such as fleeing the scene. It had to be a cautious departure.

The two walked to Thomas Cooke's travel office where Slater arranged ship tickets for the Lusitania bound for New York on December 26, two days later. Slater had chosen the Atlantic ship journey no matter the wintry swelling of the waves and gale-force winds. In New York, Anderson the American could begin anew, albeit cash-strapped. When questioned by police early the next morning, December 25, Cameron falsely claimed he did not know if Slater expected to skip town.

Thomas Cooke Travel Office in Glasgow

Did Cameron believe Slater was the murderer and planned to leave Glasgow because he had scored a successful haul from the victim's flat? Was there something in it for him?

Second-class passage was £12. Cooke's Liverpool office, closed by that hour, required Slater to return the next day, December 25, to complete the transaction. He left his name and address as Oscar Slater, c/o Anderson, St. George's Road, Glasgow. Hugh Cameron heard the following details: Thomas Cooke's, Lusitania, Liverpool, New York. He also knew Slater's alias.

Slater and Cameron veered towards a few more stops. Slater sent a £5 note ($24) to his parents as a Christmas present. There was no evidence of how much or whether Slater sent money to his parents in the past.

The men stopped for tea. What was Cameron thinking, having told his wife he'd be back home for tea? He apparently was mining Slater for information.

At this point, Cameron was not yet a police informant. The police charged into Cameron's home before dawn the next morning, December 25. They wouldn't have done so had Cameron been working with them. Sauchiehall's gaudily attired Moudie was both a greedy accessory after-the-fact as well as a police informant.

Their last stop was to a butcher where Slater bought meat for his household, a conspicuous errand with borrowed money. His purchase affirmed his alibi of always eating dinner at home with the ladies (as he allegedly had the night of the murder, December 21).

Before going home with the meat, Slater stopped at Central Station. He had been giving much thought to the police pursuit and the need to move more quickly than he'd planned. He telegrammed his friend in London, David Freedman, urging that "his girl" (Luise), i.e. a "working girl" and supposed stepsister of Mlle. Andrée's, *come quick* to Glasgow and take over his flat at 69 St. Georges Road. She and another step-sister, Elsa Huppe, were duly sent by Freedman and arrived from London the following afternoon, December 25.

CHAPTER 36

Lightning Strikes December 25

St. John's United Free Church

Marion Gilchrist's funeral was held at St. John's United Free Church. A large crowd attended to bid farewell to the blameless victim. The minister said she had lived her life fully as a good Christian. Her impressive granite tombstone today stands mute at Glasgow's Necropolis cemetery. When tourists visit, these many years after her death, they can be assured her murderer was not wrongfully convicted.

December 25--- Oscar Slater's delusion about not being outed as the murderer was the product of a steely sense of self. That is why he resorted routinely to a getaway when problems arose. This time, in Glasgow, he found himself pinned to a crypt.

Slater visited his barber for a shave that morning. He needed to close his eyes in a comfortable chair and plan his leave-taking. The barber told police he noticed that Slater's mustache was reappearing in its usual stage of thick growth.

12:30 p.m.---Mrs. Luise Freedman and Miss Elsa Huppe arrived from London to take over the flat for a few weeks. In the Record, Luise was designated with an aura of legitimacy as Mrs. Luise Freedman, wife of David Freedman. She was in fact Luise Klebow, a 20-year-old German-Russian émigré who understood little English. Freedman sent her to Slater's flat, a favor of one pimp to another. Luise and Elsa could work Glasgow streets during their habitation. The young women arrived even sooner than expected in response to Slater's telegram that they *come at once if convenient, and if inconvenient, come all the same* (paraphrasing Sherlock Holmes, "The Adventure of the Creeping Man.").

2 p.m.---Newspaper accounts of the murder were unrelenting. This particular afternoon, another feature of the suspect appeared--Mary Barrowman's description of the twisted nose, clean-shaven, and well-dressed man. From the twisted nose detail, Slater's telltale heart pumped a beat audible to his ear.

At the flat, he frantically began packing his bags, ready to flee and without the inconsolable Andrée. This was no ordered plan of leaving permanently for America. Musing on the tension in his flat that afternoon, with Andrée sobbing and pleading, Katerina stricken, and the young women sent by Freedman wondering what fresh hell they had entered, one can honestly conclude that Slater was desperate to escape. He was desperate because he was the murderer of Marian Gilchrist and soon to be exposed as such.

These were four streetwise, foreign women. The papers—English, German, Yiddish-- were filled with headlines about the murder of a wealthy elder lady in Glasgow. She had lived in walking distance of Slater's residence. Some of the published descriptions fit the features of the career hustler and diamond dealer.

Remorseless but panicked, Slater ordered Luise to take Andrée back to "her people in Belgium," *and, by the way, let me £25.* He wasn't her hustler. That was Freedman. She refused him the money unless he agreed to take Andrée. Oddly, he didn't mention the pawned brooch at Liddell's. He kept the pawn ticket in his coat pocket. If the brooch were actually his, or Andrée's, he could have arranged an exchange. He could have redeemed it with a larger extortion from Luise. Slater had shared details of the brooch with Hugh Cameron, even after the murder but he was not so forthcoming with the ladies. They could not be easily deceived by the aggressive Slater, now furiously packing his bags to skip town at the last minute and badgering Luise for money.

Nor did he leave behind the stained waterproof coat or the hammer. Should Luise need to break apart a few coals for the fire or nail a hook, she'd have to buy her own.

Was Slater so callous that he would continue to wear a coat which he'd worn when murdering Marion Gilchrist? Yes. Accept his indifference; it equated with his brutal hammering of an old woman. He treated the stains himself rather than going to his laundry where his bill remained to be paid. On December 25, Slater wasn't thinking when he packed. He took what was his, and let the devil take tomorrow.

Some of Slater's obdurate defenders concluded that it was Patrick Nugent who murdered Miss Gilchrist. That would have meant that during Slater's hurried packing, Nugent heard about it—though none of Slater's landsmen knew. Then, Nugent arrived, unseen by the ladies or neighbors at the Slater/Anderson residence, bringing with him a stained fawn waterproof and a hammer so that Slater would pack it in his luggage. The problem? Slater admitted to the New York police that the fawn waterproof and the hammer were his. And, in the chaos at the flat, how was Nugent able to get Slater's consent and then leave without being noticed? Truly an impossibility. Glasgow bettors wouldn't play the Nugent odds.

Christmas Day's Flickers of Light

December 25, 6:10 p.m.--- The denunciation by Allan McLean. McLean, a Scotsman, bicycle dealer and gambler, arrived at the Central Police Station to identify a man, a "German Jew," he said, whom he knew only as "Mr. Oscar." He believed the man was the Gilchrist murderer. McLean was a member of the Sloper Club where Slater was recently admitted upon Hugh Cameron's reference.

Glasgow's Central Police Station

Four days after the murder, the police still had no clue of the suspect's identity but here it was-- delivered on Christmas Day. At the time McLean appeared at the station, Slater was ready for his getaway from Glasgow to Liverpool where he would board the Lusitania bound for America.

McLean's statement exposed a nativist antipathy toward Jewish immigrants. We see it critically in a modern ethos. But McLean did not identify Slater to police simply because he was Jewish. He confirmed the description of his twisted nose about which McLean read in the newspapers. He added that Mr. Oscar needed to borrow money from him and from Gordon Henderson at the Motor Club late the night of December 21. That same December 21st night, Slater also tried to sell a pawn ticket for a brooch. What did McLean know of brooches? Nothing, except that an old lady with a jewelry collection had been murdered. An old lady! Mr. Oscar was a jewelry dealer, a fence, and a gambler. The murder was within a few streets of Mr. Oscar's flat.

McLean didn't come forth to report him to police until he'd read the Christmas afternoon news description of a suspect with a twisted nose who wore a fawn or grey coat. Mr. Oscar wore a fawn waterproof. According to McLean, it was no secret among the gambling crowd that in late November or December, Oscar bought that coat from a thief who had heisted outerwear from a Glasgow haberdashery, McPherson & Johnston. So it came to pass that Oscar scouted the Gilchrist neighborhood wearing a new fawn waterproof in mid-December.

McLean led police to Mr. Oscar's residence at 69 St. George's Road. A plaque hanging outside read "A. Anderson, Dentist" with no indication of an Oscar residing at the premises. They left.

7 p.m.--- Detective Inspector William Powell returned to the flat at 69 St. George's Road and questioned tenant, Mabel Bernstein and her maid, Ruby Russell. They lived below the Anderson dental flat. They knew him from the sign hanging outdoors as dentist A. Anderson. Ruby told the detective that Dr. Anderson left the flat an hour before. There was no connection made to a "Mr. Oscar" and Detective Inspector Powell returned to the police station. Anderson the dentist was not a suspect. His leaving the flat could have meant he was making a call on a patient or going out for dinner.

December 25, Midnight---Detective Inspector Powell and two constables returned to the Anderson flat where they were met by Katerina Schmaltz, the maid who spoke very little English. They searched the place and among the discarded items found a torn piece of envelope stamped "registered and fragile." It was addressed to Oscar Slater, Esq., c/o A. Anderson, Esq. The police stumbled on his alias. They would soon learn that the envelope had contained Oscar Slater's repaired watch sent expedited from London by Messrs. Dent.

Katerina, the sharpie, misled the police. She told them the torn envelope belonged to "Madame" (Andrée) who was out with a gentleman. Katerina knew however that Slater and Andrée were already en route to Liverpool and beyond.

Residents below, awakened by the rattle, told police, as they stomped down the wooden stairs that the dentist and his wife left... with their luggage... about 8 p.m. The police had missed them. Oscar Slater had fled.

Detective-Inspector Powell immediately directed his two constables to the Sloper Club mentioned by McLean and there seek information about Oscar Slater, the alias found on the envelope. He was possibly the same "Mr. Oscar" reported by McLean. The constables learned about Slater's companions, including Hugh Cameron, the Moudie who referred Oscar for membership in the Motor Club.

At the Motor Club, which was next door to the Sloper Club, police questioned Gordon Henderson, the manager who lived on the premises. Besides Slater having asked him for a loan December 21 at 9:45 p.m., Henderson added to the growing evidence. He told police that a *"German"* (i.e. a Jewish acquaintance of Slater's), Max Brooks, told him that Oscar Slater murdered the old woman. Slater's landsman, Max, sought no reward. He made that conclusion from talking with Slater and from the remarks swirling among the gambling crowd.

CHAPTER 37

The Heat is On, December 26

At 2 a.m. --- Police moved quickly to Hugh Cameron's house, rousing him from his bed. They questioned him about his friend, Oscar Slater, and the brooch—a brooch reported by McLean earlier that evening and the brooch Helen Lambie reported as missing from the Gilchrist flat. Cameron told them about his December 24th errand run with Oscar, including details about the Thomas Cooke Travel Office, Liverpool, the Lusitania, New York, and Slater having surprisingly asked him to sell a pawn ticket for a brooch held at Liddell's Pawnbrokers.

The orderly sequence of guilty circumstances was remarkable:

Oscar Slater + diamond dealer + alias + missing brooch + twisted nose + dark-haired + fawn waterproof coat + witnesses + pawn ticket + on the lam.

This was no suggestive profile nor fishing expedition by the police but solid probable cause.

4:30 a.m.---Inspector Powell and two officers arrived at the home of Liddell's clerk, Peter McLaren. The trio rousted him, demanding he take them to the pawnshop and show the brooch which was possibly stolen in the Gilchrist murder. McLaren did so but refused to turn over the brooch. No warrant.

With Slater in transit, the police were pressed for time. They focused on three witnesses who could identify the pawned brooch at Liddell's and confirm their suspicion that Oscar Slater was the killer:

1. Police took Helen Lambie to Liddell's. She was shown the pawned brooch with three rows of diamonds. As she told police on December 22, the one stolen the night of the murder had only one row of diamonds.

2. Later that morning, Liddell's clerk, Peter McLaren, took the brooch to Sorley's Jewelry Shop, Miss Gilchrist's jeweler of many years. He was accompanied by Detective-Inspector Allan Campbell and Constable Gordon.

3. William Sorley examined the brooch held by McLaren. He said it wasn't Miss Gilchrist's.

None of these witnesses were qualified to render an opinion about whether or not the pawned brooch belonged to Marian Gilchrist: Helen Lambie, a dim maid with no knowledge nor expertise in diamonds; Peter McLaren, whose only connection had been with Oscar Slater in the pawn of the brooch and the advance draws; or William Sorley, who could not reliably state that he had examined all of Miss Gilchrist's jewelry, nor produce a record of the entirety of her collection.

The police weren't quite finished with the three ladies at 69 St. George's Road, Katerina, Luise, and Elsa. That morning they returned to the flat to question them further. Katerina said she knew Oscar Slater only as "A. Anderson," the dentist whose sign hung outside, but this time added that both he and the Madame left the night before for Piccadilly in London. With the London destination, the police focused on the Liverpool train bound for that city, or, as Cameron had reported, the Liverpool train towards the dock for the Lusitania. Luise and Elsa also lied, saying they knew the man as "Anderson." Their misstatements were not attacked at trial. Luise's hustler, David Freedman, received two urgent telegrams from Slater, days before, requesting that "his girl" be sent to take over his flat. He was known to the women as Oscar Slater.

Whether they were protecting themselves from being connected with the horrible crime, or whether they were protecting a suspected killer, was never developed. Both Katerina and Luise lied to police when they said Slater and the Mademoiselle were traveling to Nice and Monte Carlo for several weeks.

Luise helped Andrée pack. Hearing from police that Oscar Slater was a suspect in the Gilchrist murder, Luise told them that Andrée had a great deal of jewelry but it was not Marion Gilchrist's. She said nothing about a brooch because she knew nothing about a diamond brooch.

As Katerina was leaving 69 St. George's Road, headed back to London, Hugh Cameron, whom she knew through Oscar Slater (known to her, she'd claimed to police, as "Anderson"), stopped by unexpectedly. He had come to see about Slater, or to learn Slater's whereabouts having been awakened by police early that morning. Cameron told her Oscar Slater was a suspect in the Gilchrist murder. To his surprise, Katerina said that he and Madame had left for Monte Carlo.

CHAPTER 38

FLIGHT

"One foot in sea and one on shore"

Oscar's travel preparations were orderly through the day of the murder, December 21. All his savings and investment account monies were requested. He arranged that Luise Freedman travel from London to sublease his flat. He gave Katerina her notice.

After the murder, Oscar's measured calm evaporated. He was short of money, desperate to sell the Liddell pawn ticket, and, once he read the December 25 afternoon paper, he was in the spotlight: a description of the murder suspect—a man with a broken or twisted nose who stole a diamond brooch. A murder charge was a hanging charge. He had a few hours within which to disappear from Glasgow. The telltale coat and hammer were packed. No items that could connect him to the murder were going to be left behind for the papers to publish and the police to pursue. He fled Glasgow as it became increasingly obvious that the police and newspapers were identifying a suspect by physical characteristics and trade—Him!

December 25, 8-8:30 p.m.--- While police were trying to make sense of "A. Anderson," Slater concentrated on a speedy exit. Hurrying to the nearby Central Railroad Station, he paid porters to pick up nine trunks and several suitcases. Once the porters left in their lorry, Slater and Andrée met outside in the street and spoke for some time. They were watched by Ruby Russell, maid to Mabel Bernstein. Away from Luise, Elsa and Katerina, Slater prepped Andrée about her name, their destination, and other deceptive specifics. They walked, separately, to Central Station, minutes away, headed for the train to Liverpool.

9:05 p.m.---The couple boarded the train bound for Liverpool. Slater spent nearly four hours during which his tension would have kept him wide awake. Slater and Andrée spent the night at Liverpool's North Western Hotel where he illegibly signed (the fifth line of the ledger) his true name, Oscar Slater, since his luggage was engraved with the initials "O.S."

North Western Hotel ledger

Oscar's signature is #5 on the North Western Hotel register

December 26--- At Liverpool's North Western hotel, Slater remained awake. The Lusitania was setting sail that day. He wrote his friend, Max Rattman, a postcard—in a mix of Yiddish and English. He told Max he'd left Glasgow for good, and "Forgot to say goodbye." He wrote that "Freedman's girl" had taken his flat and that his French girl would be returning to Paris.

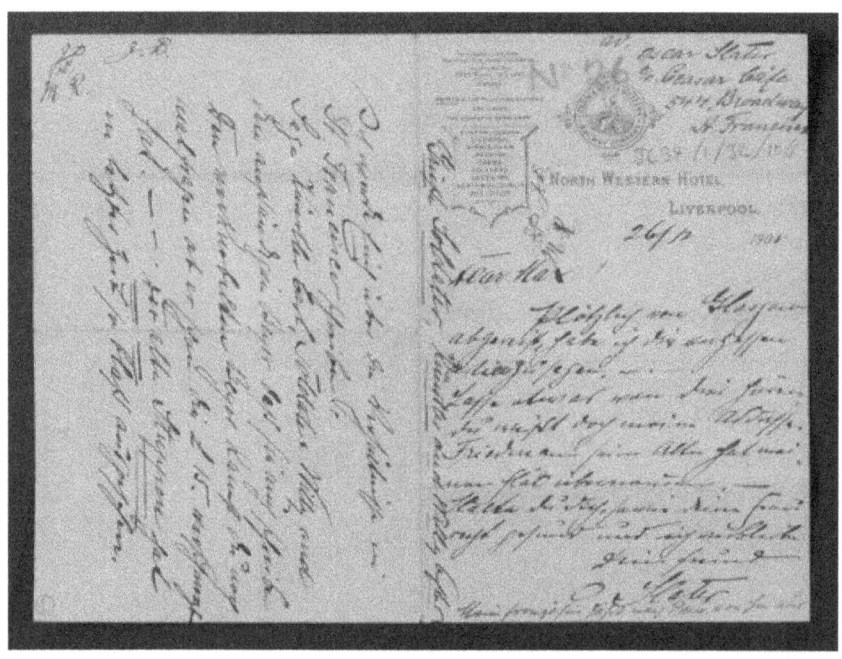

Oscar Slater Dec. 26, 1908 correspondence to Max Rattman from the North Western Hotel in Liverpool

What was irregular about the postcard was that, at the last minute, from a Liverpool hotel, Slater was letting Max know that Slater and his French girl had already left Glasgow with no plans to return. No fare-thee-well party, no parting with possessions, and no proper exchange of business and personal contacts. The postcard was sent December 26, 1908, six days after the murder. Slater was giving the impression of calm, to dispel any notion that his overnight disappearance was connected to the murder or that he was escaping the police hunt for a dark-complexioned suspect with a twisted nose. Slater's implication was that all arrangements had been orderly--like the sublease of his flat.

Slater described for Max a supposed San Francisco business, presumably in the event of police inquiries. Thus, Slater realized the police had him in their sights about the murder and from which consequences he had fled. He was aware; all the indicia of flight and consciousness of guilt were apparent.

The return address he gave Max was "Oscar Slater c/o Caesar's Café, 544 Broadway in S. Francisco." Slater wrote about his friendly walkabout with Cameron on December 24 to Thomas Cooke's for ship tickets and during which errand, Slater exchanged £15 notes for £5 English.

Slater and Andrée left the North Western hotel in the pre-dawn hours. He purchased second-class tickets at the Cunard Line office in the names Otto Sando and Anna Sando for the Lusitania leaving that day. He used the German strongman's surname (Eugen Sandow) as an alias because of the "O.S." engraved on his luggage. He was leaving the "Oscar Slater" name behind.

Oscar used an alias on the ship tickets *because* he was escaping. His luggage contained evidence of a crime. He included an American address of 30 Staate (*sic*) Street in Chicago. Not only did he misspell his purported address but it was another intentional deflection.

Cunard Line Ticket Application

> F (5) APPLICATION FORM to Cunard Co., for Contract Tickets.
> CUNARD LINE.
>
> (1) Steamer, 'Lusitania,' sailing from Liverpool on the 26.12.08; (2) Name in full, Otto Sando and Anna Sando; G (3) Age 38 years; (4) Sex, ; (5) Married or single, Married; (6) Calling or Occupation, Dentist; (7) Able to read and write, Yes; (8) Nationality (country owning political allegiance or of which citizen or subject), Germany, U.S. citizen, American address, Chicago, 30 Staate Street.

State Street was a hub of department stores and not residential. 30 State Street was a block south of the Marshall Fields. In 1909, Jeweler's Row, of which Slater may have had passing recognition, lay a block east, on Wabash Avenue.

Cunard liner; baggage hold below deck

Flight as an Indicia of Guilt

In law, the flight doctrine applies to a person's behavior after the commission of a crime. An inference of an individual's consciousness of guilt may be logically drawn if he or she skips town.

Here are factors that build an inference of guilt:

> Fleeing from the crime scene or jurisdiction
> False Alibi
> Hiding Evidence
> Changing or altering physical appearance

The value of such elements increases where the interval between the murder (December 21) and Slater's flight and assumed name (December 25) was short. "Do the math."

Previous authors equated Slater's December 25-December 26 departure as part of his ordinary course of travel. He'd dropped hints, during his short respite in Glasgow from October to December 25, that he planned to relocate...to Queensland, Australia, to Monte Carlo, to Nice, to San Francisco, to London, to Chicago, and to New York. He did so because of the substantial haul he anticipated from his residential burglary. The proceeds would smooth his relocation and even solve the American citizenship problem. In his conversations, he was leaving the impression of prosperity and an ability to travel at leisure.

Slater moved to Glasgow temporarily from London that October. If not the Gilchrist burglary, why and what for? On November 29, he wrote to his business acquaintance, David Jacobs, that he was leaving Glasgow the "end of January" and that he had "only two months' time here" (in Glasgow).

Slater planned the date of the heist for December 21, and a departure date, with a day or so of diamond selling. The orderly departure for the end of January 1909 did not go as planned. The newspaper headlines of the description of a man closely resembling Oscar Slater circumvented the orderliness. He blew out of Glasgow on December 25.

Slater knew he'd been observed by two witnesses at the scene of the crime, still another as he fled down the steps of 15 Queens Terrace on the night of the murder, and then two more witnesses as he ran towards the Kelvinbridge train station. Police, witnesses, fellow gamblers, and newspapers circled like vultures overhead, ready to prune Slater's wings.

All these evasive actions were taken by Oscar Slater. His was not a planned relocation but a flight...in legal parlance, a flight to escape justice. He saw his description in the news as the suspect and chose to escape across the ocean. He left with such speed that he made no arrangements for the resale of his furniture for which he'd paid £178, yet he was extremely short of cash.

December 28---Unaware that Slater was gone from Glasgow, David Jacobs had written to him (two days into Slater's overseas journey) that he required cash before sending him emeralds to sell. Slater had written November 29 about having made a score with sales of emeralds. Jacobs must surely have read the papers about the murder and, by this date, the suspect's name. A fellow fence and heister, Jacobs figured the jewelry theft left Slater with disposable cash.

The police returned to question Luise and Elsa at the flat. In broken English, the two persisted in having known Slater only as "Anderson." They knew him and his livelihood from his partner, David Freedman. Both were diamond dealers. Neither of the women knew where Slater and Andrée may have traveled. Five days later, Detective-Lieutenant John Trench would strike out on his own to interview the women.

CHAPTER 39

Detective-Lieutenant John T. Trench

Detective-Lieutenant John Thomson Trench appeared in this dreadful saga in the guise of saint abiding mournfully beside the near-martyred Oscar Slater. Along with author William Roughead, Trench was an enabler of the Oscar Slater Innocence Campaign.

Trench inserted himself into the Slater case at its earliest stages. He had not been assigned to the case. Though he was answerable to his superiors, Trench's interviews with witnesses were unauthorized and witness statements were fabricated or altered. He was not "the lead detective" in the case as many authors erroneously assumed.

December 31--- Trench traveled to Carfin, about 16 miles outside central Glasgow, where Patrick Nugent lived. He was not on official assignment. He professed to having been accompanied by Detective Andrew Keith—the latter having no recollection of the Nugent interview.

It was New Year's Eve, the Scottish celebration of "Hogmanay," and exactly a year since Nugent and Lambie attended the party where they weighed the profits in pinching Marian Gilchrist's jewels. Trench visited Nugent's home on a day which may have stirred his memories and his conscience.

Trench questioned him about his friendship with Miss Gilchrist's housemaid. Nugent said he was friendly with Helen Lambie for only a few months, beginning in January 1908. He ended it in September because of her religion. Shortly thereafter, on November 25, Nugent, a widower with three children by his late wife and two other women, married a Roman Catholic girl. He was living in a rented house with two of his children, his new wife, and his four brothers. In the 1909 trial list of witnesses, his occupation was that of "commercial agent." Had he appeared to testify on behalf of the prosecution, his reputation would have been scrubbed for the jury.

Trench did not journey to visit Nugent in private merely to come away with a family biography. He had his suspicions and police know-how that Nugent was somehow connected to the crime.

Nugent had visited the Gilchrist flat, dined there, met Barney the terrier, surveyed the premises, and sorted through jewelry in the spare bedroom. Lambie showed him the locked box and the jewelry. Did Trench believe that neither of them had stolen even one gem? What was it Nugent offered in exchange for Trench exonerating him (which Trench did with the assistance of William Roughead)?

Trench may have inquired whether Nugent was acquainted with Oscar Slater. Sauchiehall was a small world. But it wasn't Slater upon whom Trench was fixated. It was enough that Glasgow police were on to him and knew where he was headed aboard the Lusitania. Trench believed there was something in the Gilchrist flat that Slater was after. That was Trench's interest. What was it in the flat that tempted the trio? Slater had been able to enter the flat with such ease. *How was that possible*, Trench would have chimed into Nugent's burning ears?

Nugent had little reason to be apprehensive. Lambie wasn't about to confess and, with Slater's escape to New York, both he and Lambie were safe. Nugent would have repeated Lambie's story that Miss Gilchrist had become paranoid in her old age, hiding jewelry in odd places. Slater was a shifty bookie and gambler. Nugent became acquainted with him at the racetrack or at a gambling parlor.

Trench reported his visit to Carfin to his superior, omitting the jewelry inquiries.

January 2, 1909---Slater having been arrested in New York, Trench resumed his independent investigations. He went to Slater's flat where he questioned Luise, haplessly caught up in a serious criminal investigation. She said again that Andrée packed jewelry but that it belonged to her and not the murder victim. Neither she nor Trench discussed the brooch at Liddell's.

After interviewing Luise, Trench went to inspect the grounds outside the Gilchrist flat. At Slater's trial the coming May, Trench was asked as follows:

> **DEFENSE: Have you heard that old Miss Gilchrist was a resetter? And that she had got uncut diamonds in her house which she had got from thieves?**
> **TRENCH: I have heard that frequently.**

Setting aside that there was no objection to the Defense's cheapening of Miss Gilchrist's fate, there was both a rhetorical inference in the remark that she was an 82-year-old fence and consorted with fellow thieves, but also that there was truth to the report of uncut diamonds found in her house. Yes, Trench had heard these rumors. He did not refer to the uncut diamonds and the Defense didn't press him (*never ask a question to which you don't already know the answer*). Trench denied hearing about people digging under the floors of the flat and finding diamonds. Yet, months before the trial, on January 2, after visiting, without authorization, Luise and Elsa, the opportunistic Trench returned to Marian Gilchrist's building where he made a thorough inspection of the outside perimeter--the stairs, the window sills, and a recess outside the flat. What was he looking for? In the course of his speedy exit, had Slater dropped a diamond? Just one uncut diamond was worth £1000. Trench's outdoor search had come up empty.

January 3---In New York, Slater was under arrest and detained. In Glasgow, Trench visited Helen Lambie at the home of her aunt with whom she now resided.

Police had reported that a tray of diamonds was found in the Gilchrist flat. The diamonds were worth £5000 (the existence of this tray and the uncut diamonds were never reconciled). Trench had access to the police files. Superintendent Ord and Detective-Inspector Pyper confirmed the accounts of police searching the premises after the murder and finding jewelry. The accounts must have proved galling to any policeman who hadn't been at the discovery.

Someone then leaked the information about the tray of diamonds to *Reynolds News*. The leak's publication did not rouse the prosecutor to include the tray of diamonds as a viable motive for the burglary.

CHAPTER 40

The Sinking of Oscar Slater on Board the Lusitania

January 2, 1909---Oscar Slater stood on the ship's deck beneath a cold January sky as seagulls shrieked from above. Breathing in the invigorating salt air, he was confident he'd made his escape. Ahead was proof--the Statue of Liberty. Liberty was what absorbed him after the frightening escape by train, the sleepless exhaustion at the North Western Hotel, the nerve-wracking Cunard ticket application, and the loading of his luggage, followed finally by a comforting sleep, night after night, as he and Andrée sailed seven days across the Atlantic.

Still, the biting wind left him shuddering. How could it not? Slater was hardly free of the aggressive chase by police dogging him after "the affair" (as he referred to the murder of Marian Gilchrist).

> *For the sky and the sea, and the sea and the sky*
> *Lay dead like a load on my weary eye,*
> *And the dead were at my feet.*
>
> **RIME OF THE ANCIENT MARINER,** Coleridge

Just two nights before, the ship was alight with New Year's Eve baubles, champagne flutes, ballroom dress, dancing, and, at midnight, a joyful chorus of *Auld Lang Syne*. His and Andrée's eyes were misty with merriment. They were just a day before landfall. The Sando/Slaters would begin life anew. He still had the pawn ticket. Liddell's was not about to forfeit his claim to the brooch.

Oscar Slater's anticipation of a new life upon New York's golden pavements was not to be. Telegrams from Glasgow alerted U.S. officials to an escaping murder suspect on the Lusitania. Slater's aerie thoughts of freedom collapsed as New York Port Authority police and U.S. Marshals confronted him on board ship at the Sandy Hook port.

At first, Slater believed they were with Immigration...an inconsequential matter. He met them with a mixture of wily laughter meant to conceal a sudden anxiety. "The affair" had turned serious. The officials were there to arrest him on an extradition warrant for the murder of Marion Gilchrist in Glasgow.

Slater, ever the charlatan and accustomed to encounters with police, replied to the New York officers with mock curiosity. "Who is Miss Gilchrist?" What a frivolous riposte about the murder and hardly the reply of an innocent man. Slater vaguely recalled reading about the highly publicized murder. The discussion among Cameron, Rattman, and Aumann while they were shooting billiards the week before escaped him.

Slater called across the room to Mademoiselle Andrée: "Hilary (one of Andrée's sobriquets), do you know of this Gilchrist?" It bears repeating: *"This Gilchrist."* He was alerting the girl. His December 21 dinner alibi was going to lie again for him. Andrée, traveling as Mrs. Anna Sando, wearing a chic hat and ready for New York temperatures in a long, fur-trimmed coat, predictably answered *"Non."* How craven a young woman.

A gentleman, and one who professed innocence, would have reacted to the American officials with horror about the murder of an elderly woman in his community. Or even asked for details out of morbid curiosity. Slater believed he was safe having landed in faraway New York and with his dubious claim of being an American citizen.

In the interview with the U.S. Marshals, confronted with a grievous crime in which he was the suspect, the Oscar Slater of numerous aliases came across as a fabulist. Imagine a poetic exchange, courtesy of Shakespeare and Sherlock Holmes.

NY Police: "The game is up, Oscar Slater."
Oscar Slater: "The game has just started. The game is afoot"

"Henry V, part 1," "The Adventure of Abbey Grange"

Slater's pawn ticket was in his pocket when he was searched. The Marshals asked "Oscar Sando" why he used the name "Anderson" on the pawn ticket. "Because it was a Scottish name and easier for business." Understandably in this age, Jews resorted to aliases to avoid the prejudices attached to them.

Slater explained to the Marshals that, notwithstanding the "Sando" and the "Anderson" aliases, he had a true name and it was Oscar Slater (omitting "Leschziner/Leschzinger"). He and his wife, Andrée, married since 1901, arrived from Glasgow where they'd lived for only three months. He said he had a dental practice in New York. Here, he used the name "Anderson" because he was a witness in a murder case and for security reasons, he'd changed his surname.

For the five years he claimed to be living in New York as "Anderson," he had no criminal charges. Slater said he was a U.S. Citizen and had applied for a declaration of citizenship as "Anderson." Without the alias, his record in Great Britain and Germany would have barred him from legal residency. Of course, Slater was in Scotland and London many of the years he said he was in New York, and in those cities, and in others, as Oscar Slater, he did indeed accumulate criminal charges.

Slater denied knowledge of the victim and the murder but then admitted that he may have read or heard of the crime. To the officers, Slater was a man fabricating every detail of his life. Conan Doyle would one day also sense this inescapable trait.

When she was questioned by the Marshals, Andrée remained loyal to her "Oskarcheen." Disbelieving, she said Oscar, her husband of seven years, came home routinely at 7 each night, including the night of the murder. She knew nothing of the murder of Marion Gilchrist nor of the murderer.

His florid explanations of no consequence, Slater was hustled off the ship, parted evermore from Mademoiselle Andrée Hilaire Juno Antoine. The winter sun was setting at Sandy Hook Port as the handcuffed Oscar Slater was led down the gangplank. A horde of photographers awaited the seaside perp walk. They saw a gentleman dressed nattily in a grey wool coat, bowler hat, and gloves.

He kept his face downward, trying to shield it from photographers. His nose and dark eyes were clearly visible—just as they were when Mary Barrowman saw him beneath the street lamps at 15 Queens Terrace on December 21.

A blast of cold air wafted up from the wood pilings. They jutted up from the icy water like gnarled and angry teeth...foreboding symbols of what lay ahead for Oscar Slater.

Evidence in Oscar's Luggage

Walking behind Slater, porters hauled his luggage, the contents of which were examined by the Marshals: these included a stained fawn waterproof coat, stained trousers, and a claw hammer with blood specks and the appearance of having been scrubbed.

Detective-Inspector John Pyper testified at the trial that the coat, trousers and hammer pulled out of Slater's luggage were blood-stained. Pyper testified that "Each parcel was sealed with the Government seal." Slater admitted the clothing was his. The clothing was blood-stained. Authors who attributed the murder to Patrick Nugent, or a Gilchrist relative discounted these riveting proofs of Slater's guilt. One law gent was unmoved: "Nugent did it!"

A further problem with Nugent as the murderer—aside from his missing front tooth—was that Slater made an admission to the Marshals. He said the clothing and hammer were his.

The Marshals counted the reddish stains on the coat. There were 25. This was physical evidence. Physical evidence has no motive. In addition, Slater admitted the stained coat was his.

Recall that removal with kerosene left an orange tint to a blood stain on fabric. The officer said the fawn coat had stains "on the left shoulder, on the inside and outside of the right sleeve, down the front beside the buttons, and on the skirt."

When John Trench was questioned about the fawn coat, he identified it at trial as "Label 43" in evidence. The coat—the most significant and real piece of evidence-- was not photographed. Roughead, who presumably was in the courtroom, offered no elaboration.

The Crown barrister was focused primarily on the identification of Oscar Slater without proving the elements of the crime. As to the most serious details connecting Slater to the murder, the Crown's attempts were haphazard.

Forensic specialists examined a *too small swatch* of the stained waterproof delivered to them by Edinburgh and Glasgow police. Still, they concluded that the stains had been diluted. Each and every stain had been treated. A purposeful act. The solvent—whether water or kerosene-- turned the blood a tinted orange. These 25 tinted stains appeared on Slater's waterproof coat.

CHAPTER 41

Oscar Slater Enters the American Criminal Justice System

Slater was escorted to the criminal court in Manhattan and then across the Bridge of Sighs to Tombs Prison to await his hearing for extradition to Glasgow in the matter of Marion Gilchrist's murder.

Manhattan Criminal Courthouse (right); Bridge of Sighs (center); Tombs Prison (left).

In 1842, after a visit to the United States, Charles Dickens published *An American Tour* in which he described Tombs Prison: "Such indecent and disgusting dungeons as these cells, would bring disgrace upon the most despotic empire in the world." Dickens' temperamental review of American prisons did not improve the facilities—not during Slater's residence nor to the present day.

Oscar Slater's New York arrest. Pitchfork *(left corner, above Oscar's head)* may be 1909 Spiritualist ectoplasm; Slater sits at left. U.S. Commissioner Shields, seated. U.S. Marshal Henkel, standing at right.

New York and Extradition

In 1909 New York, a polyglot city with a population of 3 1/2 million, 12% of whom were Jewish, Slater was not likely fingered as a murderer because he looked Jewish. If anti-Semitism figured—if at all in his murder conviction—it was in Glasgow or Edinburgh. Jews were newcomers to the British Isles, 1% of a much smaller, insular population.

Oscar Slater elected his right to a hearing before extradition. He reiterated his American citizenship, hoping that only America had jurisdiction once he had landed. However, the place, the *locus*, where a crime is committed, is the place of jurisdiction.

January 6—Beginning in January, someone in the Glasgow police department was regularly leaking to the newspapers. This began after Trench's interviews with Luise Freedman, Patrick Nugent, and Helen Lambie. One newspaper reported January 6: "Authorities yesterday afternoon received important and unquestionable information which will of a certainty run the murderer to earth. *One of the suspects* turned King's evidence." There was more than one person involved in the murder. "One of the suspects" turned informant. The informant was never disclosed. Slater had been arrested in New York. He was the charged murderer. Could it have been Nugent? Trench was decidedly protective of him after the December interview. He assured William Roughead and Conan Doyle that Nugent had been absolved of any connection with the murder.

CHAPTER 42

Verisimilitude in Oscar Slater Descriptions

Witnesses Bound for New York

January 13--- Witnesses Ellen aka Helen Lambie, Mary Barrowman, and Arthur Adams, accompanied by Detective-Inspector Pyper and the Chief Sheriff of Glasgow's Criminal Office, William Warnock, were on board the RMS Baltic bound for New York. Two years hence, the Baltic would be unable to reach the sinking Titanic in time to save its passengers. In frigid January, ships sailing across the Atlantic were in for turbulent waves and blasting wind. One can imagine the queasy *mal de mer* passengers endured as the Baltic rolled and tossed. Despite the gales as well as a collision during this voyage, the ship arrived safely in New York with its celebrated passengers. Pyper and Warnock were confident their witnesses would insure Slater's return to Scotland to face trial for the murder of Marion Gilchrist.

Lambie and Mary shared the same cabin, an economical measure in a murder case costing Glasgow and Edinburgh hundreds of pounds. Subsequent reviewers of Slater's conviction found the arrangement a purposeful scheme to incriminate Slater because it enabled the two young women to exchange information. And, some said, police were able to get the comparable descriptions they wanted.

The police and the Crown determined the woman and girl were credible. Helen Lambie was not inclined to be forthcoming with Mary Barrowman nor the police about the description of the murderer. She was as yet unsure whether Slater would implicate her. Not until the days of Slater's release in 1927 was Helen Lambie prompted to publish her damning accusation that Oscar Slater was THE man who murdered Marion Gilchrist and if he denied it, he was a liar.

January 25--- Arrival of the RMS Baltic. The ship journey across the Atlantic lasted 12 days. Slater's trip was only seven. The experience of overseas travel must have been of great enjoyment for two Scottish girls who had traveled no further than a few miles from home. They arrived as important witnesses in the identification of the hunted murderer now held at Tombs Prison in New York.

Descriptions of Oscar Slater

The problem Slater faced, his defense and defenders believed, were suggestive lineups. His descriptions, taken from police and witness statements, were published in all the newspapers.

The defense improbably expected the admissibility of only exacting details of Slater's looks and garb on the days preceding the murder and the night of December 21. It was in the defense's hands to disprove the eyewitnesses as unreliable, an overwhelming task in this case. In all the Oscar Slater books, there would follow tilting, musing, dissembling, and diffusing of each witness's observations and recollections. The objections were without merit. Witness descriptions were close enough to identify Oscar Slater conclusively.

A number of witnesses watched the same man walking the nearby streets—Cumberland, West Princes Street, Grant Street, and St. Georges Road—day after day, night after night for two or more weeks. Some witnesses, including Helen Lambie, remembered the peculiarity of his gait. One maid waited to spot him through the window of her house, so accustomed was she to his routine. Euphemia Cunningham and William Campbell passed him walking twice in daylight on Cumberland Street. Robert Bryson was another who looked directly into his face.

Only a few months elapsed from late December to the May trial. Witness recollections weren't rendered foggy from an aimless drift of years. They were concentrated on a Christmas tragedy that befell an elderly neighbor.

As Oscar walked down the Lusitania's gangplank, it was not difficult to get a fix on his looks even though he kept his head down. The face, nose and eyes; the gaze; the complexion; shape of the body; and his manner of dress all conformed closely to witness descriptions.

Definitive Identifications

Oscar Slater's facial features were apparent at the crime scene. As he exited the spare bedroom, he was caught unawares by the appearance of the downstairs tenant, Arthur Adams, and Slater's inside contact, Helen Lambie.

Short-sighted Arthur wasn't wearing his spectacles. However, he had no difficulty climbing the stairs twice and peering through the side windows of Miss Gilchrist's flat. He knew the first time he walked upstairs that he wasn't wearing his glasses. If he needed them so badly, he would have put them on the second time he went upstairs.

Arthur's recollections of the man's face were fuzzy. We can attribute his hesitation to a timorous nature, but he was aware of colors and of mien as he described the man as looking like a commercial but common sort, wearing a fawn or grey coat, about 5'7" and clean-shaven.

The "clean-shaven" observation was significant. Slater's beard was such that his barber often shaved him twice daily but only trimmed his mustache. Over two weeks before the murder, Slater was himself shaving off his mustache. His maid, Katerina, and his barber affirmed this in their trial testimony. This was an intentional alteration to prevent identification. Otherwise, he was always mustached. When he returned to his barber the morning of December 25th, it was growing back.

The other witness at the Gilchrist door, Helen Lambie, improbably and impossibly declared she did not observe any aspect of the suspect's face. Though there were loud noises within, she was tentative about opening the door with Mr. Adams standing beside her. Lambie had a set schedule in the scheme; she'd kept to it. Regrettably, the man was still inside. It was 7 p.m. She had to open the door because Mr. Adams wouldn't leave until she did so. The lights were on. A man came out of the spare bedroom, crawled along the right wall of the lit hall, crouching so that his spattered coat wouldn't be visible, and looking directly at the two standing at the open door. He wore a soft cap which didn't hide either his face or his hair.

Both witnesses had a commanding view of Oscar's glissade along the wall. Mr. Adams said that as the suspect neared them, he stared straight ahead, then stood upright, passed between the two, and ran down the stairs "like greased lightning."

Lambie didn't shout nor scream. The suspect's manner, which Lambie clearly saw, was not of a proper visitor. Yet she let him pass without a word.

Slater's face wasn't lowered down into his collar. How could he have crept out unless he looked ahead? Lambie didn't out him because it would have involved her participation. Lambie couldn't recall, for a good long time, a single facial characteristic of Oscar Slater's.

Witness Observations

๏ OSCAR HAD NO MUSTACHE

On the night of the murder: Arthur Adams, Annie Armour, Mary Barrowman, Hugh Cameron, Rowena Adams Liddell, Allan McLean, Katerina Schmaltz.

Allan McLean, the bicycle-dealer and gambler, reported to police his suspicions that a man from the gaming halls named "Mr. Oscar" was the probable killer; he saw him the evening of December 21 and he was clean shaven.

Two weeks until the day of the murder: Dr. John Adams, Euphemia Cunningham, William Campbell, John Clunes, Alexander Gillies, his barber, Frederick Nichols.

⁑ DARK COMPLEXION; ETHNIC

Annie Armour, Robert Bryson, Alexander Gillies, Euphemia Cunningham, Mrs. McHaffie, Allan McLean. The suspect was dark-complexioned. The look of a "German Jew" per Allan McLean and Annie Armour, the Kelvinbridge railroad ticket agent. Euphemia Cunningham said he'd looked "foreign." Constable Walker mistook Slater, loitering in the neighborhood, for a Jewish merchant familiar to both, Isaac Paradise, and had waved to him. The ethnic look of a man did not raise suspicion in the officer. Constable Walker and Isaac Paradise were friendly.

⁑ SALLOW COMPLEXION: (*sallow*, dusky, dark; yellow or brown in tone) Alexander Gillies and Euphemia Cunningham said the man had a dark and sallow complexion. Euphemia said he was "heavy featured."

♣ THE NOSE

Mary Barrowman, Hugh Cameron, Rowena Adams Liddell, Allan McLean, Frederick Nichols. Slater's nose was prominent in witness identifications. Outright recognition of this facial characteristic was assuredly persuasive. The twist of his nose had been Mary Barrowman's instant recollection.

At 7:05 p.m., as Slater bolted down the stairs of 15 Queens Terrace, he was observed by 15-year-old Mary on an errand from her brother's shop on the High Street. Slater had the unexpected benefit of a bright lamp post about three feet from the Gilchrist building. According to a policeman's testimony, the electric street lamp threw a bright light. In this light, and a second light across the street, Mary saw the man who paused twice. He looked in her direction. She was the first to identify a prominent feature of Slater's face--his "twisted nose."

Author Peter Hunt went so far as to suggest the we "bar the nose" in describing the suspect because, Hunt claimed, it had been an after-arrest identification *introduced by the police*. Not so. Mary's description was reported immediately to her mother and to the family neighbor, a policeman. It was independent of the police and witnesses Arthur Adams and Helen Lambie. The police received no such facial characteristic from either Arthur or Lambie. Neither one described Slater's face in such detail. Yes, the police had this description; it had been fortuitously provided by Mary Barrowman to the police.

That Lambie, without Arthur's vision issues, could not point out the twisted nose of a man who crouched upright several feet, face forward, and then walked out of the murder scene, was another factor in her complicity.

Slater did indeed have a twisted nose. The bridge had been broken in a fistfight some years prior. A police report confirmed it. The immigration examiner in America included the broken nose in the description portion of Slater's application (as A. Anderson). The informant and gambling club manager, Allan McLean, described his twisted nose.

Awaiting Oscar's trial in Edinburgh, a reporter wrote:

"The deformed nose, of which so much has been made, is a feature which, once noticed, is not likely to be forgotten. It is not so noticeable on a front view of the face, but is the most conspicuous feature when looking at the profile."

❧ HAIR

Euphemia Cunningham, Alexander Gillies, Mrs. McHaffie. The McHaffie family lived across the street from Miss Gilchrist. Mrs. McHaffie looked through her window to observe a strange man walking the street near Miss Gilchrist's flat. As Miss Anne Elliott said: "We cannot help ourselves. We live at home, quiet, confined..." (*Persuasion* by Jane Austen). Mrs. McHaffie watched him in the afternoons over the course of a week. He had very dark hair—corroborated by stockbroker Alexander Gillies who also lived across from Miss Gilchrist. On his way home from work, Gillies had seen the same man for several evenings prior to the murder. Sometimes he would be wearing a bowler hat. Mrs. McHaffie said the man seemed to have no other intention but the looking up and down around the street and the Gilchrist flat.

Even more revealing was cousin Annie McHaffie's description of a man, in that same time period, who had come up to the McHaffie door. He had asked if a man named "Anderson" lived there. This was Slater's crafty self, engaging the women he saw watching him out their windows.

Some witnesses could not accurately describe the suspect's hair because, in the December weather, he wore a soft cap or a bowler.

❧ PECULIAR WALK

Madge McHaffie and Helen Lambie both saw Oscar Slater walking and both described his peculiar gait. Detective-Inspector Pyper testified about Slater's walk and his hen toe.

Mrs. McHaffie talked about the man with her daughter, Margaret, who said she had passed the man several times in the street. Their cousin, Madge, said she'd seen the man, wearing a fawn coat and a black bowler hat, about 7 p.m. two weeks before the murder. On an afternoon, Madge encountered the man yet again, and noticed he shuffled as he walked. Oscar Slater's peculiar walk was also mentioned by Helen Lambie.

> *And they (Joseph's brothers) brought[it] to their father and they said, "We have found this, now recognize whether it is your son's coat or not."*
>
> **GENESIS 37:32**

❧ THE FAWN WATERPROOF COAT

Arthur Adams, Dr. John Adams, Mary Barrowman, Alexander Gillies, Helen Lambie, Madge McHaffie, Oscar Slater.

The suspect's coat drew as much consternation just as, biblically, what Jacob experienced with Joseph's brothers over a coat of many colors. What colored the biblical event and Oscar Slater's was the gravity of deception and trickery. Slater did indeed own and wear a fawn weatherproof. He admitted this to the U.S. Marshals on the Lusitania. Slater apologists attached little importance to his admission, his possession of this coat, witness observations, intentional dilution, and that the fawn waterproof coat packed in Slater's luggage revealed 25 diluted reddish/blood stains on its front. Like Joseph's coat, the fawn waterproof had assumed various hues.

There were also blood-stained trousers which, after the trial, were handed over to the Prison Aid Society which displayed this Oscar Slater evidence at its fundraisers.

It was indisputable that Oscar wore a fawn waterproof coat both during his neighborhood walks and on the night of the murder. Short-sighted Arthur thought the coat was either fawn or grey, but Lambie said it was fawn-colored. The police, taking no chances, reported that the suspect wore either a fawn or grey coat.

♪ SOFT CAP

The police, and later authors, made much of the suspect's cap: that it was "soft," a "Donegal," or "tweed," as if they were markedly distinctive. They were soft caps. A Donegal cap had a rim around its entirety. Arthur, Lambie, Mary, and Agnes Brown saw a man wearing a soft tweed cap. A variety of soft caps was found in Slater's luggage. As he was led out of the Lusitania, Oscar wore his great coat and a bowler.

Hoist on His Own Petard

Oscar Slater was caught in an inescapable net at the scene of the murder: beneath the electric street lamps, Mary Barrowman saw the face and twisted nose of the fleeing man who wore a fawn waterproof. She watched him because she was a young girl and spooked by this character. She watched Slater take a right turn from St. Georges Road to Grant Street. Who but an eyewitness could vouch for this detour off St. George's Road? Slater could have continued down St. George's Road toward his flat in time for the alibi dinner. Instead, he made a turn onto Grant. He did so because another man waited, holding another of Slater's coats. This was Nugent. The two men ran from Grant Street towards

Cumberland, where they made a right turn. This route up Cumberland led to another witness sighting, that of the night school teacher Agnes Brown.

Mary Barrowman's was the most telling identification simultaneous with the murder when compared with the obstructive Helen Lambie and the questionably vision-challenged Arthur Adams.

Then came Agnes Brown on Slater's getaway path immediately after the Mary Barrowman sighting. Miss Brown saw Slater's back when he and Nugent—the man waiting on Grant Street-- raced past her on Cumberland Road. She saw Slater's coat flapping in the wind and also that he'd been carrying something in his right hand as he ran.

Annie Armour was the train's ticket taker and described the overheated face of a gent scrambling for the train minutes after Agnes Brown's sighting on Cumberland Road.

CHAPTER 43

Gilchrist Jewelry Back in the News

While Slater awaited New York's extradition proceedings, the American prosecuting attorneys assisted the Glasgow officials. They had traveled a long distance to collect the suspect and charge him in a gruesome murder.

Initially, the Americans believed Slater's stories. He presented himself as a U.S. citizen who had lived several lawful years in New York. The authorities were unsure whether to release him to Scottish law enforcement.

January 4, 1909--- From London, the *Reynolds Newspaper* reported that a tray of "unset" diamonds worth £5000 had been found at the Gilchrist flat. It had been in a hidden corner. Police had continued searching the flat. Why? Had policemen filched a gem or two? Who had valued the diamonds? How many were there? How had the police uncovered a hidden corner in the flat?

Marion Gilchrist may have purchased uncut diamonds. If so, she had added to her collection. She may have been waiting to see if prices would rise or fall. David Dick's Inventory did not include uncut diamonds nor the jewelry tray. He testified that when he arrived to inspect and value the collection, jewels and gems were scattered haphazardly around the room. Some jewelry was found in tied pouches.

The tray wasn't discovered, according to the news article, until a week after the murder. What appeared from the *Reynolds News* article, from John Trench's inveterate inquiries, and from the ongoing police searches within the flat, was a motive not dissimilar from that of Oscar Slater and his companions, Helen Lambie and Patrick Nugent. Diamonds.

CHAPTER 44

Extradition Proceedings

Lineups and Contrivances

January 26, 1909---Slater was still in New York weeks after his arrest on board the Lusitania. While in custody, he asked for regular shaves and his requests were approved.

Had Slater remained in Glasgow rather than fleeing the scene, he and his lawyers could have used the time to prepare. As it was, they weren't ready for a prosecution so inadequate that it skirted the element of motive. Oscar Slater's motive for the murder lay unproven. The purloining of Gilchrist diamonds, which had so ruthlessly absorbed him in the burglary, was a motive corrupted by the possibly acquisitive Glasgow police.

So it was that Oscar Slater was escorted, handcuffed, to the New York Courthouse between two cheerless U.S. Marshals towards the chambers of a hearing officer.

As the three men walked through the hall, they encountered King's Counsel Charles Fox and the three Glasgow witnesses waiting for the lineup. They had arrived in New York the day before. Helen Lambie testified at trial that May that when she saw Slater led into the courthouse, she spontaneously declared "That is the man!" Helen Lambie, the insider in the Gilchrist scheme, was going to prove Slater's most vocal accuser. The KC--who had never before seen Slater—then repeated that Oscar Slater was being led in. All three witnesses recalled they independently recognized the man:

Lambie: because she knew him.

Arthur: because he had seen the man walk from the spare bedroom.

Mary Barrowman: because she had looked right into Slater's face and reported for posterity the singularly definitive nose.

Oscar Slater's anxieties were compounded on seeing the Glasgow witnesses. The game was afoot and it was a serious one indeed. Prior to the lineup, he was met by his New York attorneys, Hugh Gordon Miller and William A. Goodhart. He retained them with his sole possession of value-- the gold watch he'd had fixed by Messrs. Dent. All of these individuals sat in one room. In defending Slater, authors argued that both KC Fox and Slater's defense counsel were at fault for allowing the lineup to proceed.

The conduct of the lineup was within the jurisdiction and authority of the state of New York. An eventual "identity parade" in Scotland was likewise required. For a procedurally lawful lineup, authorities could not persuade nor prompt a witness to identify a suspect. Only one witness at a time could attend a lineup. The Scottish authorities were unfamiliar with procedures in the American courthouse, and, for this cause célèbre, were hesitant to object.

Photo identification was admissible so long as the suspect's photo was shown among several photos and the witness was asked to select the suspect from the photos displayed. Authorities improperly prompted the witnesses with a police photograph of Oscar Slater: Arthur was unsure. Mary was sure. Lambie refused to look at it.

On February 2, 1909 after the lineups and while sitting in Tombs Prison, Slater sat down to write a letter to Hugh Cameron in Glasgow. Predictably unnerved by Lambie's remark as "the man," his instinct and recognition of his guilt, led him to take evasive action. The extradition hearing was not going his way. The Americans were going to return him to Scotland. Worse, his lawyers were agreeing to his voluntary departure.

He had no money to pay them to represent him further and to file appeals. In the letter to the Moudie, Slater's hindsight and promptings were too transparent. Mice wouldn't swallow that cheese.

Letter written to Hugh Cameron while at Tombs Prison

New York
Centre Street
Tombs
2/2/1909

Dear Friend Cameron!

To-day it is nearly five weeks I am kept here in prison for the Glasgow murder.

I am very down-hearted my dear Cameron to know that my friends in Glasgow like Gordon Henderson can tell such liars about me to the Glasgow police.

I have seen here his statements he made in Glasgow telling the police that a German came up to him and had told him Oscar Slater had committed the murder, and also that I have been on the night of the murder in his place asking him for money, I was very excited and in hurry, I didn't think it was very clever from him, <u>because he like to make himself a good name by the Police to tell such liars.</u>

I don't deny I have been in his place asking him for money because I went broke in the Sloper Club. Only I will fix Mr. Gordon Henderson I will prove with plenty of witnesses that I was playing there mucky, and I am entitled to ask a proprietor from a gambling house when I am broke for money.

He would not mind to get me hangt and I will try to prove that from a gambling point, I am right to ask for some money. I hope nobody propper mindet will blame me for this.

The dirty caracter was trying to make the police believe I done the murder, was excitet, asking for money to hop off.

I think you know different remember when have been in the Cunard Line office trying to change for a £5 note, we have been in three or four differend place after found some change in the Grosvenor have posted with you on Hope Street office a registered letter.

I shall go back to Glasgow with my free will, because you know so good than myselfs that I am not the murder.

I hope my dear Cameron that you will still be my friend in my troubel (*sic*) and tell the truth and stand on my side. You know the best reason I have left Glasgow because I have shown to you the letter from St Francisco from my friend, also I have left you my address from St Francisco.

I reely was surprised I don't have seen your statement because I think you was too strait forvard for them. They only have taken the statement against me and not for me. Likely I will be in Scotland in fourteen days and so quicke your hear that I am in prison in Glasgow send me the best criminal lawyer up you get recomendet in Glasgow I stand on your dear Cameron.

Keep all this quiet because the police is trying hard to make a frame up for me. I must have a good lawyer, and after I can proof my innocents befor having a trial, because I will prove with five people where I have been when the murder was committed.

Thanking you at present, and I hope to have a true friend on you, because every man is able to get put in such a affair and being innocent. My best regards to you and all my friends. — I am, your friend,

Oscar Slater

The letter was strategic. He knew the authorities read his correspondence. It was Slater's entreaty for a character reference. He wrote that the matter would be resolved "before having a trial." Though Slater read the Glasgow newspapers and knew the specifics of the Gilchrist murder far better than anyone, he avoided reference to the victim or her name.

Oscar Slater's Extradition Hearing

Slater did not testify—not at the extradition hearing nor at his coming trial in Edinburgh though his very life was in jeopardy. He submitted written "not guilty" pleas in New York and in Edinburgh. He was experienced in courtroom challenges having been arrested on numerous occasions in many British towns. In New York, he voluntarily chose not to testify because he believed his ambiguous American citizenship would protect him from the jurisdiction of the Scottish courts.

The prosecution began its case with the deposition taken in Glasgow of Luise Freedman. She had been visited and questioned two or three times by police at Slater's flat where she and Elsa Huppe were staying. The two women had been rushed from London to his flat sooner than agreed and witnessed Slater's frenzied packing the afternoon of December 25. Their testimony was relevant to the issue of flight.

Slater supporters made excuses that his travel to New York was just another of his routine business trips. However, Luise was forced to lend him money. He couldn't wait. He had to leave. The £25 was just enough to give him breathing space upon arrival in New York. He told the ladies he was going to Monte Carlo for three weeks. The money was Slater's price for not abandoning Andrée to whom he was not married.

For the defense, Slater's friends testified as to his good character. Among them were his diamond dealer associates, including David Jacobs, Solomon Miller, fka Solomon Biler, and Henry Wrone. The men, refugees from eastern Europe who spoke broken English, shared a common expertise in the diamond trade. In the New York courtroom, Slater's fellow fences and fellow Jews faced the American brand of anti-Semitism in their impeachment as his character witnesses.

On cross-examination by the New York prosecutor, Mr. Wrone denied he was a "resetter", or fence, for Oscar Slater in dealing with loose stones. A similar denial was made by Solomon Miller. David Jacobs was cross-examined as to whether he and the defendant had a joint practice of fencing contraband jewelry, on both sides of the Atlantic. Jacobs, alias "Sticks," protested that he and Oscar Slater were legitimate jewelry dealers.

Following his testimony on February 9, poor "Sticks" was arrested while visiting Slater at Tombs Prison. Here's where one might venture to say that Tombs Prison's (Irish) "keepers" observed with disdain Oscar Slater's Jewish *mishpocha* (family friends) coming to visit. *Oscar Slater—the killer of an old woman for her diamonds. During Christmas!*

Telegrams flew back and forth with London. The American authorities learned that "Sticks" was wanted-- for a 1904 burglary of a pearl stick pin worth £600 from the 10th Earl of Chesterfield. A reward may have been in the offing for the expensive extradition, overseas, over a minuscule stick pin missing for six years. David Jacobs was shipped off to London.

CHAPTER 45

On Scotland's Soil

The Edinburgh High Court situated in Parliament Square

In February, Slater's hearing ended in his extradition. He pontificated: "I fought against extradition because I am not a murderer. I did not know and never heard of Miss Gilchrist. My one regret is that I have been treated shabbily by America, my adopted country. I hope to prove my innocence." He spoke of his cosmopolitan life, having traveled the world over, and that he had not practiced dentistry for a number of years.

He was put on the ship Columbia headed for Scotland. Andrée boarded a ship bound for Liverpool and from there, returned to Paris. On the first of May, she was in Edinburgh awaiting Oscar's May 3, 1909 trial.

When Slater deboarded the Columbia, handcuffed, he was met by a sea of faces, a populace stirred by newspaper headlines swirling about the brute arrested for the murder of Miss Marion Gilchrist. He was oblivious to the boos and taunts. The only unfortunate experience, he claimed, was that a crew member kicked him as he left the ship.

The mood of the public was judgmental. Oscar Slater was guilty even before the trial; the newspapers had resolved that issue. Besides Andrée, only a Rabbi of the Glasgow community (then titled "Minister" or "Reverend"), Eleazar Phillips, maintained deep sympathy for Slater's plight. The Rabbi believed Slater was being scapegoated because he was Jewish. He could not believe a Jew would commit such a heinous crime. Accusations of blood libel hadn't died in the Middle Ages. Pogroms arose from superstitions and bigotry about Jews. In Britain, "The Jew's Daughter" endured as a jolly folk song about the Lincoln blood libel of 1255.

Rabbi Phillips' congregants, however, were not of the same predisposition. Not only would they not contribute to a legal defense fund for Oscar Slater, they informed the Rabbi that any money for Slater would be out of his own pocket with not a penny from the congregation. It would be Rabbi Phillips' unrestrained loyalty to one of his people that would seize the public imagination along with the publicity raised by Conan Doyle, William Roughead, and John Trench.

Glasgow Lineups

Slater was held at a Glasgow jail to await trial at the Edinburgh High Court. For witnesses, Glasgow was convenient.

Lineups in Glasgow were in their shaky early stages giving Slater reason for hope. As in New York, legal protocols were not yet stringently applied. Police showed his photo to witnesses prior to the lineups. It was not as if the witnesses hadn't become familiar with the face and description from the newspapers.

Detective-Lieutenant Trench testified at Slater's trial that every precaution was taken so witnesses did not see him before the lineup. Witnesses stood outside the room and were led in, one by one. There were struggles in identifying someone who faced death by hanging. Alexander Gillies, the stockbroker, no longer remembered if Slater was the same man he *repeatedly encountered* in the close at 46 Princes Street (adjoining 15 Queens Terrace) between December 15 and December 17. Someone had shut off the gaslight in the close during those evenings. He couldn't be sure.

Slater was able to choose where to stand in the lineup. The other men were police officers and railroad men in plain clothes. All were Scotsmen, pallid, ruddy, or as dark as Slater. But he, well-dressed and "foreign-looking," had been publicized worldwide. Author Philip Whitwell Wilson, in his 1928 article, "But Who Killed Miss Gilchrist?" himself referred to Oscar Slater racially as "the dark-skinned prisoner." With his now-haunted dark eyes, fearing the trial, he stood out prominently.

CHAPTER 46

The Burden of Proof

> "It is a capital mistake to theorize before one has data. Insensibly one begins to twist facts to suit theories, instead of theories to suit facts."
> Sherlock Holmes, *Scandal in Bohemia*

A Nutshell of the Law

The golden thread, or Sherlock Holmes' scarlet skein, that runs, sometimes not tautly enough in a criminal case, is the "presumption of innocence": the doctrine that demands the prosecution must both *produce* evidence of guilt and *persuade* the fact-finder that proof exists "beyond a reasonable doubt." The legal concept is "Elementary." William Blackstone, in his *Commentaries on the Laws of England*, coined this adage: "Better that ten guilty persons escape, than that one innocent person suffers." The "fact-finder" can be a judge or a jury who reviews the facts produced by both sides and from which makes a determination of guilt or innocence.

In his book, *The Proof: Uses of Evidence, Law, Politics, and Everything Else*, author Frederick Shauer writes of the probity and truth which must derive from the evidence produced. Slater's trial failed to forcefully present material physical evidence and of a scheme—circumstantial evidence-- that traced back to Helen Lambie and Patrick Nugent beginning January 1908 until Marion Gilchrist's murder December 21, 1908. There were powerful bits of evidence ignored by the assembly of post-trial sleuths.

The elements of the crime of murder that attached to Oscar Slater were ascertainable facts: His propitious return to Glasgow for two months during which he immediately began selling diamonds under-the-table. Slater's meandering in the Gilchrist neighborhood for several weeks. Katerina's testimony that Slater had himself shaved off his mustache two weeks prior to the murder. His daily barber, Fred Nichols, corroborated her testimony. Slater shaved off his mustache to alter his appearance as he reconnoitered Marion Gilchrist's neighborhood. The description of a suspect, at the murder scene, who had a twisted nose. His stained fawn waterproof and hammer packed in his luggage. The legal inference of flight as consciousness of guilt.

Elements of the crime of Marion Gilchrist's murder

a criminal act--Murder

criminal intent—a dwelling burglary

causation—hammer and chair

harm—indisputable

The fact finder in Slater's trial was a jury. In 1909, the male jury listened to the facts of the crime and heard evidence that the defendant in the dock committed the crime.

Intent to Steal From Marion Gilchrist

- Oscar Slater's sudden return to Glasgow from London in October, for two months, during which time he found a nearby temporary residence.

- Once he arrived in October, Slater's repeated remarks about relocating from Glasgow to a variety of distant locales.
- Slater's October diamond sales, savings, and payment of his bills.

Premeditated Intent to Murder Marion Gilchrist

Intent to kill may be implied from the suspect's actions.

- Did intent to murder arise when Slater bought the hammer early in November? The intent was either to recklessly pound the back of Marion Gilchrist's head, rendering her unconscious or to kill her outright.
- Bludgeoning her repeatedly with the claw edge of a hammer was indicative of his intent to murder her.
- The hammer was a standard model---to pound nails or break coals. It was not a "wee," miniature model with which to fix tacks. He had lived in Scotland for over eight years yet had found no need to purchase a hammer.
- Extreme indifference to human life, e.g., the vicious hammering of the elderly woman's face and skull, would fall within the "depraved heart" rule where intent was implied from the conduct of the act.
- Marion Gilchrist was elderly. Even a blow to the skull intended to render her unconscious could have resulted in her death.
- Slater's panic when opening the dining room door and seeing Marion Gilchrist facing him did not deter his readiness to murder her. The panic and fury of this assailant was a repeat of

his conduct--his "m.o."--in prior altercations, only this time, with a far more compelling motivation.

Preparation and Planning

The murderer had unobstructed access to the flat.

Knowledge of the layout of the flat.

Knowledge of the spare bedroom and its contents.

Knowledge that Marion Gilchrist was elderly, alone at the time, with no visitors nor dog.

Knowledge that no tenants lived upstairs.

Knowledge that Miss Gilchrist was not on friendly terms with the downstairs tenants.

Knowledge there was piano playing downstairs during music lessons for young students.

Knowledge that Miss Gilchrist owned a valuable store of diamonds.

Breaking and entering aka Burglary

The offense began with the breaking and entering into a dwelling at night with intent to commit a felony. The offense was considered particularly serious because people were likely to be within. The doors were left unlocked, but they were left unlocked without authority, consent or knowledge of the owner of the premises.

From the testimony of local witnesses, Slater took precautions—observing routines and the evening light, passers-by including police constables, the outside door and steps to 15 Queens Terrace, the comings and goings at 14 Queens Terrace, the window lighting from the second story flat, and the ease of access.

Circumstantial Evidence

Circumstantial evidence-- where crucial determinations of guilt or innocence rested, arguably, on ambivalent identification, such evidence nevertheless gave rise to a reasonable inference of Slater's guilt.

Helen Lambie had motive in her imprecise identifications, but what she did divulge was good enough. Arthur Adams dithered at trial though in the early investigation, he confirmed Lambie's account of the color of Slater's coat, his commercial look, and that he ran out of the flat. Years later, Arthur admitted to friends that he knew at trial that Oscar Slater was the man he saw the night of the murder. He said he had been reluctant to identify him because he feared the man would be hanged.

Slater ran "like greased lightning" from the murder he had just committed (again, flight as consciousness of guilt), down the stairs and outside, bumping immediately into a surprised Mary Barrowman. She never wavered in her description. She was the first to mention the suspect's twisted nose. That detail set Slater on track for the scaffold.

Helen Lambie waited until Oscar Slater's release from prison in 1927 to identify him positively as the murderer. In her published letter, she called him a liar. Only a person acquainted with Slater could mark this trait 20 years after the murder. She knew he was a liar because she had been the insider in the plot to rob Marion Gilchrist.

Inferences from the Circumstantial Evidence

• Witness statements:

Jurors in Slater's trial heard compelling descriptions and about his identity and livelihood. It was useless to pretend the jurors didn't form conclusions about Slater's gambling, his seedy friends, and his scarlet women. The jurors, as did Judge Guthrie, formed reasonable conclusions about Slater's business of diamond brokering and resetting. Stealing diamonds was a logical motivation for the burglary and murder.

• Flight:

1. Running from the scene of the crime at the instance of its occurrence, and
2. From Glasgow to New York.

• Statements made by the accused before or at the time of his arrest, inconsistent with the story:

1. Slater knew or heard nothing of the Gilchrist's murder.
2. His departure to New York was planned.
3. Intentional discrepancies about his destination on leaving Glasgow.
4. Slater's business was that of a dentist.

• Altering appearance--Shaving his mustache several weeks prior to the murder in preparation for casing the neighborhood.

• Alibis—His unsupported alibis were that the night of December 21, he played billiards in the late afternoon and early evening, and at 7 p.m., the time when Mary Barrowman spotted him outside the Gilchrist flat, he was having dinner at home with Mlle. Andrée and the maid, Katerina.

• His career as gem dealer—a motive for robbing Marion Gilchrist of diamonds worth "in the thousands."

• Physical fitness—Did Slater have the physical strength to beat an old woman to death, race from the scene and run all the way to the Kelvinbridge Station without stopping? From all accounts, this inference was reasonable and likewise damning.

• Aliases—A habitual name-changer with the intent to evade police, file for U.S. citizenship, and safely operate brothels.

• His violent past—Did Oscar Slater have the inclination to beat an old woman to death? Fisticuffs, fights with his feet, beating up women. Admissible? Yes.

Admissions

To the U.S. Marshals that the stained fawn waterproof coat and the hammer were his.

Physical Evidence

Two brooches

Broken nose

Two coats worn by Slater: fawn waterproof coat (in evidence) and navy-blue Merton coat with black velvet collar (which he wore to court)

25 reddish/orange stains on coat; blood stains within hammer

Dilution of stains

Hammer

Forensic Evidence

Hammer

Stains on fawn waterproof coat

Blood spatter on hammer

Dilution of stains

CHAPTER 47

TRIAL – May 3 to May 9, 1909

"Data! Data! data!" he cried impatiently.
"I can't make bricks without clay."
The Adventure of the Copper Beeches.

Slater's Arraignment and Trial began May 3, 1909 at the Supreme Court for Criminal Matters in Scotland, the High Court of Justiciary, in the capital of Edinburgh. The court had exclusive jurisdiction over serious crimes such as murder. Oscar Slater arrived to court wearing his navy-blue Melton coat with a black velvet collar, unaware of Agnes Brown's description of a coat worn by one of two men who ran past her on Cumberland Road minutes after the murder.

In Slater's written arraignment statement, he pled as follows: "My name is Oscar Slater. I am a native of Germany, married, thirty-eight years of age, a dentist, and have no residence at present. I know nothing about the charge of having assaulted Marion Gilchrist and murdering her. I am innocent. All of which I declare to be truth."

Slater sat in the well of the courtroom between two mustachioed policemen no less dark than he. Slater appeared dour and pallid having been out of sunshine and fresh air since January. The gloom of his embittered face and his downcast posture spelled resignation to his anticipated fate. He may have thought to say "I may be peccant in small ways, but Gentlemen, why must I sit through this trial, the details of which are about an affair of which I have no knowledge?"

He had kept himself at a distance from traditional life because, it would be argued by the Crown, he gamboled day and night in locales where his ladies of pleasure walked, where he played at billiards, where he took bets, and where he sold his reset gems.

His mustache had grown back. Katerina Schmaltz would testify that Oscar had shaved off his mustache for about two weeks before the murder and on the day of the murder; though she noticed this stark change, she did not know why he did so.

For the past 12 years until the 1909 trial, the Scottish and British public lived with the exploits of Sherlock Holmes. Public interest in murders and in solutions to crime was as rabid as was the rise in reading about them. Conan Doyle was a literary phenomenon, and a rich one.

The police investigation of the Oscar Slater case was near to the truth of Sherlock Holmes' offhand remarks about the incompetence of Inspector Lestrade and company. The public had grown to expect Holmesian perfection in the real world of criminal trials. Instead, the hurried and imprecise investigation and the abbreviated trial left the Oscar Slater case open to eternal scrutiny.

To Oscar Slater's right is a table on which sits a rolled-up bundle with attached labels. It is the evidence in his case.

The physical evidence against Oscar Slater was rolled up and fastened into a bundle within the Persian rug onto which Marion Gilchrist had bled. If there was a fawn waterproof coat enclosed within that jumble, it is not visible.

Choosing Not to Testify

Slater's choice was not to testify. It could not be used against him. There was no lawful compulsion that an accused expose himself to the perils of cross- examination. He had the right not to incriminate himself. However, in summing up, the judge could comment on the failure of the accused to give evidence on oath. The jury would assume the defendant's silence was evidence of his guilt. Subsequent authors preferred the excuse that Oscar Slater –a multilingual defendant-- would have been judged unfavorably because of his foreign accent.

Newspapers vaporized Oscar Slater into something less than a human being: he was a foreigner, a German and a Jew, a violent pimp, dishonorable card cheat, bookie, gambler, and street dealer of gemstones. How then would his court testimony have been detrimental to his already tarred persona?

His defense counsel, Sir Alexander Logan McClure, may have suspected Oscar was the murderer and didn't want him testifying falsely. Many a criminal defense lawyer can sense a client's guilt. It can be a look from the defendant, a misstatement, an averted eye...something that just clicks. It was unclear whether McClure ever spoke with Slater. Counsel for the prisoner received instructions from the solicitor; seldom was there communication with a prisoner. McClure's instructions about putting Slater on the stand would have come from the solicitor.

Before the Criminal Evidence Act of 1898, a prisoner could not take the stand in his own behalf. He could instead make an unsworn statement to the jury from the dock. In practice, Slater could have addressed the jury or presented his statement.

In every single book, article, correspondence, and statement of Oscar Slater, not once did he refer to matters in the crime, nor of the brutality, and certainly not about Marion Gilchrist's diamonds. Instead, his was an ambiguous "you know I could never do such a thing."

His defense counsel chose to put on Slater's landsmen and fellow dealers as witnesses. All were foreign-speakers with heavy accents. They could not testify to his character, or risk "opening the door" for the Crown to eviscerate Slater. They testified peripherally in support of his shaky alibi. What must the jury of Scottish Presbyters have discussed, while deliberating Slater's innocence or guilt, about his companions? It would not have been a pretty parlay.

The defense should have brought forth—even dragged forth-- a few Glaswegians with credit and credibility for the few months of Slater's/Anderson's residence, e.g., an observant Jew, a rabbi, the butcher about Slater's purchases including on December 21, a librarian (Slater was a reader), the skating parlor proprietor--people who could present, for example, Slater's favorable attributes such that would support the account of his buying and eating dinner at home routinely and on December 21.

⁎ Could Oscar's violent or tawdry lifestyle be used as evidence?

Britain's Criminal Evidence Act of 1898 allowed only past criminal convictions to be admissible. Slater's conduct or lifestyle could not be admissible. Prior bad acts as evidence, though appearing relevant, were excluded by Scottish courts for reasons of policy and humanity. Why unearth a defendant's past life and allow a jury to say "Well, the police and the Crown think he did it, and he sure was a disreputable sort. So, he must be guilty."

Slater's past involved repeated acts of violence against women. The complaints were brought by prostitutes who were given short shrift by police and no charges nor convictions resulted. Slater's prior acts of violence were inadmissible at trial. His propensity to commit such acts was inadmissible. Here, in the court of public opinion, we can cast a gimlet eye over his malfeasances. In modern cases, is the propensity to beat women probative?

Pursuant to the precedential Act during Slater's trial, the Crown's imputations would instead be cast upon the character of Slater's witnesses. The seedy underworld could be impressed upon the jury by the appearance and testimony of the ladies: Mlle. Andrée, Luise Freedman, and Katerina Schmaltz, as well as Slater's gambling and resetting cohorts. Colorful but malign and immoral.

The Brooches at Trial

Neither the Crown nor the police knew what to do about Slater's motive for the fatal break-in. Had it been to steal one diamond brooch from Marion Gilchrist?

Authors subsequently extolled his innocence because he had no motive and that he didn't know the victim. He could have used the £25 from Luise Freedman to stave off privation. Instead, he used the money to flee to New York that same afternoon. He didn't disclose to Luise that he was the owner of a pawned brooch with three rows of diamonds.

⚜ The Brooches Were Not the Motive for Slater's Break-in

No brooch was produced at trial even though one remained at Liddell's Pawnbrokers.

On December 26, Liddell's clerk hadn't been forthcoming with police when they woke him early that morning at 4:30. Later that day, the police, with Helen Lambie in tow, went to Liddell's where Lambie was shown the brooch. She said the brooch with three rows of diamonds was not the same as the one she reported stolen on December 22. The clerk, Peter McLaren, reminded police that the brooch at Liddell's was pawned by Slater on November 18, a month before the murder. At trial, neither the pawned brooch nor its sketch were produced.

Miss Gilchrist's jeweler, William Sorley, testified from a catalog sketch about a crescent-shaped brooch with one row of diamonds-- this was the small brooch, Brooch #1, reported missing by Lambie on the morning of December 22. No brooch had gone missing on December 21. Lambie stuck to what she'd been instructed--laying a "blind" for police, and blinded they were.

Sorley testified that the sketch of the small brooch "was like the one" purchased from him by Miss Gilchrist. Marion Gilchrist had been to Sorley's shop the previous March to have that brooch cleaned. The conclusion must be that it existed through October at which point Slater got it, reset it and sold its diamonds separately. He didn't break in to Marion Gilchrist's house on December 21 to steal one brooch. Lambie had been able to pilfer single pieces of jewelry that hopefully went unnoticed…so she thought.

In January 1909, still unclear about the pawned brooch, the police brought Peter McLaren from Liddell's to William Sorley's shop. There, Sorley was shown the brooch pawned by Slater.

At trial, Sorley offered no account of his March 1908 conversation with Marion and the prosecution didn't press for one. Sorley's testimony that Miss Gilchrist had no other brooch but Brooch #1, the stolen crescent-shaped, single-row diamond brooch, left a suggestion that a three-row diamond brooch, pawned by Oscar Slater on November 18, a month before the murder, was his legal property.

Sorley produced no list of jewelry purchased from him by Miss Gilchrist, nor a list of jewelry held by Miss Gilchrist prior to Helen Lambie's employment, nor a list of jewelry he'd stored for Miss Gilchrist when she went on holiday. Sorley testified that the three-row brooch (Brooch #2) wasn't Miss Gilchrist's. How would he have known that? No foundation nor corroboration for this testimony was laid. Sorley was not her only jeweler. Marion Gilchrist's Last Will and Testament included jewelers Messrs. Dent of Glasgow (Slater used the same jeweler based in London).

Hearsay evidence was approached cautiously. The risk of error in hearsay evidence was thought to be exaggerated. The courts were not so stringent about its admissibility. It could be corroborated by other evidence. Here, Sorley's evidence was uncorroborated. It did little to explain the world of two brooches and the Gilchrist murder. Miss Gilchrist, a jewelry collector and customer of 20 years, owned numerous brooches.

The dismal performance of the prosecution omitted the particulars of the two very important diamond brooches, relying on the word of Marion Gilchrist's 22-year-old, uneducated housemaid and on William Sorley's account of her jewelry collection. Both had been stolen before the murder. The motive for the break-in was something else entirely.

Slater's defense offered Slater's version of Brooch #2 via Mlle. Andrée's willingness to give false testimony, not once but twice. The jury of 15 men, though titillated by her furry and flattering ensemble, nonetheless doubted the veracity of her statements.

Andrée' testified that Slater bought her the brooch two years' prior. Slater requested this "blind" to be affirmed by Andrée because he was guilty; and she complied. Slater had instructed Helen Lambie in a similar blind in misleading police about a missing brooch on December 22. Andrée was lulled into this moral compromise just as Lambie had been: Andrée because she wanted Slater notwithstanding his murder charge, and Lambie because she feared being connected to the murder.

Andrée lied for her lover and murderer of an old woman --that he had been eating dinner with her the night of the murder. She lied to the U.S. Marshals that neither she nor Slater knew anything about the Gilchrist murder though they left a Glasgow plastered with publicity about the murder. Mademoiselle Andrée was less a coquette than a perjurious accessory after the fact.

After the trial, nothing more was heard of Brooch #2 held at Liddell's. It disappeared from the Record and from the Oscar Slater books. In his list of personal possessions for which he sought recompense upon release from prison, Slater did not include the value of that brooch.

Lambie Persists in Identifying Oscar Slater as the Murderer

The police and the Crown were so sure of their suspect's guilt, that they took short cuts at trial, primarily emphasizing Slater's identification. Twelve different witnesses swore to tell the truth and identified the man.

Police Constable Christopher Walker testified he had seen Oscar Slater on three occasions: early in December and the 17th. On the 18th, he again saw Slater at 6:45 p.m. standing at the foot of West Princes Street, near St. George's Road, opposite the chemist's door.

Helen Lambie testified that when she saw a man walking between two other men into a New York courthouse hall, she recognized him as the man who crept and ran from Miss Gilchrist's. She recognized him by his height, the part of his face that she'd glimpsed, and the manner of his walk. His shoulders shook as he walked and he kept his head bent down.

On the second day of the trial, Lambie, suddenly revelatory, told the packed courtroom, "I *did* see his face!" When challenged by the defense as to why she had not mentioned this before trial, and with the passing of two-and-a-half months since her testimony in New York, Lambie defiantly exclaimed, "I am saying it now!" The defense meekly demurred. Lambie didn't fear a counter-accusation by Oscar Slater. Who would believe him? His life was exposed as that of a pimp and swindler. The judge and jury groped around the testimonies, unwilling to see him as anything but a murderer. He was done for.

Helen Lambie held to the fiction that she knew nothing except that Oscar Slater was the murderer. The public would eventually read more of her scathing accusations, but not until Oscar Slater's release from Peterhead Prison in 1927.

Helen Lambie at the trial

CHAPTER 48

Parsing the Evidence

The police and the Crown were so convinced of Oscar Slater's identity and guilt that a proper investigation and prosecution lay fallow. There was little attention given to the connective elements of the crime: the conspiracy and scheme, the periodic pilfering and subsequent sales, and the accessible entry to the flat. A motive must fit in order to complete the puzzle: the lure of the Gilchrist diamonds by a dangerous diamond dealer and his two fellow scroungers.

So why did the Crown and professional police forces fail to prove a case where investigating detectives and medical and forensic experts were at their disposal?

Once they fixed upon a swarthy fellow with a twisted nose, the police and Procurator-Fiscal brought the investigation to a swift conclusion. The trial was just as swift. These abbreviated procedures, with patches of disorganized and commingled evidence, were among the reasons that the murder of Marion Gilchrist remained "unsolved." In 1927, when Oscar Slater was released from prison, the public, sleuths, authors, a rabbi, and scholars remained steadfast in Oscar Slater's innocence. It was Conan Doyle who came to recognize the folly, albeit too late.

Fascinating Forensics

"Guilty as charged!" to quote an old friend who, after watching a true crime show, would render this uncompromising verdict.

The victim must be defended. Marion Gilchrist was dead and unavailable to accuse the killer. In a capital case such as Slater's, the judge was sworn to direct a jury upon circumstances and statements scrupulously proven before deciding whether or not to take away a life.

Forensics had been first applied in a murder case in China 3000 years ago. It was in an agrarian setting, but murder would still out. A farmer's sickle, which was the murder weapon, was placed beside other sickles within a venerated and immaculate temple. After a few days, the weapon was identified from the flies sticking to the dried blood on the sickle. The murderer was tied to a post and endured his fate of "death by a thousand cuts"...*lingchi*, a slow slicing of his body with a knife. In the 13th century, China's Sung Tzhu wrote *The Washing Away of Wrongs*, a manual of murder clues in drownings, tramplings by buffalo, demonic possession, sexual excess, and tiger bites versus venomous snake bites.

Glasgow's investigatory team was preceded by established, ancient traditions of attention to forensic details. Law, rational proofs, and justice were a consuming imperative for thousands of years. Yet, inefficiency and dishonesty infected the proceedings in Oscar Slater's case.

Forensics and the Hammer

Helen Lambie testified that when she left the house that evening to run her errand, Miss Gilchrist was sitting down, her back to the fire. She'd been reading and wearing her spectacles. Lambie said she remembered this because, after checking the time on the kitchen clock, she went round to the front of the dining room and told Miss Gilchrist she would be back for the half-sovereign on the table. If this was how Miss Gilchrist was situated when Slater entered, she would have turned to her left towards his entry. Her spectacles were not broken by the hammer attack. She hadn't been reading her magazine nor had she been sitting down. The magazines and spectacles lay untouched on the dining room table.

Dr. John Adams was the first on the scene—no more than 15 minutes after the murder because he lived across the street. He saw no weapon and determined that, from the blood and flesh on the bottom of the chair legs, Marion Gilchrist was attacked with the chair. He was not called as a prosecution witness because his conclusion had been made before all the evidence—of the hammer—had been collected. Otherwise, his examination of Marion Gilchrist's corpse was invaluable.

The prosecution's medical witnesses were two renowned forensic experts: Dr. John Glaister, Professor of Forensic Medicine at the University of Glasgow and the Glasgow Royal Infirmary, and a foremost authority in this developing science. Among his publications was *A Textbook of Medical Jurisprudence, Toxicology and Public Health.* Dr. Hugh Galt was also a professor of Forensic Medicine and Pathology at the University of Glasgow, an early expert in diagnosing malignancies and of the analysis of toxicity.

Dr. Glaister and Dr. Galt both testified that Miss Gilchrist had been standing before the fireplace. She may have instinctively held onto the chair with her right hand for protection. No blood was found on her right hand, but there was blood on the left.

The hammer's momentum moved with the strength of Oscar's swing. As he struck repeatedly with his right hand, the claw end of the hammer pushed the orbit of her skull further back and into the posterior. One of the blows was driven into the left eyeball.

The body was found outstretched. Dr. Glaister testified that upon viewing the body the next day, December 22, he determined the manner of the striking through the eye and then into the skull was from the claw end of a hammer--the pointed end:

"The claws of the hammer corresponded to the spindle-shaped wounds found in the skull and this instrument accounted particularly for the eye mischief."

The body was removed by police to the Royal Infirmary where on December 23, Dr. Glaister performed a complete post-mortem, e.g. time of death, tissue samples tested microscopically, extent and location of physical injuries.

The physicians said Marion Gilchrist had been struck 30 to 40 times. "He was that set on making sure she was dead," Dr. Glaister reported.

"It was one of the most brutally smashed heads I have ever seen in my experience."

Both physicians signed the report "upon their soul and conscience." Slater was not yet on the Lusitania, and his luggage, which contained a hammer with blood specks, had not yet been seized and searched.

At trial, Dr. Glaister testified that though he could not be certain, he reasonably believed the hammer recovered from Slater's luggage "bore the appearance of having been probably washed and scrubbed or sandpapered." And said "This hammer could, in my opinion, in the hands of a strong man and forcibly wielded, have produced the injuries found on that body." And "I can only say that this instrument accounts most easily for the different classes of wounds, and particularly the eye mischief."

The forensic evidence was damning. The forcible use of the hammer, the velocity in wielding the hammer, and the attacker's strength, culminated in the lethal blows to Marian Gilchrist's skull. On viewing the typical, household hammer—and not the "tack hammer" nor "toffee hammer" subscribed to by numerous authors-- a man wielding enough force, in an aggressive state of adrenalin and a loss of mental control and sensibility, would cause Marion Gilchrist's fatal hammer-attack injuries. Dr. Glaister and Dr. Galt testified that Oscar Slater's hammer was the murder weapon which had been used 40 to 60 times on the elderly victim.

Believe it or not, Reader, there continue to be male critics—callow in maturity—who reject the idea that Slater's hammer, even applied with force, could have caused the injuries to her face, eyes and skull. There are women alive today who survived hammer attacks. They know that if he's carrying a hammer, he means business.

Overkill: Hammer Attack, Chair-Cracking, and Foot Stomping

As first determined by Dr. John Adams at the murder scene, Drs. Glaister and Galt also found that Marion Gilchrist suffered fractures to the bones in her face, jaw and skull. An internal examination revealed her brain to be

> "greatly torn and disorganised with several pieces missing. The right eye was partially torn out of its socket by the deep fractures of the right side of the brow. There was much blood on and among the hair of the head. On the carpet rug beneath the head on both sides was a considerable amount of clotted blood, and fluid blood had soaked into the substance of the rug.

> Within her chest, "the breast-bone had been fractured completely through its entire thickness about its middle and on the right side, … her third, fourth, fifth and sixth ribs were all fractured, some multiple times, whilst on the left side, the fourth rib was broken."

The chest breaks indicated to the physicians that the killer knelt on top of the chair placed atop Marion Gilchrist's chest to subdue her, even though she was incapacitated. Then, in his dominant position, he inflicted further wounds to her face and head. Dr. Glaister testified that it had been a "furious assault." He'd kept hammering!

Dr. John Adams determined the killer stomped upon her with his feet. Was this not the work of a man with a habit of punching women in the face, of stomping on men who'd fallen in a fistfight, and whose aggression was fueled with a rise in anger and adrenaline? Common sense must overcome human stupidity and obtuseness.

Oscar Slater, the Hammer and the Chair

Once Slater hammered Marion Gilchrist through her face, and into her eye and skull, both of their bodies--the chair between them-- crashed onto the floor. Slater lifted himself upright, knelt on the chair and, using his weight, cracked her rib bones with the chair legs.

When at Peterhead Prison, Slater was twice written up for assault: once he used a hammer against a warder. Inmates used hammers in their daily, 12-hour, hard labor at the quarries pounding granite blocks. Slater was among those inmates—exhausted and overworked; his aggression kicked in.

Blood Stains on Oscar Slater's Fawn Waterproof Coat

Dr. Adams, arriving minutes after the murder, found the back of Marion Gilchrist's left leg drenched in blood. The blood had pooled beneath her. Because of her backward fall and the chair and the killer atop her, the blood gravitated down onto the carpet. The downward flow and the shielding of the chair kept the blood on Slater to a minimum—***only* 25 stains** on the front of his waterproof.

When his waterproof coat was discovered in his luggage, there were 25 reddish blood stains on it. 25 stains just two weeks after the murder. The U.S. Marshals at the New York port, and then the Glasgow police when Oscar's luggage was returned, numbered the stains on the front of the coat: "on the left shoulder, on the inside and outside of the right sleeve, down the front beside the buttons, and on the skirt." The coat was worn by a killer frontally facing his victim.

Here was physical evidence. The Crown's neglect of the coat and its telltale stains was inconceivable. It does not appear from the examination, direct or cross, that the coat was displayed. Nor were there photographs for such a devastating piece of evidence and cameras were in the room.

The defense did not suggest an alternative for the appearance of those remarkable stains on Slater's fawn waterproof. A cardinal trial rule prevented it: "Never ask a question to which you're not prepared for the answer." (example: asking Orenthal "O.J." Simpson to try on the gloves.)

The forensic experts testified the stains on the front of the waterproof were intentionally diluted and turned reddish-brown from a solvent. They varied in shape and size from 5/8" long by ¼" wide, some pinhead size, and "many of them having the appearance of splatters."

All 25 stains were of the same reddish/brown color, i.e., *they happened at the same time* and each stain had been (intentionally) diluted. Because they had been diluted, leaving "too small an amount of material," the forensic experts could not reach a conclusion beyond certitude. In those early days before DNA, at least two teaspoonfuls of blood were required for testing.

The two forensic specialists were joined by a third, Professor Harvey Littlejohn. Here was their statement: "After treatment of the brownish-red stains, and on microscopic examination, corpuscular bodies resembling **in general appearance mammalian red blood corpuscles** were found on certain of the stains." (author's emphasis). The reason they could not come to conclusive terms on the "mammalian" (human...warm-blooded vertebrates) was, again, because of the dilution and therefore, too "small amount of material" to test.

Dr. Glaister: "I have no doubt in my own mind that these were blood corpuscles."

Forensic Blood Tests

The guiacum blood test was discovered for forensic use in 1860. It was already centuries old. Developed in China in 1250 C.E., a blood test appeared in the first known treatise on forensic science, *Instructions to Coroners.* By 1908, the guiacum test was in accepted use to examine blood, mud, or rust stains. Old bloodstains could be diluted or treated with vinegar or kerosene, but would result in remnant tints, as occurred on Slater's waterproof. A blood stain could not disappear entirely.

To detect dried blood, the Teichmann test could have been used but that would have involved heating of the suspected blood sample with acetic acid (vinegar) and a chloride compound leading to the production of hematin crystals detected microscopically.

According to the expert opinion of cardiologist Franklin Saksena, M.D., it would have been impractical to use this test for the dried blood on Oscar's coat. Why? Because if you heat the clothing, it's going to be scorched and useless as an evidentiary sample. Dr. Saksena cited the availability of a better test, available since the early 1900s. This was the Fluorescein test. It would react with the hemoglobin molecules and glow when exposed to UV light.

On appeal in 1927, Dr. Alexander Veitch, Master of Surgery at Edinburgh University (Conan Doyle's alma mater) had not personally viewed the evidence—had it still been available. His testimony during the appellate review of Oscar Slater's case affirmed what he'd read in Dr. John Glaister's reports for the trial held 27 years earlier: there were 25 blood spatter stains on the coat and there was blood within the hammer. Each of the coat stains had been diluted. The hammer had been scrubbed but blood particles remained. Such expert hearsay is still in use today by police and the FBI but subject to contradiction by counter-experts offered by the defense.

Weren't the Blood Stains Apparent to Investigators?

- The 25 diluted, red/blood spots found on the front of Slater's fawn waterproof were coincidentally aligned to the murdered body of Marion Gilchrist, and profound in quantity. According to the testimony of the forensic specialist: "*I cannot say here that the appearance of the stains was due to their being washed, but I am clear that it was due to the influence of water...*" This was a purposeful contrivance to conceal by Oscar Slater.

- The number of blood stains on the coat, two weeks after the murder, was that of the man who killed Marion Gilchrist.

The waterproof coat should have been displayed for the jury. The directive did not appear in the trial transcripts. It was convincing evidence of his waterproof coat's

- fawn color,
- numerous stains,
- stains on the coat all occurring at the same time,
- stains on a fawn waterproof coat soon after the murder,
- Slater's attempt to wipe each stain and the solution used,
- the orientation of the coat stains with Slater's position on the chair and Marion Gilchrist's body,
- Slater's admission that the coat was his.

Blood Stain Opinions in Oscar Slater Books

Conan Doyle: In his book about the Slater case, written in 1911, years before Doyle sat in at the 1927 Appeal hearing, the reference was peripheral: "The Crown never attempted to prove either blood-stains in a pocket, or the fact that any clothes had been burned." **True that the Crown's performance was sketchy, yet the forensic experts were convinced that 25 intentionally diluted blood stains on the waterproof (assuming they had the entire coat to examine) were "mammalian." Coat burning was discussed above.**

Margalit Fox: Quoting from Charles Dickens' *A Christmas Carol*: "The stains on Slater's coat could have been more of gravy than the grave." **This seasonally-inept metaphor for a grave-destined victim could not dilute the opinion of a forensic expert.**

William Roughead: "The condition of the hammer and waterproof was of vital importance to the Crown case, for these were the only links between Slater and the murder. Apart from them, nothing incriminating was found in his possession. Not any of the clothing he was supposed to have been wearing was found, and the expert scientists disagreed as to whether the bloodstains were blood or other matter. With the exception of the disputable stains on the waterproof, no article of clothing belonging to him was bloodstained." **25 blood stains. The number of stains on a waterproof coat so soon after a murder in Slater's neighborhood, must have eluded Roughead's interest. There were two pieces of physical evidence linking Slater to the crime: the waterproof coat and the hammer.**

Thomas Toughill: "Brownishred (*sic*) stains were seen on Slater's coat but close examination could not show that these in fact were blood." **Toughill subsumes the reddish/orange tint stains on the coat into one word exported from the *Alice in Wonderland* glossary. He omits the "waterproof" style of the coat. He omits the number…25 blood stains. The forensic experts were convinced the stains were human blood stains that had been diluted intentionally. Since Slater admitted the coat was his, we can presume he diluted each of the 25 stains.**

Richard Whittington-Egan: referencing Slater's defense counsel: "…no unequivocal bloodstains could be discovered on anything belonging to his client."

Philip Whitwell Wilson: "On the hammer, there were found…no traces of blood…" **The author hadn't read the forensic experts' testimony and reports. Slater's hammer had blood specks and had been scrubbed.**

CHAPTER 49

The Verdict

May 4--- During the trial, Mlle. Andrée and Katerina lodged at the Houston Temperance Hotel in Edinburgh. Katerina appeared in court to testify and to hear the verdict, but otherwise remained indoors. She was described mercilessly in the newspapers as "the grim, dwarfish servant in Slater's home" and as the one who affirmed Mlle. Andrée's alibi for Oscar Slater.

Andrée wrote to Slater while he sat in detention. She meant to cheer him with memories of the good times they once shared at that hotel. She was hope-filled for an acquittal though she did not refer to the murder of the old lady nor to the specifics of his dinner alibi. She ended with a tender Yiddish diminutive for her handsome dandy: *Oscarcheen*.

Jurors had not been directed nor misdirected by Judge Guthrie about the lineup identifications, but his acid directions left no doubt of his conclusion. None of the witnesses identified a person other than Oscar Slater. Significant time hadn't elapsed from the murder to the date of trial.

May 5--- The guilty verdict consumed all of 55 minutes for the all-male jurors and for Judge Guthrie's donning of the black cloth to indicate a sentence of death in the offing.

Upon hearing the verdict, Oscar Slater sobbed loudly, repeating "I know nothing of the affair." He exclaimed "I never knew that such a person existed!" Yes, Slater shouted: "such a person" about Marion Gilchrist.

With Judge Guthrie's imposition of the death sentence, he was as good as dead, his meager possessions forfeit to the Crown.

> For hateful deeds committed by myself.
> I am a villain. Yet I lie. I am not.
> Fool, of thyself speak well. Fool, do not flatter:
> My conscience hath a thousand several tongues,
> And every tongue brings in a several tale,
> And every tale condemns me for a villain.
> Perjury, perjury, in the highest degree;
> Murder, stern murder, in the direst degree;
> All several sins, all used in each degree,
> Throng to the bar, crying all, **"Guilty! guilty!"**
> I shall despair. There is no creature loves me,
> And if I die no soul will pity me.
> RICHARD III

Judge Charles Guthrie—grimace indicating one disinclined to be sympatico

Photo by Alex. A. Inglis, Edinburgh
The Hon. Lord Guthrie

Judge Guthrie's Command of the Case

Long-advocated, godly guidance to a judge was that he take a sip of holy water at the beginning of a case and not swallow it until all the evidence on both sides was heard. This credo would have been familiar to Judge Guthrie, a minister's son. He was educated at Edinburgh's Royal High School and College of Law-- schools dominated by religion, literature, "mental philosophy," and the law.

In British court tradition and practice, Judge Guthrie questioned witnesses and took notes. He delivered his instructions to the jury but did so without disguising his bias.

- When Mary Barrowman's testified about recognizing Oscar Slater beneath the street lights, the Court imparted: "When I say that the light is quite good I mean that by it one could read ordinary print." This was a reasonable direction intended for the jury to reflect on the sharpness of Mary's details of Slater's face, his twisted nose, his coat, and his startled pauses beneath the street lights.

- Of Superintendent John Ord, the Court asked: "Did all the advertisements or police notices in the papers contain a description with reference to the peculiarity of the nose? (Witness Ord answered "Yes.")

- Continuing with Ord, the Court refreshed the jury's recollection of the man, Oscar Slater:

Did you know him under any other name than Oscar Slater?

ORD: No.

Did you know whether he had any regular occupation or did you not?

ORD: I do not think so.

Did he appear to be a man of education?

ORD: Yes, he was very cultured.

Did he speak English well?

ORD: Pretty well.

With a foreign accent?

ORD. You would know he was a foreigner.

In Judge Guthrie's world, gentlemen and gentlewomen had reputations they maintained and protected. To lose one's reputation and to face scandal prevented gentle persons from involvement in crime. To immigrants, unfamiliar with the heritage and tradition of Great Britain, reputation extended as far as the family or neighbors. To Oscar Slater, reputation was a useless resource.

This Way to the Gallows

After the verdict and sentence were read, the newspapers and the public, not yet exposed to William Roughead's interpretation, did not protest. There was approval drawn from the solid witness descriptions: Slater's broken nose, the foreign look, the fawn waterproof coat with stains, the hammer, the testimony of fellow gamblers and diamond dealers, and his courtesan lady friends. Though the Crown failed to hammer home the blood stains on Slater's coat and hammer, a mustache that came and went, and no reliable alibi, the public was convinced that Oscar Slater was justly sentenced for a terrible crime.

Newspapers called out alarms about foreigners in their midst… imported rogues…" "European outcasts." And, "the machinery is there in the Aliens Act of four years ago and the feeling aroused by the Slater trial may strengthen the determination to apply it with the greater stringency." Borrowing from the monster in Bram Stoker's best-selling *Dracula*, "The trial has cast a lurid light…it shows a brood of alien vampires, lost to conscience and to shame, crawling in black depths at the basement of society."

Slater the condemned collapsed upon hearing the verdict. He was unable to walk on his own so deep was his shock and fear. The ordeal of the trial, the jury's crushing verdict, and the judge's pronouncement upon donning his black cap, shrank the once erect figure. Though he was not a tall man, only smallness was visibly on display as he was carried from the Edinburgh courthouse after sentencing. Someone charitably remembered to place his bowler on his head and fastened one button of his coat. Two tall, grim-faced officers of the law supported the doomed man as they walked out into the sunlight and the crowd of onlookers booing the convicted killer.

Oscar Slater Led Out of the Courthouse After Sentencing

Crowd outside Courthouse after Oscar Slater conviction

The *Glasgow Herald News* reported that as he was led to a cell, he continued to weep bitterly. In his paroxysms of fear and agony, the warders reported that Slater burst out with confessions—outside the hearing of Mlle. Andrée, Katerina, Luise, the jurors, and the judge:

> *"See here! I am not the only guilty party.*
> *When I am dead, another will be found guilty."*

He was guilty, but with other plotters. His hysteria was noted by the police who did all they could to calm him:

> *"If I have to die, the girl will not be long after me, Boys. I am going to give something away. I am not the only guilty one. That girl will also be found dead."*

In the years to follow, Slater included Nugent in the mix.

Slater was transferred from Edinburgh to Glasgow's Duke Prison. There, he would await the gallows on May 26, 1909. Rabbi Eleazar Phillips, who remained an unwavering supporter of Slater's innocence, traveled from the Edinburgh Courthouse, along with the distraught Mlle. Andrée, and Luise Freedman, and met with the condemned Oscar Slater. The two ladies then returned to their homes, Andrée to Paris and Luise to Thale, a resort community in Germany.

May 15, 1909---At Slater's request, the *Glasgow Herald* published his letter to his parents in Poland, to stave off their shame, asserting his innocence and that the people of Scotland likewise believed him to be innocent. He denied that his parents had shunned him.

May 17---Rabbi Phillips stirred up a petition for relief and commutation of Slater's death sentence to one of life imprisonment. His congregation was not supportive.

May 25---This was the day before Oscar Slater was set to hang and also the day King Edward VII—another betting man-- commuted his death sentence by way of a "Conditional Pardon." The pardon was only so far as to the hanging. Slater would serve life in prison. Judge Guthrie and fellow judges, in conference over the application for a Pardon, were convinced of Oscar Slater's guilt of the murder. Life in prison would be considered served at the conclusion of 18 years' incarceration. Slater wept in gratitude and thanked the officials who delivered the news. He was to serve his life sentence at Peterhead Prison.

Oscar's entered bleak Peterhead Prison on the northeast coast of Scotland, July 7, 1909.

December 17, 1909---Oscar would see Mlle. Andrée one last time. She came to visit at the prison where he enthused her about reports that his sentence would soon be reversed and his innocence declared. She had sat in for all of the trial and spoke at length with Luise and Katerina. She had testified falsely on his behalf. After the visit, Andrée returned to France and no more was heard from her.

CHAPTER 50

A Disquisition

Was the Pawned Brooch Owned by Oscar Slater, Mlle. Andrée or Marion Gilchrist?

- Miss Gilchrist was left a tidy estate by her father and thus the wherewithal to collect jewelry.

- There were a number of formal photographs of Marion Gilchrist, and in each, she wore a brooch.

- Slater had no brooch with three rows of diamonds (Brooch #2) before November 18 when he pawned it. His livelihood was as bookie, gambler, and under-the-table diamond dealer.

- Miss Gilchrist had many brooches. They were a Victorian era fancy. A dealer acquaintance of Slater's described a Victorian brooch as "peculiar." They were out of fashion in 1909.

- William Sorley, Miss Gilchrist's jeweler for 20 years, testified that the three-row brooch was not Miss Gilchrist's. He was not competent to so testify. He could have produced a list of jewelry which she had stored with him when she went on holiday, but he did not. He had no knowledge of whether she shopped with other jewelers. She did, with Messrs. Dent of Glasgow. The idea that she had not, in 20 to 30 years, visited another jeweler is improbable. Sorley had not been in her house in 20 years taking inventory of the brooches and other jewelry she owned.

- The manager from Liddell's Pawnbrokers did not produce the three-row diamond brooch pawned by Oscar Slater. No sketch nor photograph was provided.

- None of Marion Gilchrist's three prior maids—Agnes Guthrie, Jane Duff Walker, or Marion Galbraith Ferguson-- testified about a three-row diamond brooch or a crescent-shaped one-row diamond brooch.

- Helen Lambie, a person with little education and who worked for Marion Gilchrist about three years, described a missing brooch with questionable particularity to police the day after the murder. She was an incompetent witness of Miss Gilchrist's jewelry collection.

- Miss Gilchrist's niece, Margaret Birrell, was familiar with the jewelry and described a valuable diamond necklace missing from the collection.

- Mlle. Andrée was 17 when she met Slater and 23 at the time of the murder. She was herself a foreigner with no money. She worked as a prostitute. In one photograph, she wore no brooch nor any jewelry. She did not pawn the brooch on November 18; Slater did. She did not hold the pawn ticket. In her May 4, 1909 letter to Slater, she did not mention a brooch. After Slater's conviction, she made no attempt to redeem the valuable brooch.

- Mlle. Andrée was a young woman. A Victorian era, diamond brooch was not her style.

- Slater was a career gem and diamond dealer. He apprenticed with his uncle in his youth, learning to cut and polish gems and diamonds, and more importantly, to reset the stones from jewelry.

- Slater had no furniture, no house, no pearls nor rubies of his own, no generous store of investments. He did not include the brooch in his financial statement for the U.S. Immigration Examiner which he filed months before the brooch was stolen.

- Slater carried business cards with his several aliases so he could present himself as a respectable dealer. It was reported in several narratives that he may have visited Miss Gilchrist in the guise of a dentist or salesman. Had this been the case, he would have left a business card. None was found in the flat.

- Brooch #2 was pawned at Liddell's within a month of Slater's return to Glasgow from London.

- Miss Gilchrist posed for a formal photograph in 1875. In it, she wore a brooch with three rows of diamonds.

Failure to Communicate

- None of Miss Gilchrist's papers, which had been found scattered in the spare bedroom by the intruder, was admitted into evidence nor separately identified.

- There was no inquiry about the scattered jewelry found by David Dick when preparing the Inventory of the collection, nor about the diamond necklace described by Miss Gilchrist's niece, and no investigation into the tray of diamonds found by police in a hidden corner of the Gilchrist flat.

- The stained waterproof coat was not sketched, photographed nor displayed.

- The ease of entry into Miss Gilchrist's flat vs. the convoluted accounts of the time were not explained.

- There was no inquiry about the three padlocks on the door to the flat and why they were unlocked on the night of the murder.

Artful Dodging

Before the doubts William Roughead published the year after the trial, the Scottish public was convinced of Oscar Slater's guilt. The turnabout arose upon Rabbi Phillips' petition for commutation of Oscar's death sentence.

The infirmity of the trial, William Roughead later wrote, began and ended with the lack of connection between Oscar Slater and Marion Gilchrist. He concluded that all the eyewitness accounts were a mixed bag of descriptions and from which the Crown and Court asked the jury to trust its instincts against the evidence. Roughead's overtures to Slater's innocence, in serial, income-producing publications for several years, disrespected the memory of an elderly lady's final, undeserved, suffering moments.

Eerily prescient, in 1887 Conan Doyle wrote a Sherlock Holmes novel, *A Study in Scarlet*. In the story, an Irish terrier is poisoned and business cards are significant. The story informed readers of the development of forensic science in police investigations. It took the effort and acumen of a private detective, Sherlock Holmes, to demonstrate what a sleuth could uncover at a crime scene given scrupulous examination. Holmes was critical of two inspectors at the murder scene. Details of the story were remarkable in similarity to the Oscar Slater case: the corpse, grotesquely contorted, lay in a pool of blood and police walked all about the scene "observing but not seeing" the rooms without taking precautions or notes. Small wonder that the public seized on Conan Doyle's support of the clamor to find Oscar Slater innocent of the murder of Marion Gilchrist.

CHAPTER 51

Trench and the Course of an Innocence Campaign

Born in 1869, John T. Trench joined the Royal Highlanders at age 18. There, his service was marred by indiscipline, drunkenness, and going AWOL to such an extent that he was jailed for a number of drying-out days. Following this unfortunate military attachment, in 1893 Trench joined the Glasgow Police force. For the next 21 years, he distinguished himself as a policeman of tireless energy and investigative abilities for which he was awarded honors and promotions.

Not unlike Oscar Slater, Patrick Nugent, and Hugh Cameron, Trench tended towards the gallant, sporting a waxed mustache, bespoke suits, a bowler hat, and the multi-use umbrella, effective against downpours and hooligans, and as a walking stick. Though a police detective, he had the wherewithal to keep himself sharply groomed.

Slater apologists painted Trench with disarming reverence, but to the crabbed eye, his effort in absolving Oscar Slater of the Gilchrist murder was self-aggrandizement with a faint residue of personal acquisition.

Dates relevant to Detective Lieutenant Trench's activities:

- On Dec. 31, 1908 (Oscar was aboard the Lusitania), ten days after the murder, Trench visited Patrick Nugent at his home in Carfin. Not official business. Police hadn't connected Nugent to the crime, though they knew he was Lambie's friend. No one suspected Lambie either.

- Jan. 2, 1909, Trench went to Oscar Slater's old flat where the two German women, Luise Freedman and Elsa Huppe, were still in residence. After the interview, Trench went to inspect the outside perimeter of the Gilchrist building.

- On Jan. 3, Trench visited Helen Lambie who was living with her aunt.

- Jan. 24, *Reynolds Newspapers* reported information received from a leak: police discovered a tray of diamonds in a "hidden corner" at the Gilchrist flat. The police determined the uncut diamonds were worth "in the thousands." One valuation was £5000.

- Police continued searching the flat after the murder. Trench was not among them. Who reported the tray of diamonds and the valuation to the newspapers, and why?

- In May 1909 at the Oscar Slater trial, two references were made about the tray of diamonds. The diamonds should have figured in establishing Oscar's motive for the burglary.

- In 1910, William Roughead published the *Oscar Slater Trial Transcripts*. He and Trench became acquainted.

- In 1912, Conan Doyle published *The Case of Oscar Slater*. He spoke publicly on Slater's behalf, drawn in by William Roughead, the newspapers, and the rising tide of public disquiet about the trial and guilty verdict.

- Nov. 23, 1913, Conan Doyle presented a paper about Oscar Slater's innocence before the "Our Society," a private club of moneyed and prominent aristocrats and professionals.

- In Jan. 1914, riding the waves of Oscar Slater publicity, Trench began removing the Slater files from the police department, disclosing them to newspapers, to new Slater solicitor David Cook and to William Roughead.

- On Jan. 14, 1914, a Glasgow jewelry shop was robbed of £900 worth of jewelry. Burglars entered in the middle of the night through the floor above, an umbrella shop. Trench requested that he be assigned to the case. He arranged the return of the jewelry through an informant, and he and David Cook reached an agreement with the jeweler's insurer. Trench told the insurer that his superiors authorized Trench to accept £400 for the informant, that the attorney, David Cook, would hold the funds, and Trench would turn over the jewelry to the insurer.

- In March 1914, Superintendent John Ord identified John Trench as the leaker of the Slater files.

- April 23-25, Trench and attorney David Cook secretly moved for a review of the Oscar Slater trial at another Glasgow courthouse using the stolen Slater files.

- On July 14, Trench was charged with disclosing and communicating official documents without authority. Following a hearing, he was discharged from the police force that September without his pension.

- On July 25, Conan Doyle published an Oscar Slater article in "The Spectator," one of numerous letters and articles he wrote about the deficiencies in the Crown's case against Slater.

- A year later, on May 13, 1915, John Trench was arrested with David Cook for fencing £500 in jewelry. The judge directed the jury that the prosecution had failed to make its case and directed they acquit both. Neither Trench nor Cook ever spoke again about the Oscar Slater case.

Why did John Trench leak Oscar Slater information from police files to the press and to other individuals? Initially, he had not touted Slater's innocence.

At Slater's trial, David Dick testified about his inventory of Miss Gilchrist's jewelry. He said diamonds and jewelry were scattered throughout the bedroom. Yet, the murderer had broken open the wooden box and only splinters and papers had been scattered on the floor when police arrived. There was no jewelry in the wooden box. Therefore, the scattered gems were the work of individuals searching the premises after the murder and before the inventory. David Dick included only what jewelry was left behind.

Trench moved on to an outlet for self-promotion and his own financial reward. That was the catnip which drew Trench to leaking police information after the trial.

Trench retained solicitor David Cook for Oscar Slater, and Cook began corresponding with William Roughead about Trench's inside information. The public was keen on true crime tales and Roughead was eager to satisfy this ready market. In 1910, while Roughead was preparing his *Oscar Slater Trial Transcripts* for publication, he was also soliciting Conan Doyle's support for the release of Oscar Slater from prison.

Conan Doyle's instincts for compassion and for justice were exemplified not only in the moral tone of his Sherlock Holmes stories but in a ceaseless campaign to overturn another wrongful conviction and incarceration--that of lawyer George Edalji, beginning in 1907.

Sales and publicity about the Slater case became ever more brisk with the 1912 publication by Conan Doyle of *The Case of Oscar Slater*. When Roughead was seeking Conan Doyle's participation, he assured him that Patrick Nugent had been fully exonerated by the police. He based this errant conclusion on the word of Detective-Lieutenant John Trench. Notwithstanding, in his book Conan Doyle was brutally frank in accusing the two, Helen Lambie and Patrick Nugent, as accomplices in the murder. The accusation merited no action from the police. The investigation was completed and Slater was serving his sentence. Neither Lambie nor Nugent responded to Conan Doyle's charge.

Besides the book, Conan Doyle wrote numerous newspaper articles and persistent letters of inquiry to officials about the evidence, trial and verdict, and delivered public speeches on the Oscar Slater miscarriage of justice. Conan Doyle exposed the bias faced by a foreigner in British courts. There was George Edalji, a native-born Brit of an English mother and a Parsi father, and there was Oscar Slater, a hapless Jewish refugee.

CHAPTER 52

Trench Turned Inside Out

Trench and a Secret Review of the Oscar Slater Trial

Working with papers from the police department, Trench and David Cook secretly arranged for a review of the Oscar Slater trial in another county courthouse—to the fury of the Glasgow police. The police never doubted that Slater murdered Marion Gilchrist.

Slater was not present for the rehearing, April 23-25, 1914. There was no reexamination of the trial testimony or evidence. The court confined itself to a review of Trench's interviews, statements and conclusions. Thus began Trench's unraveling.

Trench reported that Superintendent Ord verbally authorized him to conduct post murder interviews. The Superintendent denied this claim. He did not learn of the interviews and the alleged witness statements until March 29, 1914. On that day, Ord set a tactical trap, assigning Trench to investigate who had been leaking official documents. On April 14, prior to the no-longer-secret review hearing, Ord was informed that John Trench was indeed the culprit. Trench also confessed. Ord's confrontation with Trench was fierce.

The Slater rehearing proceeded but with unintended consequences for Detective Lieutenant Trench. Trench's witnesses vehemently denied his written statements about their having identified alternative suspects in the murder.

Trench and Roughead had been fixated on the murder having been the act of two male relatives…anything to dispel the idea that Slater would have engaged in such brutality and to support their campaign. Some authors supported their exercise in hogwash. The murderer was assuredly the stained-waterproof-coat-wearing Oscar Slater.

Trench alleged that Helen Lambie and Margaret Birrell identified a Gilchrist relative by the initials "A.B." as the murderer. The women denied that such claim was made by Lambie to Miss Birrell. Furthermore, Lambie was too young and had worked for Miss Gilchrist too short a time to have become familiar enough with a visitor or relative to refer to them by initials.

Charles Cowan, Miss Birrell's lodger, was present in the room the evening of December 21 when Lambie came rushing in, weeping hysterically about the murder. He said she never mentioned an "A.B." nor had she accused Miss Gilchrist's nephew, Dr. Charteris. Lambie implicated no one, least of all herself, the night the horror of Miss Gilchrist's murder struck.

Authors of the Oscar Slater books ignored the angry denials of Helen Lambie, Margaret Birrell and Charles Cowan. They made excuses for John Trench's dubious accounts, among which were that he was performing official duties, had no reason to fabricate, and was anxious to free Oscar Slater from an unfair verdict and incarceration.

Not only did the Glasgow court presiding over the limited review of the Slater trial hear witness statements contradicting Trench…putting the Detective's trustworthiness into shadow, but Trench's trial testimony also conflicted with his 1914 objective—to have Oscar Slater declared innocent. What a coup that would have been for Slater's new solicitor, David Cook, author William Roughead, and Trench the insider.

Trench's official duties in the Gilchrist case were to conduct the lineups. He testified about the precautions taken to avoid unfair or suggestive lineups and that they had been conducted without prejudice or error. He testified, for example, that witness Mrs. McHaffie identified Slater, as did her family, all of whom lived or visited in the neighborhood. Mr. Bryson identified Slater "without hesitation."

When witness Mary Barrowman was brought to the lineup, Trench testified that she fearlessly asked Slater to pull down his hat the way he'd worn it the night she spotted him. When he did so, Mary was unflinching: "That's it, that is the way you were dressed when I saw you." Query: Where was a photographer, sketch artist, or police report of Slater's facial expression when confronted in that room with Mary's challenge?

At trial, Trench testified that every witness was certain in his or her identification of Oscar Slater as the murderer of Marion Gilchrist.

When it came to the physical evidence against Slater—the stained coat and the hammer in his luggage—Trench's testimony at the secret review hearing was likewise precarious. He admitted he'd been in the room when police searched Slater's luggage, but he himself had no authority to inspect the clothing. *He said he did so anyway* but remembered no details of what was in the luggage. He kept quiet about the stained clothing –evidence of which was sinfully evaded at trial. If anything put the finger on Slater and the bloody murder, it was the fawn waterproof coat with 25 diluted reddish stains.

On June 16, 1914, the Sheriff Principal of Lanarkshire, James Gardner Millar, sent a letter to solicitor David Cooke advising him the Commission of Enquiry found no justification for interference with Oscar Slater's sentence.

The 1914 review of the Slater trial and conviction had three consequences: Slater's conviction remained in force. Roughead published an updated Oscar Slater book. John Trench faced official repercussions.

Trench records revealed he was never cured of his serious drinking problem. It affected his performance as a young man with the Royal Highlanders so much so he had to be jailed. His conduct as a detective in assisting a defendant's lawyer, David Cook, and the defendant's publicist, William Roughead, with specious facts and untruths, misled the reviewing court, journalists, true crime authors and the public about Oscar Slater's guilt. Even worse, the toll minimized the suffering and death of Marion Gilchrist.

Trench's Police Career Comes to an End

Superintendent John Ord was a man of civil and official distinction. Even before he became a steadily promoted policeman, he was renowned as a collector and essayist. Late in the Trench controversy, Ord came to learn of the secretive goings-on in his police department and of the inconceivable violations of a policeman's duty.

Trench lied to Superintendent Ord, his superior officer, among others, and denied that he removed police files. Subsequently, he retracted the denial and admitted to the thefts. Ord concluded that Trench's theft of official documents constituted "treachery against the Glasgow police." He aimed his accusatory finger at Trench's motivation: "I know his weakness for notoriety." A hearing was launched into Officer Trench's misconduct.

In September 1914, Trench was charged with misconduct—untrustworthiness, lying to his superiors, forging documents, falsified witness statements, pursuing independent, unofficial investigations, gross indiscipline, and deliberate and subversive acts without authority. After a full hearing and unanimous opinion, he was dismissed from the force without his pension after 21 years of service.

Trench and the Jewelry Shop Burglary

Trench's troubles were not over. He joined the Royal Scot Fusiliers after his discharge but the Glasgow police continued sorting through his files. These included a January 13-14, 1914 burglary at C.L. Reis & Co, a Glasgow jewelry shop. At his request, Trench had been assigned to investigate the jewel heist. The burglary file was among those removed by Trench that January.

The police review of the Reis jewel burglary concluded with the arrest of John Trench and solicitor David Cook on August 7, 1915, more than a year after the heist. Still feeling the sting of Trench's venal conduct while a policeman and detective, the Superintendent had no misgivings about Trench's complicity.

Trench, Cook, and a third man, an informant, pawnbroker and fence, John McArthur, were accused of unlawful possession of jewelry stolen from Reis, fences for the stolen jewelry, receiving money by fraudulent means, and an unauthorized financial arrangement with the jewelry shop's insurance agent, John Buchanan. McArthur did not appear to face charges.

Trench missed departure with the Ayr Battalion of the Royal Scot Fusiliers for Gallipoli in February 1915 because of the ongoing investigation. At his September 1915 trial, in the uniform of a Royal Fusilier, Trench testified that the burglary had been the work of an expert gang and that John McArthur, a reliable informant, had access to the thieves.

Above Glasgow's C.L. Reis & Co. jewelry shop was an umbrella shop, one where Trench and other gentlemen purchased their sturdy brollies. A hole was dug from the umbrella shop floor down through which the thief or thieves entered the shop in the middle of the night and stole 2,977 pieces of jewelry. Reis estimated the value at £1700.

Trench said he was assisted in his investigation by another detective who, at Trench's trial, had no recollection.

Trench met his informant, John McArthur, at a pub. McArthur told him he had access to most of the stolen jewelry. Trench admitted receiving the Reis jewelry—but only as part of his investigation. With solicitor David Clark's assistance, Trench came to satisfactory terms with the informant and then with Buchanan, agent for Guardian Insurance Company. In exchange for £400 from Buchanan, McArthur would turn over the jewelry to him for the Reis Jewelry Company.

Instead, McArthur reportedly turned the stolen jewelry over to David Cook who was to hold it until Buchanan paid the money. Cook went to Buchanan's home to return the jewelry and was paid money in exchange. Cook claimed that he reported the investigation to the Procurator-fiscal. The Procurator-fiscal denied that he and Cook had been in contact.

The judge at Trench and Cook's criminal trial decided that though it was a serious case, it had been brought too late—with stale evidence, missed recollections, and forgetful witnesses. Trench and Cook were acquitted by the jury on direction of the judge who advised that the two men returned the goods to the satisfaction of the rightful owners and had acted with "meritorious intent."

Procedurally, the criminal case ended with a lawyer's artful maneuvering: the fence for the stolen jewelry disappeared during the trial and the complaining jeweler and his insurer were satisfactorily reimbursed.

CHAPTER 53

An Appeal for the Misbegotten

Among Oscar Slater supporters was author William Park. In 1926, seventeen years after the trial, Slater granted him an interview at Peterhead Prison. Slater was almost at the 18-year mark of the original sentence's minimum which would allow his release. Meanwhile Park reached out to Conan Doyle to become reinvested in freeing Oscar and, more importantly, for a reversal of his conviction. Park himself needed the marketing assistance of Leslie Reade, the young lawyer who corresponded with Slater throughout his imprisonment. Within months of Slater's release, William Park died from a narcotics overdose. He would not be alive for Slater's anticipated huzzahs upon release from Peterhead.

Conan Doyle was ripe for righting an unjustified conviction after his experience with police and town corruption in the appalling case of lawyer George Edalji. Doyle subsidized the publication of Park's book *The Truth About Oscar Slater: With the Prisoner's Own Story*. In the research for his book, Park relied on documents from John Trench's secretly removed police files and on Slater's late, reconstructed alibis.

Park's introduction was written by Sir Arthur Conan Doyle, M.D., LL.D.: "It is certain that the case of the alien German Jew, who bore the pseudonym of Oscar Slater, will live in the history of criminology as a miscarriage of justice of a character very unusual in the records of the Court."

Conan Doyle determined that Slater was wrongfully convicted of a murder solely because of his disreputable life and occupation—which

Doyle the gentleman himself abhorred. He concluded that Slater's defense team had been asleep at the wheel. Doyle's opinions weren't sufficient to exonerate Oscar Slater. The police and the Crown were implacable in having got the right man. Slater's incarceration continued. There was no right to a criminal appeal...not until that year, 1927.

The British public continued its clamor for Slater, interrupted by the communal tragedies of the Great War and the flu epidemic. Spiritualists, a global crowd of believers in communicating with the dead, of whom Conan Doyle and his wife were prominent members, advanced a pro-Oscar mission. One of its groups claimed contact with the deceased, Marion Gilchrist. She had called out at a séance: "He is not the man!"

Conan Doyle explained his interest in wrongful conviction cases because he was "a paladin of lost causes." The credibility and judgment of such a man—creator of the greatest sleuth of the day, Sherlock Holmes—were regarded with reverence. All these groups, famous men, and even the spirit of the dead woman protested that Oscar Slater was innocent. Slater himself joined the chorus of believers.

The ministerial lords were anxious to cure a miscarriage of the law, as the public demanded, and to satisfy the community "that justice will be done." So much so were they maneuvered that in November 1927, a law of retroactivity was passed giving Oscar Slater leave to appeal. A new appellate trial of sorts was set for July 9, 1928. Publicity from Park's book was assured. Having Conan Doyle in Oscar Slater's corner upped the market, public interest, and publicity prior to the appeal.

An Unimaginative Exercise

The June 8, 1928 appeal had restrictions imposed. There would be no new evidence and Slater could not testify. In response, Slater left the court in a snit, but subsequently returned, having been implored by counsel and by the probability of a finding of innocence.

At the appeal hearing before the newly established Scottish Court of Appeal, William Roughead appeared as an expert witness—expertise based on what he had heard in the Slater trial of May 1909 and about which he had written in *The Trial of Oscar Slater* and its updates.

Roughead testified that the hammer used to kill Marion Gilchrist was not Oscar Slater's. This "expert opinion" disregarded Slater's admission to the U.S. Marshals. The hammer in his luggage, said Roughead—a man who professed a legal education-- was actually one used by Slater in his jewelry business. Slater's jewelry instruments were not introduced at the May 1909 trial.

KC Craigie Aitchison, a renowned and expensive Scottish advocate chosen by Conan Doyle, cross-examined the testimony of Helen Lambie from her depositions given in Slater's extradition and for the May 1909 trial. Helen Lambie Gillon, having married and moved to Peoria, Illinois, was unavailable to appear as a witness during the entirety of the campaign to release Oscar Slater.

Startling issues addressed by Mr. Aitchison from Lambie's 1909 sworn testimony included faithful Barney's September 1908 poisoning. He argued it had nothing to do with Slater because he hadn't arrived in Glasgow until October.

One impervious Appeals judge recalled Lambie's specific description of Oscar Slater's manner of walking. Judge Guthrie had instructed Slater to walk in the courtroom. (No objection heard from defense counsel as to Slater's announced choice not to testify nor incriminate himself). The Appeals judge found Lambie's description of Slater's "peculiar gait" at the murder scene still compelling.

Five judges sat and listened to the six-day, fourteen-hour review of the Crown's case against Oscar Slater. So did Arthur Conan Doyle. What must have been his deductive ruminations as he heard the testimony and the arguments? Misgivings must have given way. He may have heard a distant voice "halloa" from a story he published in 1903, *The Hound of the Baskervilles*. In the book, reflecting on the Notting Hill murderer hiding in the moors, Dr. Watson recalled Sherlock Holmes's interest in the murderer's trial "...on account of the peculiar ferocity of the crime and the wanton brutality which had marked all the actions of the assassin. The commutation of his death sentence had been due to some doubts as to his complete sanity, so atrocious was his conduct."

Doyle's manner towards Oscar Slater was never again favorable. He had previously determined that Nugent and Lambie were complicit in the crime, and his proactive publicity on behalf of Slater and the Innocence Campaign came to an abrupt end.

Helen Lambie, living in Peoria, Illinois, wrote letters and newspaper articles a year in advance of Slater's appeal of his conviction. Her message of his guilt would have cleaved to Appeals Court judges before rendering an opinion, and which was limited to disturbing the Slater case only on technicalities.

In letters to her mother living in Glasgow, Lambie remained adamant that Slater murdered Miss Gilchrist. Upon his release, 18 ½ years after the trial, Lambie issued a scathing rebuke published in the *Empire News*.

Helen Lambie's Long-Distance Accusations

Here are excerpts of Lambie's scabrous letters, years after the murder, written to her mother from Lambie's home in Peoria, Illinois. She was assuring her aging mother to keep away from the newspaper pressmen clamoring for information:

Nov. 29, 1927: "So Slater is lucky to have such a smart, wealthy body (Conan Doyle) at his back, and being treated so kindly and given flowers on his return to Glasgow. Slater's lawyers might be the means of him being a very wealthy man yet, if they can go on as they are doing and gets him compensation...It's enough to cause the public to raise trouble at a murderer being set free. Innocent—if he would tell the truth that would find him out, and *he is no innocent man. He knows that, too, the coward.*" (emphasis, author).

Dec. 6, 1927: "So if Slater says he is a poor Jew and pretends he can't speak good English, he has a smart lot to speak for him, and if he proves his innocence it will be by telling lies, as I know perfectly well Slater is the man that passed me out of Miss Gilchrist's house. Slater is a coward for not telling the truth...***A mob should form up and blow Slater to pieces. Give him what he gave the old lady. Batter him to pieces***." (emphasis, author).

Dec. 18, 1927: In the *Empire Newspaper:* "I wish to put a denial to the statement recentaly (*sic*) published in the Newspapers there is no truth in that statement Connan (*sic*) Doyle used a false statement I would not blame another man. Slater is the man that I saw coming out of the house of Miss Gilchrist. I am as strong and of the same mind as I was at the trial If Slater would tell the truth he is not an Innocent man."

And What About Helen Lambie?

After the trial, Helen Lambie avoided discussion of the murder, the locked jewelry box, or the brooches. She wrote no memoir. Eighteen years later, upon Oscar's appeal, she published her letter in the *Empire News* saying Slater was a liar and that he knew he'd murdered Marion Gilchrist. How did she know Slater was a liar unless she was acquainted with him? Put paid to another of Thomas Toughill's illogical conclusions—that Lambie did not know Oscar Slater.

Lambie was living in Peoria, Illinois when she wrote that letter: "He did it." But did she ever speak of any event from that night, December 21, 1908? Not once. Like Slater and Nugent, her guilty conscience disappeared with her into the grave.

CHAPTER 54

Windswept Gloom

The Appeals Court did not overturn Slater's guilty verdict. Reversal rested upon the trial's infirmity and in assuaging Scotland's imagined guilt for having convicted an innocent man. The appeal's consequences arose from Lord Guthrie's remarks to the jury; conflicted medical evidence; conflict as to the weapon used to kill Marion Gilchrist, i.e. a chair vs. a hammer; inconsistent witness identifications during the New York extradition, the Glasgow lineups and in trial testimony; and that the legal inference of guilt from Slater's flight from Glasgow was discredited by virtue of his having signed his true name at the North Western hotel in Liverpool. The Court also reflected upon Helen Lambie's testimony, saying she was a "false and unscrupulous, untruthful and an insolent witness." Perhaps, within the lines of those accusations, the Court was suggesting that she had known the truth and, as Conan Doyle believed, was party to the crime.

The decision of the Appeals Court did not declare Slater innocent nor, to his dismay and anger, did it grant him a full pardon. He left court in buried fury. His grasp of the English language appeared in a *Sunday Mail* article he wrote upon his release: "...a vale of grief, suffering and tribulation through which an unconsciously cruel and relentless fate compelled me to tread."

On November 27, 1927, Slater was released and awarded £6,000 in restitution (today $339,000). He was also paid thousands of pounds by journalists and reporters who hounded him for photographs and accounts of the case.

Superintendent Ord died in 1928. Though he had been offered a great deal of money for a book about the murder, the trial, and the undisclosed facts, he refused all offers. Ord was unmoved by theories of Oscar Slater's innocence, convinced the Glasgow police had caught the killer of Marian Gilchrist. Further, Ord had no desire to revisit John Trench's disturbing activities with witnesses and police files.

Peterhead Bay cormorants

Oscar Slater walked out of Peterhead Prison, a bleak, granite fortress overlooking the North Sea on Britain's frigid northeastern coastline. Peterhead had been his damp home for over 18 years. Flights of sinister-looking, slender black cormorants were perched along the steep cliffs off the coast. Migratory and terroristic, the birds are uncontrolled in their greedy passion for fish, building strength from excessive feeding.

Fishermen hate this killing machine but follow the law about culling the birds.

There is more to the "birds of a feather" analogy. Cormorants have a technique of waterproofing, beating their wet-feathered chests and elongating their broad wings to dry and to fly. As they fly off, they leave behind a reminder of their presence: fecal droppings. The strong odor around Peterhead Prison paths blew in through the ventilation shafts and windows. With each breath, Slater spent 18 1/2 years sobering his December 21 memories of waterproofing, water, and the inextricable judgment wrought by his crime and his own evidentiary leavings.

Marion Gilchrist's commemoration was just as foul. It lay in lurid newspaper photos, penny dreadfuls, and in pro-Slater books, stripped of her humanity, fractured, bloodied and beaten to death by one truly Satanic hoodlum.

Oscar Slater served 18 1/2 years for a crime he did in fact commit. This book may not prove him guilty beyond a reasonable doubt—the years past have been many. Had specifics, such as interrogating accessories and scrutinizing events and correspondence, even a trial delay, been thoughtful and deliberate, there would have been irrefutable evidence of Slater's determined path to murder an old lady for a trove of diamonds, holding the Court to its duty of enforcing Slater's destiny with the hangman.

"Peace is not for wicked men." ISAIAH 48:22.

CHAPTER 55

Authors as Sleuths

Thomas Toughill's Alternative Suspects

Thomas Toughill, an author from Glasgow intrigued by this unsolved case, availed himself of government documents, including those stolen by Detective-Lieutenant John Trench. Toughill's book, *Oscar Slater: The Mystery Solved,* was published in 1989. He alluded to two anonymous letters sent to the police identifying the real killers as either the Charteris or Birrell relatives of Marian Gilchrist. After the revelations about John Trench, David Cook, Esq., and William Roughead, the identity of the anonymous letter writer might have wound around those three interested parties.

Toughill improved on Trench's fabricated investigations, pointing to a duo of Miss Gilchrist's nephews, the Charteris brothers, as having conspired with cousin Wingate Birrell --a son of Marion Gilchrist's sister, Janet, suffering from terminal tuberculosis—to kill their elderly aunt Marion.

One nephew, Dr. Francis Charteris, a distinguished physician, had been immediately brought by police to the murder scene from his High Street office a few streets away. Dr. Charteris was the relative who bought Barney the dog. Upon seeing Lambie at the murder scene along with Margaret Birrell and Charles Cowan, Dr. Charteris described Lambie as "incoherent." The other conspirator named by Toughill was another Gilchrist nephew, Archibald Hamilton Charteris, a professor of law.

These relatives were supposedly in the flat when Arthur Adams ran up the stairs. Except for the thuds and the splintering of wood, Mr. Adams hadn't heard the footfalls of several men within. Only one man exited from the flat and ran between Mr. Adams and Lambie as they stood at the open door. Toughill surmised that one of the relatives, in the cold and rainy night, in the sheer darkness, may have opened the kitchen window, spied a spindly waterpipe about 10 feet to the left of the second-story window, crawled out, reached for the waterpipe, climbed on it and noiselessly hurtled down—leaving no footprints on the muddy ground.

Mr. Adams', Lambie's, and Mary Barrowman's descriptions of Slater's exit were so specific in detail that Toughill's alternative scenario, of men rumbling around the flat, one anxiously raising open the kitchen window, dangerously reaching outside to grab hold of a fragile, soaking waterpipe—unseen and unheard by the downstairs Adams family—lapses into enthusiastic delirium. Had such an event been introduced to the jury, within the shadow of Judge Guthrie's grimace, the defense would have been hard-pressed to avoid his vitriol.

The motive of the relatives, according to Toughill, was revenge and anger, having heard (from whom? her solicitor?) that their aunt revised her Will. These men of privilege and professions were bent on finding and destroying her Will. This was a motive based on misunderstanding by the author. The original of Marion Gilchrist's Last Will and Testament would have been kept in her solicitor's office. It is still available online. As disclosed at Slater's trial, Marion Gilchrist left much of her estate to her sister, Mrs. Jane Gilchrist Birrell, to charitable institutions including her church, and to Margaret Galbraith Ferguson, her friend and former maidservant. She also left separate, specific bequests. What she executed with her solicitor around November 20 had not been a new Will but a codicil to assure benefits for the children of Margaret Galbraith Ferguson.

A physician and a professor of law desperate for jewelry and diamonds? Neither of the Charteris brothers was a gem dealer but it counted in Slater's livelihood. There were not two men who walked briskly out of the flat and neither Charteris brother had a criminal background. Toughill offered no details of how the Charteris' access aligned with Helen Lambie's timely exit from and to the flat that night. The relatives weren't identified by their fawn waterproofs or broken noses. Finally, two men didn't race out of the building smack into witness Mary Barrowman.

Steven Hines: Further Flaws

Steven Hines, in his *True Crime Files of Sir Arthur Conan Doyle* (2001), included an introduction by Steven Womack who revealed little sympathy for Oscar Slater. He "would have rotted in prison for the rest of his miserable life, except once again, Sir Arthur Conan Doyle quite literally came to the rescue."

Though Hines and Womack believed Oscar led a miserable life, they nevertheless concluded he had been wrongfully convicted in a "twisted, bizarre case." The only bizarre element was the tray of diamonds that appeared and then disappeared in the police investigation.

Statements like Hines' erroneous reference to Brooch #2, the one pawned at Liddell's, as having belonged to Slater, add to the case landing into a bizarre heap. He was another author who too lightly examined the diamond and brooch evidence, David Dick's Inventory, and Lambie's spin. Hines concluded with foggy ease that Slater's ownership of the brooch "was shown beyond all cavil and dispute." Where this brooch production and proof took place, in whose presence, and what expert witness so testified, appeared nowhere in the Record. The brooch wasn't Slater's as the facts above have proved and as Marion Gilchrist's photograph, in which she wore a brooch with three rows of diamonds, attests.

CHAPTER 56

Arthur Conan Doyle's "*Je t'accuse!*"
"The whole of Slater's story is a tissue of lies."

Arthur Conan Doyle experienced police corruption and misconduct in the George Edalji case in which he successfully defended the wrongfully convicted lawyer. Conan Doyle had been approached by William Roughead, a trustworthy, well-intentioned professional who claimed inside information about police misconduct from Detective-Lieutenant John Trench. Conan Doyle became zealously engaged, over the course of many years, in the plight of a Jewish refugee convicted of the savage murder of an old Scottish lady.

Had Slater's appeal been rejected, he would still have walked out of prison because he had served the 18 years of good conduct expected of a life sentence. Upon his release November 27, 1927 and his receipt of compensation, Conan Doyle suddenly requested reimbursement of (only) the appeal costs he expended on Slater's behalf.

Doyle had not broached the issue of reimbursement while Slater was serving his sentence. The change of attitude began after the Appeal Hearing. Doyle expected Slater, a newly released prison inmate, to act the gentleman and repay a debt…whether or not such an agreement had been contemplated between the parties. Slater refused to repay, stating that though Conan Doyle worked on his behalf, still, he and others made money from all their Oscar Slater publications, income which they had not shared with him.

Conan Doyle grew to despise Oscar Slater. Slater was no metaphor for the plight of the Jewish refugee. Doyle expected Slater to repay him from his £6000 compensation. The man had been in prison for 18 ½ years and had to begin life anew with just that sum. Doyle was in a fury on reading that Slater was holidaying at Brighton—a former haunt--sunning, bathing, golfing, dancing, attending the theater, and enjoying himself in relative comfort. Doyle then assumed with gusto the role of Dickensian debt collector. The activity fell on Slater's deaf ears.

Doyle resorted to writing withering rebukes in the *Empire News,* the *Telegraph,* and the *Daily Mail* newspapers about the man for whose release he'd fought since 1910. Slater, attempting to restore relations, sent him a silver cigar cutter, which Doyle returned.

Doyle referred to Slater as a "rolling stone of a man," an "ungrateful dog," and "a liar." He kept him at arm's length. Hardly could Doyle have taken such a contemptuous turn towards the man over his costs. Doyle published this glaring accusation: "nearly everything he says is untrue." Both Conan Doyle and Helen Lambie's newspaper diatribes appeared like ricocheting bullets, but now-famous Oscar Slater dodged them. He felt he had suffered enough as a wrongfully convicted man targeted as a murderer because he was a Jewish foreigner.

Conan Doyle avoided making the ultimate condemnation. He was held in high esteem by the international public. He would be loathe to admit that his Sherlockian reasoning failed him in this case. Instead, he continued his editorial vendetta. In May 1929, less than a year before Doyle's untimely death, he damned Oscar Slater as cautiously as he could:

"The whole of Slater's story is a tissue of lies."

Conan Doyle's accusations of guilt redeemed the facts and circumstances supporting Oscar Slater's just conviction for the murder of Marion Gilchrist.

Leslie Reade, his former frequent correspondent in matters of law, finances, and pity, moved on from Slater in 1930 with the last of his Slater letters.

CHAPTER 57

Oscar Slater in Retirement

Of All the Gin Joints....

Oscar Slater returned to Scotland and retired to Ayr on the northwestern coast. Yes, Ayr, where Marion Gilchrist had once holidayed with her family, Lambie, and Barney, and where she'd met Lambie's friend, Patrick Nugent.

In 1936, Oscar married 33-year-old Lina Schad of German (Christian) ancestry. They lived as Mr. and Mrs. Oscar Slater Leschziner in a seaside house on St. Phillans Road with a garden and the peace of Scottish country life. He resumed use of "Leschziner," preferring to forget the ugly past and an incarceration that stole from him his youth and livelihood. Townspeople referred to the celebrated Oscar Slater as the "reprieved murderer," not as an innocent.

Slater had been an expert billiards player at one time in his life, and Ayr offered membership in the distinguished Gentlemen's Club for men with a fancy for snooker, drinks, and conversation. The seaside resort had a pier, a Pavilion, and fine dance floors. Friends visited Slater at his home though Lina turned down her nose at "all the Jewish talk." During the day, when Slater wasn't gardening or listening to music, he visited the Ayr Racetrack, rated among the best racecourses in Scotland. Annually, an Antiques Fair rolled into town where Slater bought and sold antiques.

Though he had 20 years of life ahead of him, he never wrote a book or memoir, nor granted an interview detailing his activities the day and evening of December 21, 1908 from which he could have anticipated a fortune.

He remained a man of media interest and posed for a good many photographs but refused any effort to revive the Gilchrist matter. He consorted no more on Sauchiehall Street, nor pawnbrokers, nor ladies of the evening. His compensation was comfortable for retirement. He earned pocket money as an antiques dealer and from posing for newspaper and book photographs.

While Slater was imprisoned, his parents died, as did his brother and sister-in-law. One of Slater's nephews died in the Great War, another was institutionalized for nervous troubles, and the last was a businessman until World War II and the Holocaust.

During the Second World War, Slater's remaining family, his sisters Phemi and Malchen were deported to concentration camps and murdered with millions of fellow European Jews. Their names are inscribed at the Yad Vashem Memorial in Israel.

Slater died January 31, 1948, age 76, and was cremated. On his death certificate, his last occupation was listed as that of a baker (his father's occupation) and antiques dealer.

The evil that men do lives after them...
The good is oft interred with their bones.
Julius Caesar, **Shakespeare**

Oscar Slater was cremated.
No bones.
No good.

In 2018, Glasgow hosted a play: *Oscar Slater - The Trial That Shamed A City*. The Scottish legal community touted it. A great big collective penitential experience.

The Greater Shame: Marion Gilchrist was Murdered by Oscar Slater

▶--- Helen Lambie and Patrick Nugent were parties to the plot. They wanted a share of the jewels and they had access.

▶--- Both brooches were stolen from Marion Gilchrist. Oscar reset and sold the diamonds from the crescent-shaped brooch with one row of diamonds, and he pawned the more valuable brooch with three rows of diamonds.

▶--- With Nugent's description of Marion Gilchrist, the inside of the flat, the jewelry, and with Lambie's assistance, Oscar Slater entered the flat and murdered Marion Gilchrist on Dec. 21, 1908.

▶--- It was not Nugent who entered the flat and murdered Marion Gilchrist. He and Lambie were conspirators in the burglary and murder. Oscar wore the fawn waterproof coat and bought a hammer both of which he packed when he escaped on the Lusitania headed for America.

Marion Gilchrist's ashes rest in an urn atop the Gilchrist monument in the Glasgow Necropolis cemetery. A shroud covers it. "Nearer my God to thee."

BIBLIOGRAPHY

www.ancestry.com/search/collections/1093/?name=patrick_nugent. Patrick Nugent wedding photos.

Author's interviews, Nov.2022, Jan. 2023: Professor Carlina De La Cova, hammer and velocity, skull fractures; Dr. Franklin Saksena 1908 and 1909 blood testing; Mr. Alan Shaw. Billiards, gamesmanship, card games and playing.

William Blackstone, *Commentaries on the Laws of England,* Clarendon Press (4 volumes, 1765-1770), Clarendon Press: Oxford

Barnes, Julian, *Arthur and George*, Knopf, New York (2006).

Baston, Karen, "Oscar Slater: What Happened...," *Signet Magazine: The Society of Writers to her Majesty's Signet* (2012) no. 3, pp. 28-29. www.wssociety.co.uk/documents/Signet%20Magazine.

Bell, Neil and Wood, Adam, *Sir Howard Vincent's Police Code of 1889*, Mango Books: FL (2009).

Braber, Ben, "The Trial of Oscar Slater and Anti-Jewish Prejudices in Edwardian Glasgow," Vol.88, pp. 262-279, www.jstor.org/stable/24427043.

https://www.britishnewspaperarchive.co.uk: *Empire News, Glasgow Herald, Reynolds News.*

Burns, Robert, "Auld Lang Syne," "The Mouse," "My Heart's in the Highlands," "The Louse."

Correspondence of "Oscar Slater, the Jewish Prisoner Championed by Arthur Conan Doyle": to Leslie Reade, William Park, from Peterhead Prison. www.carpelibrumbooks.com/correspondence-of-oscar-slater-the-jewish-prisoner-championed-by-arthur-conan-doyle.

https://www.conandoyleinfo.com/life-conan-doyle/conan-doyles-own-mystery-cases/oscar-slater. "The Oscar Slater Case." Photograph, Conan Doyle shooting pool.

Connelly, Clare, Sr. Law Lecturer, Univ. of Glasgow, "A Great Miscarriage of Justice: Oscar Slater," *Scots Law Tales,* John Grant and Elaine Sutherland, eds., Oxford Academic: 2010. https://academic.oup.com/edinburgh-scholarship-online/book/19325.

Connelly, Clare, contributor, "An Innocent Man? *Sgeulachd* Oscar Slater." TV Movie, 2012. Writers Thomas Toughill, Richard Whittington-Egan, Matthew Watson. https://www.imdb.com/title/tt3850064.

De La Cova, Carlina, Professor of Anthropology, "Fractured Lives: Structural Violence, Trauma, and Recidivism in Urban and Institutionalized 19th-century-born African Americans and Euro-Americans," in *Broken Bones, Broken Bodies: Bioarchaeological and Forensic Approaches for Accumulative Trauma and Violence*, Caryn E. Tegtmeyer and Debra L. Martin, eds., Lexington Press, MD (2017).

Dictionary of National Biography, "William Roughead", vol. 47, 936-937.

Doyle, Arthur Conan, "The Adventure of Black Peter"; "The Adventure of the Copper Beeches;" "The Adventure of the Creeping Man"; "The Adventure of the Empty House"; "Scandal in Bohemia;" "The Sign of Four." *The Complete Sherlock Holmes Collection*: Wordsworth Editions: NY (2017).

Doyle, Arthur Conan, *The Case of Oscar Slater*, Hodder & Staughton, London (1912).

Doyle, Arthur Conan, "Who Did Murder Miss Marion Gilchrist"? *Empire News*, Nov. 13, 1927.

https://www.familysearch.org/en/wiki/Hamburg_Passenger_Lists. Hamburg passengers to Great Britain and Scotland, 1895-1900.

Fox, Margalit, *Conan Doyle for the Defense*, Random House, NY (2018).

Galton, Sir Francis, *Finger Prints*, Macmillan: London (1892).

www.gla.ac.uk/myglasgow/archivespecialcollections/consultingourcollections/.

www.glasgowlife.org.uk/libraries/city-archives.

Hepburn, Dr. Stuart, "The Trial that Shamed a City," performed at A Place, a Pie, a Pint, Glasgow, November 2018.

Himmelfarb, Gertrude, *The People of the Book*, Encounter Books: London (2011).

Hines, Steven, *True Crime Files of Sir Arthur Conan Doyle*, Berkeley Publishing Group: NY (2001).

Hirst, Damien, *For the Love of God, The Making of The Diamond Skull*, Other Criteria Books: London (2007).

www.historicenvironment.scotland. North Sea waters, wild fowl, rivers Kelvin and Clyde, Leith port.

House, Jack, *Square Mile of Murder*, Black and White Publishing: Edinburgh (1961 reprint 2001).

Hunt, Peter, *Oscar Slater: The Great Suspect*, Burleigh Press: Great Britain (1951).

Julius, Anthony, *Trials of the Diaspora*, Oxford (2010).

Kacir, Rachel, "Glasgow's Square Mile of Murder," Glasgow City Heritage Trust, 2021. https://www.glasgowheritage.org.uk/glasgows-square-mile-of-murder.

Kilday, Anne Marie, "Kilday, Anne-Marie. "'Circumstances of Unexplained Savagery': The Gilchrist Murder Case and Its Legacy, 1908–1927." *Fair and Unfair Trials in the British Isles, 1800–1940: Microhistories of Justice and Injustice*. David Nash and Anne-Marie Kilday, eds. Bloomsbury Academic: London, 2020. www.bloomsburycollections.com.

Lawson, John D. and Keedy, Edwin R., *Criminal Procedure in England*, 1 J. CRIM. L. & CRIMINOLOGY 595 (1911), at scholarlycommons.law.northwestern.edu/jclc/vol1/iss4/7.

Library-asc@scotlandspeople.gov.uk.

Mortimer, John C., "The Oscar Slater Trial," *Famous Trials,* Dorset Press: Dorset uk (1986).

www.nationalarchives.gov.uk.

National Archives and Records Administration; Washington, DC; Record Group Title: Records of District Courts of the United States, 1685-2009; Record Group Number: RG 21.

New York, State and Federal Naturalization Records, 1794-1940, online genealogical and biographical information.

www.nrscotland.gov.uk, "The Case of Oscar Slater," with photographs.

Oates, Joyce Carol, notes on William Roughead in reviewing "The Mystery of Jon Benet Ramsey," *New York Review of Books*, June 24, 1999.

Our Society (formerly "Crimes Club"). Presentations by Bernard Spilsbury, pathologist; Conan Doyle on Oscar Slater (Dec. 11, 1911, Nov. 11, 1913, May 5, 1918); Police Methods (Feb. 6, 1927). www.oursociety.uk.com/clubhistory.html.

Oxford Dictionary of National Biography, Sir (Charles Edward) Vincent Howard (1804-1908), lawyer, author of *The Police Code and General Manual of the Criminal Law* (1912 edition).

Park, William, *The Truth About Oscar Slater: With the Prisoner's Own Story*. Psychic Press: London 1927.

www.policemuseum.org.uk. Detective-Lieutenant John Thompson Trench.

Pretty Women of Paris 1883, Wordsworth edition: uk, 1996.

Random Scottish History: "The Trial of Oscar Slater--Verdict and Aftermath," 2021. www.randomscottishhistory.com/2021/12/14/oscar-slater-verdict-aftermath.

Records.Management@scotland.police.uk .

Roughead, William, *Classic Crimes*, NY Review Book: NY (2000 edition), and *The Trial of Oscar Slater*, William Hodge & Co., Glasgow and Edinburgh (1910, 1915, 1925).

Rossini, Brenda, "An Indisputable Jack the Ripper Identification" (2012), reprinted as "Jack the Ripper's Identification: Confirmed, or Not, by DNA," *The Bilge Pump*, vol.11, no.02 (Feb. 2023)

Schauer, Frederick, *The Proof: Uses of Evidence in Law, Politics, and Everything Else*, Belknap Press/ Harvard: Cambridge (2022).

scotlandspeople.gov.uk.

Scotiana Everything Scottish, "Oscar Slater is Set Free" (photographs of family, Glasgow, Rabbi Eleazar Phillips, www.scotiana.com/oscar-slater-is-set-free; "Monstrous Conspiracy that condemned the innocent Oscar Slater," www.scotiana.com/monstrous-conspiracy-that-condemned-the-innocent-oscar-slater-1909.

Scottish Jewish Archives, *Second City Jewry: The Jews of Glasgow in the Age of Expansion, 1790-1919*, Glasgow: 1990.

Signet Library, William Roughead collection, https://www.wssociety.co.uk/features.

Silesian archives of Herbert C. Scheja and Paul Scheja, 1888 – 1911; include Hamburg and Bremen; Cunard lines errata. Personal library of the author.

www.st-andrews.ac.uk/library/special-collections/photographs/.

Toughhill, Thomas, *Oscar Slater: The "Immortal" Case of Sir Arthur Conan Doyle*, Sutton Publishing: Gloucestershire UK (2006).

Twardoch, Szczepan, *The King of Warsaw*, Amazon Crossing: NY (2020).

University of Aberdeen, specialcollections@abdn.ac.uk.

Whittington-Egan, Richard, *The Oscar Slater Murder Story: New Light On a Classic Miscarriage of Justice*, Neil Wilson Publishing: Glasgow, 2001.

Wilson, Philip Whitwell, "But Who Killed Miss Gilchrist?" *North American Review*, Vol. 226, No. 5, pp. 531-544. (Nov. 1928).

Womack, Steven, *True Crime Files of Arthur Conan Doyle*, Berkley Prime Crime: NY (2001).

Yad Vashem, Israel: World Holocaust Remembrance Center, www.yadvashem.org.

INDEX

Adams, Arthur 82, 85, 86, 91, 114, 125, 175, 176, 177, 180, 184, 185, 189, 190, 193, 196, 198, 199, 200, 204, 207, 210, 211, 220, 222, 227, 238, 241, 247, 250, 252, 291, 293, 294, 295, 296, 298, 300, 317, 376

Adams, John M.D. 158, 163, 189, 223, 224, 225, 250, 295, 298, 332, 334, 335, 336

Adams, Laura 222, 227

Alexandra, Queen 36

Anderson, Adolf 55, 98, 103, 111, 125, 126, 131, 132, 137, 157, 170, 171, 172, 216, 243, 246, 257, 258, 262, 264, 265, 268, 269, 270, 277, 284, 297, 324

Anti-Semitism 21, 34, 49, 93, 94, 95, 289, 308

Armour, Annie 221, 295, 300

Austen, Jane 10, 297

Ayr, Scotland 75, 79, 87, 104, 113, 114, 115, 119, 120, 121, 169, 192, 202, 203, 218, 382

S.S. Baltic 291, 292

Barney the terrier 77, 79, 82, 86, 98, 114, 116, 120, 121, 125, 152, 153, 161, 163, 178, 195, 197, 227, 279, 368, 375, 382

Barrowman, Mary 91, 98, 168, 187, 189, 212, 214, 215, 216, 217, 238, 240, 241, 248, 249, 255, 257, 261, 285, 291, 295, 296, 298, 299, 300, 304, 317, 318, 344, 362, 376, 377

Bartitsu 73

Bernstein, Mabel 264, 271

Beuthen 20, 45, 46

Biler, Solomon, aka Solomon Miller   308

Birrell, Margaret Dawson   164, 222, 227, 352, 361, 375

Blackstone, William, *Commentaries on the Laws of England*   313, 386

blood spatter   90, 229, 320, 338

bloodstains   337, 340

Brien, Francis, Police Constable   160, 168, 177, 195, 223

Brighton   111, 112, 380

Brooch #1   38, 39, 40, 41, 57, 110, 125, 139, 140, 141, 250, 255, 326

Brooch #2   40, 41, 61, 80, 81, 89, 136, 139, 140, 141, 144, 149, 165, 170, 171, 252, 255, 327, 328, 351, 353, 377

Brooks, Max   266

Brown, Agnes   64, 106, 154, 169, 182, 218, 219, 220, 221, 251, 299, 300, 321

Bryce Pawnbrokers   127, 137, 138, 159, 253

Bryson, Robert   167, 170, 193, 292, 295, 362

Buchan, John
---*Greenmantle*   94
---*39 Steps*   94

Buchanan, John   364, 365

Burgh Act of 1892 (prostitution)   67

Burglary   13, 79, 80, 81, 86, 107, 109, 116, 118, 120, 121, 160, 167, 169, 171, 184, 205, 208, 211, 217, 218, 232, 245, 253, 276, 281, 303, 309, 314, 316, 318, 356, 364, 384

Burns, Robert   14, 34, 62, 96, 192, 386

Campbell, Allan, Inspector   268

Carfin, Glasgow   75, 76, 77, 78, 81, 87, 106, 107, 108, 115, 154, 169, 221, 279, 280, 356

Central Hotel   63, 123, 128

Central Station   63, 167, 172, 190, 193, 259, 271

Chamberlain, Houston   93

Charteris, Dr. Francis   82, 113, 227, 233, 361, 375, 377

Chesterfield, 10th Earl   309

Chicago   101, 273, 276

S.S. Columbia   311

Conan Doyle, Arthur
--Black Peter   228, 387
--*The Case of Oscar Slater*   356, 359, 387, 389
--Creeping Man   261, 387
--*Hound of the Baskervilles*   369
--Shoscombe Old Place   94
--*Sign of Four*   230, 387
--*Study in Scarlet*   23, 94, 354

Conan Doyle for the Defense   23, 152, 256, 387

Cook, David Esq.   231, 357, 358, 360, 361, 362, 363, 364, 365, 375

Cowan, Charles   222, 227, 361, 375

Criminal Evidence Act of 1898   323, 324

Curran, Martha   154, 184, 186

Cyrano de Bergerac   204, 216

Dick, David   37, 41, 145, 146, 162, 233, 234, 301, 353, 358, 377

Dictionary of National Biography   26, 387, 389

Donegal cap   299

Douglas, William, Superintendent, Western District, Glasgow Police   225, 227, 251

Dracula   346

Dreyfus, Alfred   21, 22

Dumbarton   110

Edinburgh High Court   310, 311

Edinburgh   26, 50, 51, 52, 53, 56, 58, 62, 68, 72, 73, 100, 133, 167, 220, 230, 287, 290, 291, 297, 307, 310, 311, 321, 338, 341, 344, 346, 349, 387, 388, 390

Edward VII, King   18, 36, 65, 103, 177, 349

Ellis Island   97

Emancipation Proclamation of 1809   21, 102

Empire News   30, 369, 370, 380, 386, 387

Evening Chronicle   174, 188, 199, 251

Evening Citizen News   253, 257

15 Queens Terrace
---dining room   13, 14, 33, 144, 164, 173, 176, 178, 192, 193, 195, 196, 198, 222, 224, 225, 229, 315, 331, 332
---fireplace   13, 14, 32, 190, 196, 224, 225, 332
---grandfather clock   178, 179, 180, 188, 189, 192, 194, 195, 229
---kitchen clock   180, 188, 192, 194, 195, 199, 331
---locked box   88, 110, 118, 119, 148, 173, 181, 195, 198, 199, 201, 206, 222, 230, 279
---padlocks   152, 153, 178, 180, 193, 354
---safe   76, 118, 144, 198, 204, 229
---spare bedroom   14, 76, 77, 81, 90, 109, 110, 116, 121, 144, 169, 183, 195, 196, 198, 201, 204, 211, 222, 229, 230, 233, 234, 249, 256, 279, 293, 294, 304, 316, 353
---felony murder   208

fingerprints   230, 231, 249

Fluorescein test   338

footprints   13, 198, 229, 376

Fox, Charles, King's Counsel   303, 304

Fox, Margalit   23, 152, 340, 387

Freedman, Luise (Klebow)   143, 261, 270, 290, 308, 325, 349, 356

Galt, Hugh, Professor of Forensic Medicine and Pathology, University of Glasgow and the Glasgow Royal Infirmary   225, 332, 334

Garnethill Synagogue   255

Galton, Sir Francis   230, 387

Gilchrist, Marion
--Last Will and Testament   80, 233, 327, 376

Gillies, Alexander   161, 295, 297, 298, 312

Glasgow   13, 14, 22, 23, 24, 27, 29, 31, 32, 36, 38, 39, 40, 43, 55, 56, 57, 58, 61, 62, 63, 64, 66, 67, 75, 77, 78, 80, 87, 88, 89, 95, 97, 100, 101, 103, 104, 105, 107, 108, 112, 115, 120, 123, 124, 125, 126, 127, 128, 129, 130, 131, 132, 136, 137, 139, 150, 154, 155, 156, 157, 158, 160, 162, 163, 166, 167, 169, 213, 218, 225, 227, 228, 230, 238, 239, 243, 248, 250, 251, 252, 254, 255, 257, 258, 259, 260, 261, 262, 263, 264, 270, 272, 276, 277, 279, 280, 281, 283, 284, 287, 288, 290, 291, 301, 303, 304, 306, 307, 308, 311, 312, 314, 315, 318, 327,, 328, 331, 332, 336, 348, 349, 351, 353, 355, 357, 360, 361, 363, 364, 368, 369, 370, 372, 373, 375, 384, 385, 386, 387, 388, 390, 391

Glasgow Herald News   348

Glaister, John, Professor of Forensic Medicine, University of Glasgow and the Glasgow Royal Infirmary   225, 332, 333, 334, 335, 337, 338

Goodhart, William A., New York Defense Counsel   304

Gorbals   63, 95

Gordon, William, Detective Lieutenant   227

Guiacum blood test   337

Guthrie, Agnes   75, 121, 125, 145, 151, 152, 153, 233, 251, 252, 352

Guthrie, Charles, Judge   16, 27, 90, 318, 341, 342, 343, 344, 345, 349, 368, 372, 376

hallmarks   57

Hamburg, Germany   47, 48, 49, 50, 52, 68, 387, 390

Hanson, Annie   53, 72

Harrison, Constable John   189

Hart, James Neil, Procurator-fiscal   227, 251

Henderson, Gordon   246, 266, 306

Herzl, Theodore   21

Highlandsman Umbrella   63

Hines, Steven   188, 377, 388

Holmes, Sherlock   28, 73, 93, 141, 228, 230, 261, 284, 313, 322, 354, 358, 367, 369, 387

Holytown, Glasgow   75, 76, 77, 78, 106, 107

Hunt, Peter   215, 216, 296, 388

Huppe, Elsa   259, 261, 308, 356

Instructions to Coroners (China, 1250 C.F.)   337

Jacobs, David   43, 100, 102, 108, 109, 125, 126, 127, 139, 155, 156, 276, 277, 308, 309

"The Jew's Daughter"   311

Juno, Mademoiselle Andrée   69, 285

Keith, Andrew, Detective-Inspector   230, 279

Kelvinbridge Train Station   218, 277

Kempton, William   253

La Guillotine   55

Lambie, Helen   13, 22, 23, 29, 30, 33, 38, 39, 40, 43, 59, 62, 75, 76, 77, 78, 79, 80, 81, 82, 87, 88, 90, 91, 101, 104, 105, 106, 107, 108, 109, 111, 112, 113, 114, 115, 116, 117, 118, 119, 120, 121, 124, 125, 126, 132, 140, 141, 142, 144, 145, 148, 149, 150,

151, 152, 153, 154, 155, 159, 161, 162, 164, 166, 168, 169, 172, 174, 175, 176, 177, 178, 179, 180, 182, 183, 184, 185, 188, 189, 190, 192, 193, 194, 195, 198, 199, 200, 201, 202, 204, 205, 206, 207, 208, 210, 211, 218, 219, 222, 223, 225, 227, 232, 233, 238, 241, 245, 247, 249, 250, 251, 252, 253, 256, 267, 268, 279, 280, 281, 290, 291, 292, 293, 294, 296, 298, 299, 300, 302, 303, 304, 313, 317, 326, 327, 328, 329, 331, 352, 356, 359, 361, 368, 369, 370, 371, 372, 375, 376, 377, 380, 382, 384

Leschziner/Leschzinger, Adolf   45

Leschziner, Amelie   45

Leschziner, Euphemia   45, 383

Leschziner, Georg   45

Leschziner, Oskar/Oscar (see Slater, Oscar)

Leschziner, Pauline   45

Levy, Isaac   53, 72

Liddell (Adams), Rowena   177, 181, 227, 247, 248, 295, 296

Liddell's Pawnbrokers   38, 57, 89, 137, 267, 325, 352

Lieth   50

Lincoln Blood Libel   311

lingchi   331

Liverpool   23, 258, 264, 265, 267, 268, 271, 272, 311, 372

Locard, Edmond   90, 231

London   12, 30, 53, 54, 55, 56, 58, 61, 63, 67, 68, 69, 72, 73, 78, 98, 100, 101, 102, 103, 104, 111, 112, 125, 126, 127, 128, 131, 145, 155, 156, 157, 159, 172, 206, 216, 230, 232, 252, 259, 261, 265, 268, 269, 270, 276, 284, 301, 308, 309, 314, 327, 353, 387, 388, 389

Lusitania   23, 65, 91, 210, 220, 239, 257, 258, 264, 267, 268, 272, 273, 280, 282, 283, 293, 298, 299, 303, 333, 356, 384

MacBrayne, Duncan   245

MacDonald, James   145, 162

MacVicar, Duncan, Detective Constable   227

McArthur, John   364, 365

McGimpsey, John, Detective   248

McHaffie, Mrs.
--Madge   298

McLaren, Peter   267, 268, 326

McLean, Allan   141, 166, 171, 263, 264, 265, 267, 295, 296, 297

McClure, Sir Alexander Logan, Defense Counsel   323

Messrs. Dent   101, 125, 126, 159, 172, 193, 252, 265, 304, 327, 351

Millar, James Gardner   362

Miller, Hugh Gordon, New York Defense Counsel   304

Miller, Solomon, aka Solomon Biler   308

Monte Carlo   68, 136, 170, 269, 276, 308

Motor Club   58, 246, 264, 265

Moudie   58, 62, 104, 126, 259, 265, 305

Nairn, Andrew   168

Napoleon   21, 102

Necropolis Cemetery   35, 260, 385

Neill, William, Police Constable   223, 225

New York City   56, 61, 81, 88, 89, 91, 92, 97, 98, 100, 101, 102, 108, 111, 112, 134, 135, 136, 137, 142, 155, 156, 172, 190, 216, 248, 252, 254, 255, 257, 258, 263, 267, 276, 280, 281, 283, 284, 289, 290, 291, 292, 301, 303, 304, 306, 307, 308, 312, 318, 325, 328, 329, 336, 372

New York Port Authority   238

New York Review of Books 27, 389

Nice, France 269, 276

Nichols, Frederick 137, 154, 160, 170, 181, 253, 295, 296, 314

North Western Hotel, Liverpool 271, 272, 273, 282, 372

Nugent, Patrick 13, 22, 23, 29, 38, 75, 76, 77, 78, 79, 80, 81, 87, 88, 90, 91, 101, 104, 105, 106, 107, 108, 109, 113, 114, 115, 116, 117, 118, 119, 120, 121, 124, 125, 126, 127, 140, 141, 148, 149, 150, 151, 152, 153, 154, 156, 166, 167, 169, 181, 182, 183, 184, 185, 186, 187, 190, 199, 201, 205, 206, 207, 208, 215, 217, 218, 219, 221, 232, 233, 250, 262, 263, 279, 280, 286, 287, 290, 299, 300, 302, 313, 349, 355, 356, 359, 369, 371, 382, 384, 386

Oates, Joyce Carol 27, 389

Ord, John, CID Chief Inspector 124, 146, 189, 225, 227, 255, 281, 344, 345, 357, 360, 363, 373

Oscar Slater - The Trial That Shamed A City 384, 388

"Othello" 36, 74

Paradise, Isaac 131, 154, 159, 160, 163, 295

Paris 69, 102, 104, 142, 228, 272, 311, 349, 389

Pawnbrokers 38, 40, 57, 60, 61, 62, 89, 127, 137, 138, 267, 325, 352, 383

Peoria, Illinois 29, 368, 369, 371

Peterhead Prison 24, 28, 45, 96, 117, 136, 216, 217, 329, 335, 350, 366, 373, 374, 386

Phillips, Rabbi Eleazar 27, 95, 255, 311, 349, 354, 390

plague 48, 243

pogroms 67, 102, 311

Poland 20, 45, 349

Powell, William, Detective-Inspector 264, 265, 267

Proverbs 55

Pryor, Mary Curtis 61, 67, 72, 97, 196

Pyper, John, Detective Inspector, Western District, Glasgow Police 37, 146, 197, 224, 225, 227, 234, 247, 249, 253, 281, 286, 291, 298

Raskolnikov 127

Rattman, Max 55, 101, 104, 139, 154, 171, 172, 190, 254, 257, 272, 283

Reid, Samuel 127, 132

Reis, C.L & Co. 364, 365

Reynolds News 145, 147, 216, 232, 281, 301, 356, 386

River Clyde 57, 110, 243, 388

River Kelvin 220, 221, 243, 244, 388

Rogers, Robert 55, 98, 100, 103, 126, 155, 156, 157

Rostand, Edmund 10

Roughead, William 24, 25, 26, 27, 28, 39, 89, 90, 108, 117, 148, 151, 167, 182, 183, 188, 207, 210, 278, 279, 287, 290, 311, 340, 345, 354, 356, 357, 358, 359, 360, 361, 362, 363, 368, 375, 379, 387, 389, 390

Russell, Ruby 264, 271

Russia 20, 102, 127, 156, 157, 261

St. John's United Free Church 31, 34, 260

Saksena, Dr. Franklin 338, 386

San Francisco 101, 136, 170, 171, 253, 273, 276

Sancroft, William 256

Sauchiehall Street 31, 60, 63, 78, 108, 164, 383

Schmaltz, Katerina 69, 132, 160, 181, 265, 295, 322, 325

Scotsman News 248

Scott, Sir Walter, *Ivanhoe* 34

Shannock, Oscar 111, 112

Shauer, Frederick, *The Proof: Uses of Evidence, Law, Politics, and Everything Elsa.* 313, 390

Silesia 13, 19, 20, 45, 126, 240, 390

Slater, John 54

Slater (Leschziner), Lina 382

Slater, Oscar
--Admission 287, 298, 319, 339, 368
--Appeal 30, 305, 338, 339, 366, 367, 368, 369, 370, 372, 379
--Confession 29, 348
--Engravings 56, 59, 125, 137, 143, 271, 273
--Flight 88, 89, 133, 135, 161, 270, 273, 275, 276, 277, 308, 314, 317, 318, 372
--Mademoiselle Andrée 24, 61, 69, 97, 100, 101, 102, 103, 112, 125, 127, 128, 132, 136, 139, 142, 143, 170, 173, 190, 191, 212, 240, 241, 253, 254, 259, 261, 262, 265, 269, 270, 271, 273, 277, 280, 282, 283, 284, 285, 308, 311, 318, 325, 327, 328, 341, 348, 349, 350, 351, 352
--parents 45
--Phemi 45, 383
--Secret Review, 1914 360, 362
--Trial 16, 22, 24, 25, 26, 27, 29, 31, 38, 40, 53, 59, 71, 72, 76, 85, 89, 90, 93, 98, 101, 102, 105, 106, 108, 110, 111, 115, 116, 117, 118, 119, 125, 127, 133, 137, 141, 144, 145, 152, 156, 160, 161, 163, 166, 169, 175, 186, 189, 190, 191, 206, 207, 210, 216, 220, 230, 232, 239, 241, 249, 268, 280, 281, 286, 287, 291, 293, 297, 299, 303, 307, 311, 312, 313, 314, 317, 318, 321, 322, 325, 326, 328, 329, 330, 333, 336, 339, 341, 345, 346, 350, 354, 356, 357, 358, 359, 360, 361, 362, 364, 365, 366, 367, 368, 369, 370, 372, 373, 374, 376, 384, 386, 388, 389, 390
--Verdict 79, 330, 341, 345, 346, 356, 359, 361, 372, 390

Sloper Club 58, 157, 164, 166, 167, 263, 265, 306

Sorley, William 31, 32, 38, 40, 41, 57, 110, 115, 124, 152, 268, 326, 327, 351

Spiritualists 289, 367

Starrett, Vincent 213

Stevenson, James V., Chief Constable 251

Stevenson, Robert Louis 26

Stewart, John 162

Streetlights
--electric 163, 212, 213, 214, 296, 299
--gas 63, 163, 213

Sunday Mail 372

Suffragettes 135, 213

Supreme Court for Criminal Matters, Scotland 321

Teichmann test 338

Thomas Cooke Travel Office 257, 258, 267, 273

Tombs Prison 288, 289, 292, 304, 305, 309

Toughill, Thomas 56, 216, 340, 371, 375, 376, 377, 387

Trench, Detective Lieutenant John 26, 27, 29, 92, 108, 115, 117, 154, 169, 170, 182, 206, 207, 231, 238, 277, 278, 279, 280, 281, 287, 290, 301, 311, 312, 355, 356, 357, 358, 359, 360, 361, 362, 363, 364, 365, 366, 373, 375, 379, 389

Trollope, Anthony 19, 31, 93, 94

Tschernichovsky, Shaul 96

"221B" 213

tusitala 26

Veitch, Dr. Alexander 338

Victoria, Queen 17, 18, 19, 93

Vincent, Sir Howard, Chief, CID Scotland Yard; author, *Police Code and Manual of Criminal Law* (1881) 228, 229, 386, 389

Voltaire 29, 93

Walker, Christopher, Police Constable   159, 162, 163, 213, 295, 328

Walker, Jane Duff   65, 115, 121, 122, 125, 142, 147, 198, 352

Warnock, William, Chief Sheriff, Glasgow Criminal Office   291

Washing Away of Wrongs (Sung Tzu, 13th Century China)   331

Whitechapel   54

Whiteinch (Glasgow) Murder   230

Whittington-Egan, Richard   32, 188, 252, 340, 387, 391

Wilhelm, Kaiser   47

Womack, Steven   377, 391

Wrone, Henry   157, 308

Yad Vashem, Israel   383, 391

Zadig   29

ACKNOWLEDGEMENT

I wish to thank the undue service, encouragement, advice, critiquing, assistance, skill and knowledge of my beloved friends and colleagues. From a stellar critique group including Barry Chessick, Kelley Chikos, Lyle Cohen, Richard M. Davidson, Estelle Laughlin, Sarah A. Schwarcz, and Peter Slonek. Readers: the Honored and Honorable Ron Levitsky, attorney Joseph J. Loss, and His Lordship Alan Shaw of Broadway. Pangloss Honoree: Bert M. Rossini-LeBougerée, I carry your support and friendship to my grave…or to the alternative ashcan.

May light forever shine above the Winnetka Public Library, Winnetka Illinois. The staff are its treasure.

www.ingramcontent.com/pod-product-compliance
Lightning Source LLC
Chambersburg PA
CBHW022057150426
43195CB00008B/175